THE CHORD OF LONGING

MY LIFE AS ATHEIST, MARXIST, MOTHER, NUN

Mother Felicitas Curti, OSB

Our Lady of the Rock
2016

Nuns-women's religious communities-religious life-Tristan chord-music and spirituality-conversion stories: atheist to Christian-conversion stories: Marxist to Catholic

First published by Dog Ear Publishing
4011 Vincennes Rd
Indianapolis, IN 46268
www.dogearpublishing.net

ISBN: 978-1-4575-4954-0

This book is printed on acid-free paper.

Printed in the United States of America

For

Bill and Carl,

Lady Abbess, and all my monastic family

CONTENTS

PART ONE: DISSONANCE

PART TWO: RESOLUTION

PREFACE

When Mother Abbess David Serna, the second Abbess of Regina Laudis, asked me to "write my life"—a life that has intrigued many people I have met along my path—I said "yes." That was in 2007. I had not the faintest idea of what I was getting into. I thought I would need about a year to carry out this assignment. I would write my life story for my communities: Regina Laudis in Bethlehem, Connecticut, and its daughter foundation, Our Lady of the Rock on Shaw Island, Washington, for my family and my close friends. I expected to run off twenty-four copies.

It has turned out quite differently. Many who heard about my plans, including those in my monastic communities, told me my story should have a broader readership. Mother Hildegard George at Our Lady of the Rock was my first reader, encourager, and editor. She has continued to be helpful all along the way, and I am most grateful to her.

But if the story was to have a broader readership, it needed further editing. I have had the incredible gift of editing by three friends, all professional writers and editors. Each one wanted to have different sets of things explained: about Christianity, Catholicism, Marxism, socialism, yoga, music, musicology, monastic life and customs. Helen Weaver, a former Oberlin roommate, author of *The Awakener* (about Jack Kerouac) and always a dear friend, read an early draft and made some important suggestions. Mary Lynn (M.L.) Lyke, formerly book editor and writer for the *Seattle Post-Intelligencer,* did the heavy groundwork of turning my manuscript into something that could reach readers beyond the confines of my monastic and academic milieux. Helen Weaver then went over the manuscript again, marking dozens of little details that needed fixing. Helen's understanding and supportive comments and questions helped me immensely.

I thought I was finished. I thought I had produced a perfect copy and was ready to search for a publisher. Almost at once I was forced to accept the disappointing reality that the book was far from completed. My friend Roby James, author of *Commencement* and several other books and articles, asked to read the manuscript. Within days, I began to receive emails from Roby with corrections for details such as mistaken footnote numbering, as well as probing, provocative questions. Yet another basic revision was needed.

Another challenge came in the matter of style. In school, in the 1930s and 40s, my teachers instilled in me firm adherence to various matters of grammar, punctuation, and spacing between sentences. By now these rules have become not only quaintly old-fashioned, but actually wrong. Reluctantly, I yielded to the opinions of my editors, and to my computer.

Dear Editors, all four of you, I love you and will ever be grateful to you.

One other person has been indispensable in the making of *The Chord of Longing*: Ned Griffin, computer doctor and teacher of Shaw Island. He has been unfailingly available whenever I need him. His immense knowledge, infinite patience, and good humor have rescued me from hundreds of difficulties whose solutions were far beyond my reach. Not only do I share with most of my generation the complexities of rapidly changing technology, but when my old iMac died, I had to get used to a new computer and a very different new Word program. Ned, my eternal thanks.

I owe deep thanks to several others: photographer Tari Gunstone, who provided the cover photograph and several other photos; to Jeffrey Morse, John and Jean Kekes, Chris Wohlforth, Alex Taub, and Tari, who have read and commented on all or parts of the manuscript; Robin Plotnik for providing a new Word program; and so many more for their encouragement and support.

I am most grateful, also, to Sister Joyce Cox, BVM, and the Seattle Archdiocese for a grant that enabled me to get my new computer.

The image of Saints Perpetua and Felicitas by Ade Bethune, first published in *The Catholic Worker* in 1937, is used courtesy of Archives and Special Collections, St. Catherine University, St. Paul, Minnesota.

Quotations from Scripture come either from the King James Version or from the various liturgical books used in the Catholic Church and in our Benedictine liturgy. Occasionally I have changed a word or two in a translation from Latin, and have modernized some archaic verb forms.

I am most grateful for my communities: The Abbey of Regina Laudis for getting me started and for their continuing encouragement, and Our Lady of the Rock for the immense amount of time given to me for this book, for their support, and for putting up with my single-mindedness all this time.

My son, William Wohlforth, has from the outset provided his whole-hearted support, materially and in every other possible way. He has shared my times of discouragement and my times of elation.

My thanks go to the staff at Dog Ear Publishing, who have been not only knowledgeable, but patient, helpful and kind.

Above all, I am grateful to my parents and especially to God. I hope I have made this clear.

The entrance gate to Our Lady of the Rock
Photo by Tari Gunstone

PART ONE

DISSONANCE

We begin with a chord. This chord is hauntingly beautiful, evoking infinite longing. Wagner opens his opera, *Tristan and Isolde*, with it. It is a dissonant chord, needing a resolution. Only four hours later, at the very end of the opera, is this chord resolved.

One

BEGINNINGS

I will give thanks to the LORD with my whole heart:
I will tell of all Thy wonderful deeds.
I will be glad and rejoice in Thee,
I will sing praise to Thy name, O Most High.

—Psalm 9:1,2

My life does not seem at all unusual to me. I have lived it step by step, phases overlapping, melting into other phases. It seems perfectly logical and understandable to me that I have been at various times a militant atheist, a radical socialist, a wife and mother, and for what is now almost half of my life, a Benedictine nun. Others wonder, though, how I got from one place to the other. People want to hear my conversion story, above all: from Martha Curti, atheist and Marxist, to Mother Felicitas, nun. Friends have asked me to write my story, and I have not done it. I am reluctant to bare my heart to any public, or even, it seems, to my good friends. But at my Monastic Consecration (July 11, 2007) Mother Abbess David Serna, OSB, Abbess of Regina Laudis, asked me to "write my life." Thus, out of obedience, I got to work.

The major threads of my life, radical and traditional, run consistently through every phase. As an infant, I was brought up on a strict routine. Hence I have always appreciated routine, consistency, predictability, and have not been easily accepting of surprises or sudden changes. At the same time I have always rebelled against that very routine. I have always wanted to please authority figures, yet have always had a strong independent streak. I have always loved tradition, yet favored major changes in the world and in myself. I have always sought and longed for love, yet have habitually behaved in ways that defeat the realization of that longing. I have always wanted to fit into whatever group, whatever set of values, whatever people I am with, yet I have chosen groups in which I am decisively set apart: a Trotskyist, and a Benedictine nun in a traditional habit. There is no way I can go outside the monastery without being noticed.

My love of tradition undoubtedly comes from my upbringing: the love that my parents, especially my mother, had for the past. My father chose to be an historian. My mother, though an experimental psychologist professionally committed to a scientific approach, was at the same time an incurable romantic with a strong attachment to the past and to family traditions. In college she studied Old Anglo-Saxon and Old High German. She was fascinated by the development of languages, Greek and Teutonic mythology, life in the Middle Ages and other past times. She insisted on our unchanging Christmas customs. There had to be stockings hung by the fire. There had to be the same food each year for breakfast (Stollen, link sausages, pink grapefruit, scrambled eggs) and for dinner (turkey, a salad, rolls, plum pudding with hard sauce). The tree had to come down precisely on January 6, the twelfth day of Christmas. She regretted the passing of the Nebraska prairie where she had grown up. She felt the presence of all the people who had ever lived at Flint Farm, our summer home in New Hampshire, and how they had lived. In short, she had a very strong dose of nostalgia.

I share this strong dose. So does my younger son, Bill; my older son, Carl, did to a much lesser extent. Where this comes from, I know not. Maybe it's the genes, maybe a gift of God. Many people do not have this: for example Bill's wife, Chris, who has no desire to go back to see the houses in which she grew up. I, on the other hand, have clear pictures in my mind of how our kitchen used to look in the 1940s. I can visualize the insides of all the places I've lived. At the World's Fair in New York in the 1960s, General Electric had a display that showed kitchens of three different periods. The kitchen of my childhood evoked such a longing in me, and it still does, to think of it. So it does also to look at the ads and the signs and other relics of those pre-WWII days. In no way do I wish to go back and live those days again, but my strong attachment to them has not faded.

This nostalgia, which I see as a gift, may account for my love of Gregorian chant and Latin and various liturgical and monastic practices.

My Family

At Beloit College, a small liberal arts college in Wisconsin, two young professors met and fell in love. My mother, Margaret Wooster, wearing cap and gown, was walking toward the gathering place for the academic procession at the opening of the school year. She saw a young man, Merle Curti, standing on a street corner, struggling to get his hood on. She stopped and offered to help him. Soon after, Margaret attended a dance at which she noticed Merle seeking out the neglected young ladies sitting on the sidelines. She was greatly impressed by this man's kindness.

Merle soon sent her a note, addressed to "Dear Miss Wooster." Their relationship flourished. Despite the inhuman teaching loads imposed on them, they found time for picnics and other diversions, accompanied by Merle's sister, my Aunt Jean, and other young people. On June 16, 1925, they were married in Paris, during my father's year in Europe on a Harvard fellowship. Their families back in Nebraska found out about their marriage only after the fact.

They both received teaching positions at Smith College: Dad in American history, Mother in psychology. He had yet to finish his dissertation at Harvard. She, seven years older, already had her PhD from the University of Chicago, where she did much of her work conducting experiments with white rats. Their first child, Nancy Alice, was born in 1927. At the age of eighteen months Nancy came down with an extremely high fever, about 107 degrees. She was diagnosed with encephalitis, and her brain was damaged in the area that affects self-control and judgment. She was physically impaired to some extent, with poor coordination. She was still a beautiful and lovable child, but that early disease marked her life and that of her family forever. She had a violent temper, and would explode unpredictably. One never knew what would provoke these explosions. She was very intelligent and curious about the world, but never in her life developed legible handwriting. Her life was plagued with difficulties in relating to others. Despite her handicaps, she had a loving disposition, and "wrote" (i.e., dictated) many poems, which my mother wrote down.

My parents, Merle and Margaret Curti, at Smith College c. 1929.

I came along in 1932, when Nancy was five. I have many good memories of Nancy from my childhood. We talked and played together a lot. She was protective of me, but also very jealous. I was told

Mother with Nancy and me, 1932.

later that when I was a toddler, she walked into the room where I was standing and knocked me down for no reason. I don't suppose such a thing is unusual between siblings, but I did come to develop a deep fear of Nancy. I will describe in later pages some of the major crises in our lives arising from her disability. But I can summarize here the main effects she has had on my life. I always felt, for one thing, that I had to be very very good and do everything well, and probably go into an academic career, because Nancy would never be able to do these things. I felt that I had to make up for her lacks. Secondly, I always felt guilty that I had been given so many gifts while she had so many handicaps and difficulties. Also, the jealousy to which I have always been prone must come from the childhood experience of resenting all the attention she received.

My parents had many things in common, but entirely different personalities. Both grew up in rural or small-town Nebraska families that had an array of common problems: early deaths of children, depression, poverty, alcoholism. Both were highly intelligent and well educated. Both had a great love of beauty in all its forms: nature, art, music, poetry, literature. They were among the very few people I have ever known who really listened to music: they would sit and listen to it on the radio or on records, and do nothing else. They never relegated music to serving as a background to other activities. Like them, I cannot stand music in the background.

Beauty was their spiritual food. They both wrote poetry: Dad in his early adulthood, Mother all her life. Their poems are both simple verses for each other and us girls on Valentine's Day or birthdays, and poems deep and serious, reflective, sometimes whimsical or with touches of humor. My Dad's poems, often melancholy, showed a genuine faith in God and a love of Our Lady, a faith and love that he later denied, though I am sure that in his heart he held onto them. That is why it is appropriate that the epitaph on his gravestone reads: "Now I know for certain."

My father's Vermont grandparents paid for my Grandmother Alice and her three children to go by train from Nebraska to Vermont and spend their summers on the farm in Essex Junction. My mother, who had enough older sisters to help their mother with the housework, spent much of her childhood on horseback, keeping her eye on the cows. Through these childhood experiences both of my parents gained a deep love for the land.

Dad was very sociable, and could strike up a conversation with anyone. Mother was shy and reserved with people she did not know. Her shyness often caused people to think she was severe. Actually, she *could* be truly severe. She had extremely high ideals and expectations for herself and for everyone else. Dad had tremendous energy and drive and was very efficient. He would rise early and write up to a dozen letters before he descended to fix breakfast for the family. He would get up from a meal before we were finished and start doing the dishes. In his work he was conscientious and ambitious, made himself available to students, was active on many committees and boards, and left behind a gigantic body of books and articles.[1] Mother, on the other hand, always had a low level of energy, was not efficient, and was easily distracted from a task by seeing something else that needed attention. In these ways I am very much like her.

My father was often discouraged and found it hard to make decisions. He would keep weighing one side of a problem against another, and Mother would step in to help him rationally consider the alternatives. Though she suffered from deep depressions, she always presented a brighter side. She sought to make the best of every situation and constantly encouraged my father. She concealed her depression so well that I did not even know of it until my father told me, years after her death, how much she had suffered, sometimes to the point of not being able to talk to people. She would, for example, write notes to our housekeeper, Mrs. Moor, rather than speak to her. Mrs. Moor was so discouraged by this seeming rejection that she told my father she was going to leave. He literally got down on his knees and implored her to stay.

Despite his unusual kindness and mildness of manner, Dad was a strong father. He had very high standards of morality and expected the same of his daughters. Like Mother, he was uncompromising in his principles of peace and justice. I don't recall all of the many times he courageously spoke, wrote, and acted in defense of academic freedom, but they include a 1953 address during the McCarthy period to the members of the American Historical Association, of which he was then president. In 1944, at the University of Wisconsin, the Faculty Club refused to grant a room to Arthur E. Burke, a black graduate student. My father led a successful campaign for the Faculty Club to reverse their discriminatory policy. As president of the Mississippi Valley Historical Association in 1952, he "persuaded a bitterly divided executive board to shift the organization's convention from racially segregated New Orleans to Chicago. Those who knew and admired Merle's gentle, soft-spoken manner sometimes underestimated the intensity of his commitments. Though unfailingly polite, he always made his ethical and social values crystal clear, and acted upon them."[2]

However parental traits are passed on to children, whether through heredity or environment, probably both, they certainly were passed on to me. I have always had a strong desire for justice. I have always suffered from depression and terrific anxiety with people: a dislike of using the telephone; a tremendous uneasiness in large groups of people such as a party or reception; an actual fear of seeing people. When as an adult I was alone at Flint Farm, and heard the mailman or anyone else coming down the road, I would hide so that I would not have to exchange pleasantries with them. And lo! Here I am in a Benedictine community in which hospitality toward strangers is a primary mission.

My parents were full of love for each other, and kept to themselves any disagreements they had. Only once did I overhear them openly argue. I was terrified to hear the word "divorce." There must have been many tensions between them, especially in the long period during my high school years when my mother was bedridden with arthritis and Addison's disease, Nancy was suicidal, and my father felt overwhelmed.

My parents loved their two daughters deeply and devoted a tremendous amount of attention to us. I often felt unloved, though. I felt I could never measure up to my mother's expectations. I have few memories of my father as a little girl. He was often away for considerable periods of time, and when he was at home he was always working. But the early memories I do have of him are good ones. My mother's insistence on a strict schedule, measured

Mother with Nancy and me, 1936. We don't look very happy.

amounts of food when I was an infant and toddler, on my having a B.M. not only every day, but at a certain time, and her attempts to suppress my "negative" emotions, made me feel in a deep way that she did not love me. Once, when at age three or four, I was sobbing about something, Mother was totally unsympathetic and told me most firmly to stop. Later, when I was about six, I would often be cross and stamp my feet in anger. She would say, "Martha, this is not the real you. You are really a nice, sweet girl."

Concerning religion, my parents were both secular humanists. They believed in the basic goodness of human nature, and were not able to believe in anything that could not be explained rationally. Dad had been an Episcopalian in his youth. He remembered being confirmed with his older siblings despite being younger than the normal age. He remembered the Archbishop taking him on his lap, asking him some questions, and concluding that Merle knew his catechism well enough. He told me about being an altar boy at St. Martin's Church in Omaha, and attending Mass daily during Lent. But at Harvard all this vanished from his life. He always retained, though, a great love of the liturgy, for what he called "aesthetic" reasons.

Mother bore within herself the religious conflicts of her parents. Her mother was a devout Methodist from whom she learned many wonderful evangelical songs, a basic acquaintance with the Bible, and an intolerance of swear words. But her father did not believe in God and loved to argue with others, especially a Jesuit priest he knew. Like him, Mother had very high ideals, and was very critical of church people who did not live up to these. She believed that Jesus was a very great man, but not the Son of God. She believed that human beings were capable of tremendous self-sacrifice and noble deeds. But there was another side to her. She was both scientist and poet. Her poetic side loved myths, fairy tales, and elves. She longed for something beyond what we can see—perhaps an all-consuming total relationship, never realizable in real life, perhaps something else. Occasionally she would quote lines from the Bible, and for her new husband she bought a beautifully printed and illustrated volume of the Little Flowers of St. Francis. She must have had some sort of faith. One of her favorite poems, one of the few she had been able to memorize, was Emily Dickinson's "I never saw a moor." But she and Dad both were decisively anti-Catholic.

My father wrote a succinct and insightful description of Mother:

> She tried hard to realize her many and varied potentialities and did indeed realize a great many. In somewhat different circumstances, she would have realized more. When the tension between her parents, Charles and Lillie, became too much for Lillie, she left for Portland, Oregon with her children, all but Mother, whose choice of staying with her father on the farm alienated her from her mother and siblings. The alcoholism of her favorite sibling, Charlie, was hard. It was a very unhappy family. That she saw so much beauty in the world was a great gift. Getting along with colleagues was not easy for her and for a pragmatist there was a strange residue of absolute certainty, which made her less tolerant of non-behaviorist psychologists than her relativism should have suggested. The burden and weight of problems taxed her ability to cope at times. Her health problems became more and more demanding. How much I wish I had done more to help her in the last years. She was indeed a wonderful person.[3]

Two

CHILDHOOD: 1932-1949

We possess within us a yearning for the infinite, an infinite sadness, a nostalgia, *which is satisfied only by an equally infinite response.*

—Pope Francis (as Jorge Mario Bergoglio)

Northampton, Massachussetts 1932-37

At age four I had a dream that I believe comes from the birth experience: I was sitting alone in a small boat, just big enough for me. The boat was taking me through a dark tunnel. Suddenly I came out onto a broad lake with very bright light. A man met me at the shore and handed me a banana. It was poison.

Whatever one may make of this dream, I believe everyone suffers shock from being born, and perhaps the majority of people suffer trauma as well. In any case the infant's experiences *in utero* and during the birth process have an indelible effect on one's being.[4] My mother had a difficult pregnancy and delivery. About a month before I was born, she was hit by a car while crossing a street and was thrown over its whole length. Since everyday experiences (music heard, the relationship of the parents, food eaten by the mother, even the thoughts of the parents toward the baby,) influence the unborn baby, surely this accident must have been traumatic for both my mother and me.

I have no record of the length of time my mother was in labor, but I do know that "high forceps" were used and that Mother's stay in the hospital was extended beyond the usual time and led to internal complications for her later on.

For decades now, I have had a recurring dream that causes such a terror in me that I actually wake up screaming. A man is trying to get into my room. He is so threatening I feel that my very life is at stake. I yell as loud as I can, "GET OUT OF HERE!!" and wake myself up, heart racing, body shaking with fear. I firmly believe that this dream recalls an actual experience, but I cannot recall any such thing. I have just recently arrived at the hypothesis that this dream reflects the threat of being born and the intrusion of the forceps. There is no way of knowing this for sure. Most people do not have terrifying nightmares simply from having been born. Nevertheless I think that some of the effects of this experience, whatever it was, are: A dislike and fear of people getting too close to my body; shyness, and a dislike of using the telephone; choosing relationships that are bound to fail, and helping that failure to happen; trying to provoke or prolong a fight with someone as a perverted seeking of intimacy.

My mother, a psychologist of the behavioral school, raised me as a baby in the most up-to-date manner of that time, following the advice of a U.S. Government pamphlet on the care of babies. Thus I was kept to a strict schedule of eating, being played with, naps, and bedtime. My food was carefully measured. If I cried at the "wrong" time, I was not to be picked up and comforted, lest I become spoiled and demanding. I was to be trained to conform to the schedule of the family. My Grandmother Wooster, on a long visit, subverted my mother's wishes and did pick me up when I cried. I'm sure that our housekeeper, Mrs. Moor, and others who took care of me, did too.

I remember standing by Mother's desk as she was writing something by hand. I noticed how she formed the letter "f", reaching above, then below, the line. I wanted her to pay attention to *me*, not to her writing. Much later, I realized she was probably taking notes *about* me, capturing verbatim many of the things I said, which became the basis of a chapter in her major book, *Child Psychology*.[5]

But knowing my mother, her great love of playfulness and general silliness, and her genuine love of Nancy and me, I'm sure that she paid a lot of loving attention to me. I credit my life-long ambivalence about routine—needing and wanting it, yet rebelling against it—to the rigidity of my early training. To this day I have trouble sticking to a schedule, doing what I have planned to do. I am easily distracted and a terrible procrastinator. But these are traits my mother herself had, so I could simply be imitating them.

Of our first house on Prospect Street in Northampton I have no memory. When I was three we moved to a beautiful house at 32 Barrett Place, from which my parents could walk to the college. Shortly after this move I showed a strong streak of independence. I disappeared one day. My parents were frantic, naturally, but they finally tracked me down. I had set out to walk back to Prospect Street (having no idea how to get there) to see my friend, Susie Ross, who lived next door.

The new house I remember clearly. It had three storeys, a porch on each side of the house on the first and second storeys, an entryway into a hall with a coat closet on either side. Off the hall on the right was the library, with a fireplace and a wind-up Victrola along with the books. Here we played children's party games such as London Bridge, Farmer in the Dell, and Here We Go Round the Mulberry Bush. Here we had our Christmas tree, for which we made garlands of popcorn and cranberries, and chains of construction paper. Even on Christmas morning we would hear from overhead the click-clack of Dad's typewriter as he wrote thank-you notes immediately after we opened our gifts.

The left side of the hall opened into a parlor, where we gathered around the piano to sing Christmas carols and other songs. How well I remember these gatherings, with Mother playing the piano. Once, I am told, I tried to correct the adults in the singing of "O Come, All Ye Faithful." I stamped my foot and exclaimed, "It's NOT 'adore.' It's 'sadore!' " The piano, an upright, had been a practice piano at Smith College. It sits now in Flint Farm in a decrepit state appropriate to its age and heavy use.

Further back, the hall led into the dining room. We had all our meals here. When there were guests, the children sat at a separate small table. From the dining room one entered the kitchen and then a pantry, from which a door opened into the back yard. When I passed through Northampton decades later and looked at the house, I saw that the back yard was very small. But as a child it had seemed plenty big enough for a swing, sandbox, cellar door, and room to run around in. My parents had the second floor, and Nancy and I each had a bedroom on the third floor.

Since Mother taught full time, we had a housekeeper, Mrs. Moor, whom my father called a saint for putting up with my depressive and demanding mother. Mrs. Moor was a devout Christian. Her late husband was a Lebanese Christian, probably a minister and a missionary. He had died before my time. Mrs. Moor's daughter Polly was one of my mother's students at Smith and a frequent presence in our home. Through Mrs. Moor I was exposed to Protestant religion. I spent weeks in the summers at her Northfield home. One summer I was sent to Bible school, of which only two things remain in my consciousness: being told not to run in the house of God, and the songs: "Jesus Loves Me," "This Little Light of Mine," and "Jesus Loves the Little Children" ("red and yellow, black and white, all are precious in His sight").

Various young women also came to take care of us from time to time. (The term "babysitters" did not yet exist). I recall a few snips of their conversations, including the word "Orthodox" in relation to church, so I presume they were religious. Older women took care of us, too.

Despite the conflicts described above, I was in general a happy child. It was the Depression, but I had not the slightest idea how privileged we were to live in a beautiful house and have plenty to eat. My memories are of our immediate world: my first movie at age four (Shirley Temple in "The Little Colonel"); standing in the yard with Shirley Faulkner, my best friend and next-door neighbor, hearing Hitler screaming over the radio, being scared, not understanding why; making Valentines out of the paper doilies and flower pictures from catalogs and interesting colored paper that Mother had collected, and putting the Valentines in a specially prepared box with a slit in the top; overhearing talk about Calvin Coolidge, sit-down strikes, the Lindberg baby kidnapping, the great Connecticut River flood and its lasting effects. I remember Mother explaining that you cannot tell a homosexual by his appearance; that we have not five, but eleven senses; that there are good bacteria as well as harmful ones and that our bodies are covered with them. I remember Daddy explaining clearly what a radical, liberal, conservative, and reactionary are. I well remember my first telephone "conversation." I was four. Mother was speaking with Mrs. Winn, my nursery school teacher, and asked me if I'd like to say something to her on the phone. I just picked it up and saying nothing, I just sang "There is a Tavern in the Town" straight through, all the verses.

I am very grateful for my early childhood, of which I have many more clear memories. Though my scant exposure to anything religious did not put God foremost in my awareness, I clearly grew up in a Protestant environment. More importantly, I know that those religious women who took care of me prayed for me.

Bronxville, New York: 1937-42

When I was five, we moved from Northampton and Smith College to Bronxville, New York, and Teachers College, Columbia, where Dad had a professorship and Mother had a research position. Had they known then that in Bronxville a Jew could not buy property, they would never have chosen to live there. They were drawn by the excellent reputation of the public school. I doubt if any really poor people lived in Bronxville. Most people seemed to be very wealthy. I did know some kids who lived in apartments or townhouses, but that was the exception. The rich people all had uniformed maids, even butlers. In school, the usual kids' threats like "I'll tell your father," or "I'll beat you up!" came out as "I'll sue you!"

When I wore a new dress to school, the girls would look at the label to see if it bore a famous name. It never did, of course.

At five and a half I was shown how to walk to school. On the first day of school I walked there by myself, bursting with pride to be in the first grade. Back in the Smith College nursery school we were weighed periodically, completely naked, boys and girls together. This did not bother me then, but anticipating the new school in Bronxville, I flatly refused to go if we had to get weighed naked with boys. My mother called the school in my presence and received the assurance that no such thing would happen.

I loved school. I remember all my teachers' names and those of many of the children. We all did boy things, like make chairs (I think the little red chair I made in first or second grade is still at Flint Farm), and ant houses, and girl things like making marmalade. We caught polliwogs and raised them, identified birds, made marionettes and put on a Gilbert and Sullivan operetta with them. In the fifth grade we created a newspaper for the school, taking on the various positions and functions the paper demanded. For some strange reason, I was chosen to be the business manager. In music class we sang and played "melody flutes." And there was an orchestra!

Mother had taught me the names of the notes, how they looked on the staff, and how to find them on the piano. I spent hours at the piano, teaching myself how to read music by playing cowboy songs from one book and all sorts of old songs from another. I also learned to play the Bach prelude to which Gounod added his "Ave Maria." Many children consider learning to read music as a dreaded chore. To me, it was a fascinating and enjoyable way of spending time.

In the third grade, when I was eight, Mother and Dad were in Jamaica for several weeks while Mother was doing research. During this time Nancy was taking piano lessons from a woman who also taught violin. She offered a reward to any of her pupils who brought in a new child: one dollar for a piano student, two for a violin student. These were the amounts that she charged for lessons. Nancy asked me if I'd like to learn to play the violin, and of course I said yes. My parents came home to find a bill for lessons in their mail, and an invitation to a student recital. The following year, in the fourth grade, I was sent to the class lessons given at school instead of private lessons. In the fifth grade I was in the elementary orchestra. A girl in the orchestra played the string bass. I was thrilled to feel the vibrations of her instrument in my feet.

Like most children, I didn't always feel like practicing. My parents set up a rule: I had to practice for a half hour before I could listen to "Captain Midnight" on the radio.

In these Bronxville years Nancy's problems either became more serious or, more likely, since I was older, more noticed by me. She often attacked us physically, once breaking my father's glasses. I remember clearly the time she had Mother pinned to the floor and actually set her clothes on fire. Thank God our housekeeper was around: she got Nancy off Mother and put out the fire. I think I helped in this, but am not sure. Not long after this, Nancy tore a lot of her own and Mother's clothes hanging in a closet. I had a recurring dream which must have arisen from my fear of Nancy: An unknown and very dangerous being was looking for me. My mother would hide me (she was very good at hiding things) in a drawer, on a closet shelf, or somewhere. But wherever she hid me this creature would always find me, and as he got closer and closer, I found myself lying on my stomach in bed, pounding the pillow with my fists as hard as I could, and this would make him go away and would wake me up.

Nancy was interested in many things that she was learning. She was curious about religion, for a time claiming that she was a Buddhist. She and I played Princess Elizabeth and Princess Margaret Rose, who were our ages. Mother told us funny stories and played with us. But Nancy had a hard time in school. Other children were often very mean to her. Once she was thrilled to be invited to a birthday party in our neighborhood. She had a nice present for the girl, all wrapped up, and went at the appointed time. A maid answered the door and said, "There is a mistake. There is no party." I am still angry about this incident. Did such things increase Nancy's feelings of frustration? How could they not?

My best friend, Carol, came from a rich family, a very nice and special family. Carol was the youngest of the five Henderson children. Mr. Henderson worked in the city "in advertising." Mrs. Henderson had majored in English at Smith or Wellesley. Each night at dinner, the family recited together Blake's poem "Tiger, tiger, burning bright, in the forest of the night." I never understood these words. At breakfast the maid would often serve grapefruit halves, each on a doily-covered plate, the sections all cut, a maraschino cherry in the center. Carol would answer the telephone so politely, saying, if she was the one being asked for, "This is she." These customs impressed me greatly.

We played pirates outdoors, and in the third-floor playroom with soldiers that had belonged to Carol's older brother. We wrote secret invisible messages with lemon juice or milk. We took hikes along the Bronx River, sometimes carrying a little lunch or snack. We were marvelously free compared to the children of today. We could play at each other's houses on the spur of the moment, without it having been arranged by adults. I just had to call home to let my folks know where I was. I had to be home at five, but walked everywhere by myself.

As early as the first grade I continued the independent streak already manifested in Northampton. One day, as I was walking home from school with my friend Dick Morrill, the son of our doctor, we went up to his house, a few blocks away from my route, and played with water pistols in the gutter for quite a while. It was noon; we only had school half a day. When I arrived home, my mother was frantic. When asked where I had been, I answered simply, "I was detained." She was furious, but later thought it was funny.

I was very interested in cowboys and Indians. (Little did I know then that one day I would live in Washington state, where cowboys and Indians are everywhere.) I was given an Indian suit and insisted on wearing it to school. I learned lots of cowboy songs. In the second grade, toward the end of the school year, we had a visit from my mother's cousin, Fred Wooster, who lived on a ranch in Lewiston, Idaho. Here was my chance! I packed toothbrush and pajamas in my little doctor's kit bag and went to the station with my family to see Cousin Fred off. I tried my darndest to get on the train, intending (without having revealed my plan to a soul at home) to go and live with him. But I had told my teacher. She called my mother and asked her if it was true that I had permission to leave school two weeks early to go out West.

I picked up an interest in the Bible and in religion from my friend Carol, whose family belonged to the Dutch Reformed Church. I began to say the Lord's Prayer every night before going to sleep. I would ask the Lord for some rather unlikely things. I asked Him to turn me into a boy overnight. Boys seemed to do more interesting things than girls. For years I worried about this wish, but my worries vanished when I read, in Maya Angelou's memoir *I Know Why the Caged Bird Sings* that as a child she, too, had prayed to become a boy.

In the summer when I was seven or eight, we stayed at the home of the historian Howard Beale in Thetford, Vermont. In the living room was a Bible, an old edition with the curious word "Selah" appearing now and then. I started reading this Bible, starting quite naturally at the beginning. I got at least as far as the story of Joseph and his cloak of many colors.

Nancy was with us there some of the time, but was in camp for several weeks. I had memorable and treasured times with each parent. My mother and I would take walks, exploring the woods, one time seeing a fox! Daddy would take me, of many an early evening, on a wide path leading uphill. Halfway up the hill was an arbor over the path with a bench on either side. We would sit there and sing the echo song from *Snow White*: "I'm wishing ... for the one I love."

In my ninth summer Nancy was in camp, Dad was some place doing research, and Mother was to teach in the summer session at the University of Oregon extension in Portland. This gave her the opportunity to take me on an exciting and memorable trip by train. On the way out we went through Nebraska, where we saw the farm where she had grown up in Silver Creek, and the houses where my father had lived, in Papillion and Omaha. We stayed with Grandmother Alice in Omaha and visited Aunt Jean, Uncle Carl, and Cousin Jean in Columbus. From the train we got views of a large portion of the USA. I wanted to soak up all that I saw. I pictured myself in the fields, farmyards, villages, and woods that flew past our window.

While in Oregon I was sent to Highbanks Camp, where I was in my element. Mother took me off two times, once for a day trip up Mt. Hood and another to Seattle, where we saw the docks and visited Mother's old family friend from Nebraska, Tonie Ebmeyer, who lived in an apartment on Marion Street. I decided that Oregon was where I wanted to live when I grew up. Food was the main reason: good beef, seafood, abundant produce, and something very important to me: real cowboys and Indians! I sat on the lap of a real Indian in Glacier Park, where we stopped on the return trip.[6]

The Flint Farm house.

Two momentous events took place that summer. We acquired Flint Farm and we also moved to Madison, Wisconsin. For years my parents had spent time each summer in Vermont or New Hampshire, staying in the homes of friends or renting places. They kept looking for a house of their own. At last they found one in tiny Lyme Center, New Hampshire, sixteen miles

On my first visit to Flint Farm on return from my trip West. I'm sitting under an apple tree, still wearing my tag from Highbanks Camp.

north of Hanover and Baker Library at Dartmouth. For $1200 borrowed from a colleague they became the owners of eighty acres and a house built in 1794, with beautiful views of nearby mountains: Smarts, Winslow Ledge, Holts Ledge, and Bear Mountain. The house needed much work, but the walls and floors still had their original wide pine boards. Many close friends were already summer residents nearby, in Lyme, Hanover, Thetford and Norwich, Vermont. After we came, several other acquaintances acquired places, forming a wonderful circle of professors and their families. The summers there were unforgettable, with mountain-climbing hikes, picnics, and surprise visits (since we had no telephone), all of which called for lots of singing.

The Second World War dominated our attention in these years. On December 7, 1941 I was sitting on the floor of the living room with the radio on. I heard the announcement that the Japanese had attacked Pearl Harbor. I experienced the war as a nine-year-old, through my parents' conversations, and through rationing, recycling, and school, where we lustily sang all the popular war songs. Perhaps my lifelong devotion to recycling traces back to those years. All the children brought newspapers to school, creating an enormous pile at the end of the hall. At home, we saved fat and made soap. We flattened our tin cans. We children took air-raid drills as an occasion for excitement: we loved blackouts. Some of my friends and

I formed a British Victory Club (evidently before the USA entered the war), but I have no recollection of what this club did.

My parents were selective pacifists. Dad had written a book, *Peace or War*, about the history of the peace movement in America. Mother was active in the Women's International League for Peace and Freedom. But the horrors of Hitler's regime called for their support of our war effort. Mother cried when Paris fell. Dad worked hard to find a university position for Ernst Posner, a German Jew who had escaped from a concentration camp and, thanks to my father, was able to come to America with his wife.

I had a dream of people as thin as sticks, eating their feces from the gutter and drinking their tears. How could a child imagine this? It must have come from overheard conversations.

Nancy had imaginary friends as a child. My son Carl had them too. Perhaps the first-born children are more likely to have them. (Two of Carl's were Dannyake and Hoo-hoo-dada.) I did, however, have a constant companion on my walks to and from school. I sensed that there was a being under the sidewalk, a kind of shadow of myself. About him I knew nothing at all, but I sensed his presence as comforting and benevolent. I also had frequent dreams of flying. There were two kinds. In one, I sort of skimmed over the ground just a few inches above the surface. In the other, I really flew, usually swooping downward over a hill, pumping my arms as in swimming to keep me up. In the fifth grade I wrote a poem entitled "Miracles:"

> I was looking out my window,
> One bright and summery day,
> My little friend was calling,
> Calling me to play.
> So I jumped right out the window
> And found that I could fly.
> Higher and higher
> I mounted to the sky.
> O'er all the village streets I flew
> With people looking out,
> Wondering why a girl like me
> Was flying all about.

I made this poem into a book, properly bound and illustrated, as a project we were doing in school. The poem came out of my experience of being sent to my room for being a Bad Girl, and wishing to escape by flying out the window.

My parents and their circle of mostly liberal intellectuals were mildly anti-Catholic: that is, not actually bigoted, but certainly suspicious of and very ignorant about the Church. I recall hearing them speak of Monsignor Sheen's[7] well-known success in the conversion of several famous people, remarking that one would not want to be in his presence lest he convert you! But we had in our very home a strong Catholic presence in the person of Hildegard Thielen, a young German woman from Minnesota. She was our housekeeper for several years, and listened faithfully to Monsignor Sheen's "Catholic Hour" on the radio. Once she asked if she could take me to Mass with her. I remember sitting next to her, kneeling when the others knelt, standing when they stood. She reported to my parents that I'd been "a good little Catholic." Hildegard never talked to me about her faith, but it spoke more strongly than words. And I know she must have prayed for me and for all of us.

Madison, Wisconsin 1942-49

The move to Madison just before the start of the sixth grade was a shock to me. A new house, a strange school, new classmates, a new accent and unaccustomed slang words—a new cultural environment with a huge increase in the number of Norwegians. I prepared for this move by singing the major scale with solfege syllables, which we had not learned in school. Since Bronxville Elementary was a progressive school, I was afraid I'd be behind in everything. Actually the only make-up work I needed to do was to learn cursive writing, for which I was sent daily to a fourth-grade class.

Dad had been invited to join the History Department at the University of Wisconsin. Mother could not teach there because of nepotism rules then in effect. She commuted by train to teach part-time in Milwaukee at the UW extension there. Their social life revolved almost entirely among University faculty. Many people dropped by to get acquainted with these newly arrived professors. The silver dish on the front hall table was filled with their calling cards.

Madison stretches out between Lake Mendota and Lake Monona, the narrow isthmus between them bridging the East and West sides of the city, and containing the downtown: the State Capitol, and state and county government office buildings; department stores, professional offices, and Grace Episcopal Church, where a sign on the door read "Come in. Rest and Pray."(In those days churches did not need to keep their doors locked.) State Street linked the Capitol Square and the University of Wisconsin. The street ended at the bottom of a steep and grassy hill lined with University buildings. On top of this hill sat Bascom Hall, the home of the History Department and my father's office.

The East Side was for us almost foreign territory. Most of the academic people lived on the West Side. My parents bought a beautiful brick house on Ely Place in University Heights. I think lovingly of that house, sturdily built in the 1920s. It had wondrous features like a little door in the kitchen, at floor level, into which one could sweep the dust and crumbs that could be forgotten after they landed in a basement bin. Both the first and second floors had doors opening to a laundry chute, which again led to the basement. There was a special built-in nook for the telephone in the wall between the kitchen and the back hall.

The winters were long, fierce, unrelenting. The wind swept up the hill from Lake Mendota to our house and penetrated even the storm windows. The milk, in bottles left on the back porch by the milkman, rose up and popped the bottle tops off. We often walked to school in twenty below zero temperatures. The summers were hot and sticky. Spring and fall, each in its way, were glorious.

The war went on. In school, boys and girls alike knitted Red Cross squares to be made into afghans for the soldiers, while our teacher, Miss Rule, read to us. My efforts at knitting were not successful: my squares inevitably ended up as trapezoids. In Wisconsin the war had a less direct effect on us than in the East: no air-raid drills or blackouts, but rationing, shortages, gold stars in windows to announce the death of a soldier, uniformed men coming and going, women going to work in factories, Victory gardens. Boys could identify by name and number all kinds of airplanes used in the war. We heard constant radio reports and announcements: "Don't repeat rumors" (I thought this meant that if you had a roomer in your house, and he left, and then wanted to come back, you couldn't let him); and "Loose lips sink ships."

One of the scariest things in my whole life occurred during our first year in Madison. I was walking home from school on a warm and sunny October afternoon. My father was waiting in front of the house to meet me, and suggested we walk down to the drugstore to get an ice cream cone. All this was highly unusual. Before we returned home he told me that Nancy had tried to kill Mother with a butcher knife. Mother had managed to throw a blanket over Nancy's head and get into her room and lock the door. This door now had a huge gouged-out place where Nancy had attacked the door with that knife. Nancy and I habitually did the dinner dishes together, she washing and I drying. For months after, I had chills and tingles up and down my spine when Nancy passed that very knife to me.

Mother and Dad had done everything they could to help Nancy. They had always had her examined and thoroughly tested by all sorts of medical professionals; they arranged for experts in movement and relaxation to work with her; they sent her to small private summer camps where she could receive special and loving attention. They poured themselves out for her. Lying in my bed upstairs, I would often hear from downstairs Nancy's agitated voice and Mother's calm one as Mother tried to get Nancy to look at situations reasonably. Sometimes this helped. But throughout Nancy's life, she habitually turned against the people who were trying to help her. Mother was top on this list.

Most of our time in Madison Nancy was not home, except for summers and vacations. Mother always tried to have her live as normal a life as possible; but her one year at Wisconsin High, a private school run by the University, was so difficult that she once attempted suicide. She finished high school at a strict Methodist boarding school in Beaver Dam, Wisconsin, tried Goddard College, which lasted only three days, then got a job in the office of a married Unitarian minister in Boston. With him she fell in love, but thankfully was rejected, resulting in another suicide attempt. She spent the next two years in Hartford, Connecticut, at the Institute of Living, which cost exactly half my father's salary; spent some time at Rockford College, but did not finish; spent some time as a patient at a Wisconsin State Hospital for the mentally ill; then got a clerical job in Milwaukee.

It must have been in our first year in Madison that she began to attend Saint Andrew's Episcopal Church regularly, and was baptized there. My parents went to the baptism. For some reason they found the situation very funny, and it took great effort for them to keep their mirth from being noticed. Nancy persuaded me to go to church with her for a while. We had a children's choir, wore white albs, and processed into the church singing "Onward, Christian Soldiers." I quit the Sunday school after bringing hot dogs to a picnic and being told "We don't eat meat on Fridays."

These Madison years—sixth grade through high school—were turbulent for me, as they must be for nearly everyone. There was the violin and very intense involvement in music. There was lots of tension and worry over Nancy, and over my mother's illness. She had rheumatoid arthritis and adrenal cortex glandular deficiency, now called Addison's disease, and was bedridden for years. At the time, total bed rest was considered the proper treatment for arthritis. I can only imagine what this must have done to her body and her spirits. For the Addison's, she had to inject herself daily. I would sterilize the needle in boiling water. I often prepared dinner at Mother's direction, though for much of the time we had a young woman, a University student, working for her room and board, who would make the dinners.

My relationship with my mother was more complicated than ever. We were very close in one way, having long and wonderful conversations, singing and laughing a lot together. Yet there was also great tension. Sometimes I would do something displeasing to Mother without realizing it, and she would not speak to me at all for days. I could not imagine any punishment worse than this. I would have to apologize to break the silence, even though I might not know what I had done to displease her. It was not enough to say, "I'm sorry you are so upset." I had to say, "I'm sorry I did..." whatever it was. With my father, too, there was a lot of tension. When Nancy was at boarding school, Dad and I did the supper dishes together every day, and fought or bickered constantly. I have no memory of what it was all about. I do remember one day telling him that I wished I had someone else for a father, which brought him to tears. I wish like anything I had not said that.

My future was a big concern. I felt that a woman had to choose between a career and marriage. I did not know any women who had successfully combined them. My brilliant mother, who my Dad believed was a better scholar than he, had basically sacrificed her own career for her family. She did a lot for Dad: edited all his writings, encouraged him, and at the same time resented him. (I did not know until decades later that some of this lack of success had to do with Mother's depression, her forthright criticism of her colleagues, and her poor health.) I had an ardent desire to be a musician—perhaps to play in a symphony orchestra. I wanted to be a terrific violin player. At the same time, I very much wanted to get married and have children, though I feared that no one would ever want to marry me because of my sister.

Friends

Socially I was shy, awkward, inept, and uncomfortable with small talk. I tried to fit in, to belong. But when kids talked about comics I was out of it—we got *The New York Times*, which had no comics. Radio programs? Except for classical music and news, they had a minimal part in our family life. Clothes? I had no good model. My mother, who had such a keen eye for beauty in nature, art, and music, did not apply this to her own person. I wore a lot of hand-me-downs that Aunt Jean sent, of excellent quality, but not what I'd have chosen. The ever-widening gap between my front teeth, which childhood braces had not helped, and frequent sties in my eyes, reinforced my conviction that I was ugly. The only place where I did not feel inferior to other girls was gym, where we had to wear identical ugly blue gym suits. There we were equal.

For a while, my Bronxville friend Carol Henderson and I kept in touch by mail. We attempted to play checkers by laboriously drawing the board in each letter, showing our latest move. But gradually we drifted apart and no longer wrote to each other. I am grateful for having known Carol, for the good times we had, and for her exposing me to the Bible.

I took school, and music, very seriously. I got good grades, which automatically ruled out being popular. Except for a few blind dates I did not go out with boys, not by my own choice but because they did not invite me. The sole exception to this aridity was Bob. I had a crush on someone or other most of the time I grew up, but Bob I truly loved, and he loved me. Our relationship began as friends. We were in many of the same classes, including four years of Latin. We often worked together on Latin over the telephone. We passed lots of notes to each other in study hall. We both worked on the school paper. We both loved music and the arts in general. He knew a lot more than I did about modern music, about the visual arts, and dance, in which he was especially interested. We spent hours downtown in the record store, where we could listen to records in booths. In our junior and senior years we went together to movies, concerts, and even a cocker spaniel show. We sunbathed in my back yard, talking. We wrote wonderful letters to each other in the summers when I was back at Flint Farm.

But the relationship had a dark side. I don't remember many details, but I suffered a lot of agony. Bob was rather unpredictable and sometimes would take someone else out or simply not show up. One evening when we were sitting on the grass in my front yard, he told me he thought he might be a homosexual. I knew not how to respond to this. I was not aware of my feelings about homosexuality. I didn't ask him anything about it, how he knew, what its implications were for our relationship. I wanted us to have sex (we never did). I imagined a life together with him.

At our senior banquet he declared to me, "You will be my wife." Like an order. But during the summer after graduation I heard that he was seeing another girl, actually a fairly good friend of mine. I was devastated. I asked my friend Louise Munson to help me. We ceremonially burned all his letters to me, and then took his bright, clear, abstract paintings off the wall of my practice room (a 7x7x7 former coal cellar) and marched over to my rival's house. She answered the door. I knew Bob was inside. I just handed the pictures to her and left.

We were not in any contact after that, and went off to our separate colleges. The following summer, when I was going to the UW summer school and living in a co-op dorm, Bob dropped by to see me once, and we had a friendly chat. That was the last time I ever saw him. Several years later he called my parents and told them that he had valued our relationship, that I had been a good influence in his life, that he appreciated the warmth of our love. He also told them that he had kept a promise we had made to each other that we would never vote for the presidential nominee of either major party.

Even after I was married, I kept thinking about Bob, reliving so many things. On a visit to my parents in Madison, around 1960, I heard that Bob had married, that it had been disaster, that he had worked making window displays for a department store, and that he had committed suicide. Thinking of his sad life still brings me to tears, and I keep him in my prayers.

I did have some good girlfriends, without whom I would not have survived. My best friend was Helen Bryan (now Helen Smith of Toronto). Her father was a professor of botany, her mother a lovely, genteel woman who grew up in the South. She made their bread, had a sewing room, and had strong literary interests. The family was Presbyterian and politically conservative. Helen and I shared our inmost thoughts, our diaries, our loves and likes and dislikes. She was amazing in her literary knowledge and sense of humor.

We drifted apart after I became conscious of being a radical and a bohemian, and after she left for her junior and senior years to attend a girls' boarding school in the East, where they translated fifty lines of Virgil a day, to our twenty.

I had good musical friends, too, especially Eva Perlman, a cellist, whose father, Selig, was the first Jewish professor in the economics department at UW and a friend of my father. He was a brilliant and famous economics and labor historian. Now, I would love to be able to talk with him about his difficult and fascinating life as an immigrant from Poland. Then, I knew him as a kind man who, like my father, rose early and prepared breakfast for the family, and who walked me home if it was dark when I left the Perlman house. Mrs. Perlman would bring cookies and milk upstairs for us when Eva and I were playing music together.

Another good friend was Marilyn Siker, a pianist whose father owned a furniture store on Capitol Square. Eva told me about some of the Jewish customs, and Marilyn introduced me to matzo. Danny Jahn, also a pianist, and Louise Munson, a fellow student of my teacher, were other good friends. With these friends I played music. With them, I felt comfortable and my real self.

At West High, where I spent grades seven through twelve, most of the kids formed social groupings—we called them "gangs"—arranged in a hierarchy of popularity. I was part of one such group, on the lower end of the hierarchical scale. I was rather a fringe member of the group: we went to school football and basketball games together, preceded by pot-luck suppers at each other's houses; we usually sat together for lunch and took walks afterwards. But where boys were concerned, I was left out.

The girls were mostly from Lutheran or Congregationalist families; one Catholic girl joined us regularly at lunch. I heard talk of Advent and Epiphany, but had no idea what they were; of giving up things for Lent; of singing in church. No real talk about God or Jesus. These girls liked to sing, and in seventh and eighth grade chorus (a required subject) we enjoyed sitting in the back row and singing the bass line. Miss Huxtable, our teacher, did not seem to notice. We sang informally while going places in the car, camp-type songs like "My Gal's a Corker" and "Show Me the Way To Go Home." We also sang rounds: "Dona Nobis Pacem" and "White Coral Bells." We knew how to add harmonies to the songs, which nowadays very few kids can do.

My true friends, however, were the ones with whom I could share my deepest feelings and interests: Helen Bryan and my musical friends. These are the ones who have had a lasting influence on me, and most of us still keep in touch after six decades.

Body Fear

When I was in the eighth grade, my Grandmother Alice came to visit us. In the middle of one night, out of a deep sleep, I heard her calling: "Martha, Martha, go call the police! There's a burglar in the house!" At once I went downstairs and into the back hall where the telephone was. It was pitch dark. I sensed a presence. A man shone a flashlight into my eyes, cut the phone cord, and threw a blanket over my head. Thinking my mother was in her bed in the adjoining sun porch, I tried to scream, but in my terror no sound would come out of my mouth. The man left, saying, "I'm coming back with more men."

Back upstairs, I went into Grandma's room and got into her bed with her. She told me that Dad had left with Mother, who needed to be taken to the hospital. The burglar had told Grandma: "Give me your money." She told him she had none, and that's when she called me. We got up, trembling, and checked downstairs and all around to see what he had taken. Apparently he had been surprised that there were people in the house, having probably seen my parents leave in their car. So his attempts had been thwarted. We put a chair up under the doorknob at the top of the basement stairs, as we had no way of locking that door. We locked ourselves into the upstairs bathroom, fearing the burglar would really return with more men.

Soon we were more scared than ever to hear that someone was trying to open that door at the top of the basement stairs. Then we heard footsteps coming up the stairs to where we were. It turned out to be my father, who immediately called the police. He must have had to rouse our next-door neighbors to do this, since our line had been cut.

This story came out in the morning papers. I was famous at school that day. For months afterwards, at night I would see visions of the bright light of the flashlight shining into my eyes, and I felt my bed tremble as if someone under it was shaking it.

It was only decades later, during my religious formation at the Abbey of Regina Laudis, that I came to appreciate the seriousness of that burglar experience, possibly as important as my mother's accident while pregnant with me, and my sister's unpredictable violence, in causing the deep fear I have of anyone coming too close to me, or of any violence to my body.

Politics and Religion

In the eighth grade, I already considered myself a radical. I thought, for one thing, that the discrepancy in incomes should be wiped out, and that no one should be allowed to earn more than $10,000 a year. I was anti-religious at this time. My parents made me attend the Unitarian Sunday school along with Eloise Barton, my second best friend, the daughter of good faculty friends of my parents; and Tommy Groves, another faculty child, who came from a Quaker family. We three were the class. We pretended not to like it, but underneath, I think we did. I remember little about the class itself, but I did like the teacher, Mr. Taliafero. What I really enjoyed about Sunday school was that we joined the adults after our class and got to sing some good old traditional Protestant hymns with Unitarian words.

I actually learned something about Christianity from my mother. She thought, in Unitarian fashion, that Jesus was simply an exceptionally good man. She disapproved of mainstream churches, having observed the hypocrisy of the many so-called Christians who did not behave as such, businessmen who were pious on Sunday and cheated people the rest of the week. But she had very high ideals of self-sacrifice, and of a just distribution of goods. It was from her that I first heard the Communist motto: "From each according to his ability, to each according to his need." This corresponds exactly to the description of the early Christian community in *Acts* chapter 4, but I did not know that then.

Later, in senior high, my mind was seething with questions about life, the universe, justice, my own identity. I was not thinking, really, about God; but I was deeply concerned with the matter of infinity. I could not comprehend it. Yes, in abstract numbers: we can always add "one" to any number. But in terms of time or space, I could not imagine either that there was a beginning and an end, or that there was no beginning and no end. Was the universe created out of nothing? How could that be? But if it was created out of something, how did *that* something come to be? I wrestled with this for a long time, talking with friends about it. I never did come to a conclusion. I still cannot imagine infinity, or its opposite. But I no longer worry about it. I know that God has it figured out and I do not need to understand.

My violin friend, Louise Munson, tried without success to convince me of the miracles of Jesus. Though my thoughts on religion were not at all developed in my Madison years, I did have a strong curiosity about the Catholic Church. My beloved violin teacher, Marie Endres, was Catholic, and I would try to get her to talk to me about her faith at our lessons, but she was very professional and would not get involved. She directed the choir at her church. In my junior year I went to Midnight Mass on Christmas Eve to hear her choir and orchestra. In my senior year I played in that orchestra and afterwards went to the home of an older student of Miss Endres, also a Catholic, for a little party. My parents highly disapproved of my not staying home on Christmas Eve.

My parents and most of their friends were very suspicious of Catholics. I had the impression that one could not be both a good scholar and a Catholic. Catholics believed in the "supernatural," and that was a bad word in my parents' minds, equivalent to "superstitious." I could hardly believe it when I discovered that Haydn and Mozart had been Catholics. How could they be such great composers and be Catholic? Yet Teacher (as many of Miss Endres's students called her) was obviously a highly intelligent and good person. Her sister Olive, who taught piano, also impressed me tremendously. The Endres sisters were simply intelligent, gifted women, as were many of the women I knew. But nuns and priests, who in those days always wore their clerical clothes or religious habits, seemed mysterious, exotic creatures. Once when I was younger, maybe ten, I was hanging onto a strap on a packed bus on the way home from my lesson, violin case in my free hand, and a nun, sitting on an aisle seat, invited me to sit on her lap, which I did. It turned out she was a good friend of my teacher. Thus, in many little ways, the seeds of interest in the Church were planted.

During the later high school years I became increasingly interested in politics, not in the sense of elections or current events, but in a desire for a more just and peaceful world. When the school had mock elections, Bob and I supported Norman Thomas, the moderate socialist candidate for president. I was thrilled by the famous and eloquent words of Eugene V. Debs, founder of the Socialist Party in America:

"Years ago I recognized my kinship with all living beings, and I made up my mind that I was not one bit better than the meanest on earth. I said then, and I say now, that while there is a lower class, I am in it, and while there is a criminal element, I am of it, and while there is a soul in prison, I am not free."[8]

But being a Norman Thomas socialist was hardly a radical stance. The radical side of my nature came out in my playing the role of Being a Bohemian. This I did not alone but with two friends, Jo and Bourtai, who were virtual nonentities in West High's social structure, but very interesting people. They were involved with modern art and poetry, and were friends of the surrealist painter Marshall Glazer, for whom they posed, much to the distress of Bourtai's mother. Glazer depicted Jo as a monkey and Bourtai as a lion, and I did indeed see a resemblance. Through Jo and Bourtai I heard about Ezra Pound, John Cage, and others in the avant-garde. Primarily, though, bohemianism meant for me a lifestyle. We sought to emulate the stereotype of the starving artist in a garret, totally impractical and unconcerned with middle-class values. We imagined a future of living together in the dark red Victorian house next door to my family home on Ely Place. It had an enticing tower with round rooms on three levels. We had no plan about how to get money, but we did know what we wanted to do with it when it magically appeared: each of us would put whatever earnings we had into what we called a Communist Money Pot. We would devote ourselves to Art: I to music, Jo and Bourtai to poetry.

The Violin

These were the years when I became seriously devoted to music and the violin. In my senior year I obtained permission from school to attend classes only half a day so that I could practice three hours daily. I came to school in the afternoon on the days when there were orchestra rehearsals. I also played in the Madison String Orchestra run by my violin teacher, which met on Saturday afternoons. Miss Endres had built a very good string orchestra, and her choice of music was admirable. She included many works by contemporary composers such as Ernest Bloch, David Diamond, Samuel Barber, Percy Grainger, and Vaughan Williams, in addition to Baroque, classical, and romantic composers.

In addition, I played in the Madison Civic Symphony Orchestra, which met one evening a week, and in a trio with two boys about my age, Danny Jahn and Jerry Fox. My piano friend Marilyn and I spent many pleasant hours working on pieces that I was studying, and sight-reading other pieces. I made a little money as a soloist—people would call the Wisconsin School of Music to hire someone to play at events—and with the trio.

In my fifteenth summer I was introduced to Jean Chan, a girl my age and an excellent pianist. Her father, W. T. Chan, was a Dartmouth professor of Chinese philosophy and culture. Jean and I had wonderful times for the next few years, playing together and listening to music in the record store. She and one of her friends, Patsy McKenna, introduced me to singing rounds, especially Elizabethan ones. From this experience I gained a lasting love of Elizabethan music. Through Jean I was invited to music sessions at the home of the Ballard family in Norwich, Vermont. We played a lot of chamber music, and sang. I remember singing Kodaly's *Te Deum* there. Mrs. Ballard also invited Jean and me to a week or more at the Tanglewood Festival in the Berkshires, where they had a second house.

Here we gathered around their picnic table after breakfast singing Palestrina[9] and Elizabethan madrigals. What a discovery!! I wrote to Teacher: "I have discovered a wonderful composer named Palestrina. Have you heard of him?" At the Tanglewood Festival concerts I was introduced to many other great works of music. The Ballards were exemplary music lovers. They had the scores of the works they would be hearing at the Festival, and would study them in advance of the concerts.

I observed that I went through alternating phases. One phase was a taking-in, absorbing phase; the other was a phase of creative output. I called these phases "The Muse of Apollo" and "The Life of the Single Purpose," which meant, I think, total dedication to the violin. Louise Munson introduced me to the pleasures of oil painting, and one that I did illustrates The Life of the Single Purpose. I painted myself wearing shorts (!), standing on top of a pile of discarded Material Possessions—jewelry, books, clothes—holding my violin and gazing nobly into the distant future. For some strange reason my parents put this painting over the mantelpiece, replacing a large stylized picture of Indians on horseback chasing buffaloes. I think, and hope, it did not stay there for long.

Flint Farm

Even during the war, we spent all summers but one at Flint Farm. Then, and for much of my adult life, our summers there were my refuge. I spent many hours alone, exploring the woods, looking for springs and ruins of old apple orchards, old cellar holes, crumbled stone walls and other signs of human habitation, keenly aware that it was probably not possible to step anywhere that had not been stepped on by others who came before me. I remember scrambling through brush to get to the hidden Trout Pond; or, several times, taking a route in the saddle between Winslow Ledge and Holt's Ledge looking for traces of an old cemetery in Tinkhamtown, a remote and short-lived settlement of a few families during the Civil War—and finding a rusted old stove, some apple and lilac trees, some roses, but no trace of the reputed cemetery; often getting lost, but always finding my way back; lying on grass or moss and looking up through the trees, relishing the green of the trees against the clear blue of the sky; listening to the hum of bees, the crickets, the birds; trying, many times, to follow the little stream on our land leading to Grant Brook, but never finding the connection because the heavy brush and swampy areas defeated my attempt; lying under the tamarack tree by the house with our cocker spaniel, Brownie, who I felt was the only one in the world who really understood me, my only solace in the lonely, troubled times of adolescence.

Dad, having spent the summers of his youth in Vermont, was deeply attached to the land of northern New England. As soon as we arrived in Lyme Center each year, even in his eighties, he would immediately go out to cut brush. He loved the open meadows, and struggled year after year to keep them from growing into brush, then shrubs, then woods. It was a losing battle, but he kept trying. He was always anxious for our neighbor, Charlie Clark, to come and cut our shrinking hay fields. He and Mother would always start a flower garden, with zinnias, phlox, peonies, orange day lilies, lilacs. Dad was the most un-mechanical person I have ever known. He had to lug his heavy typewriter to the store to have them change the ribbon, because he could not figure out how to do it. In spite of his deficient mechanical ability he taught me, in those summers, two of the most useful skills in life: driving and typing.

Mother, on the other hand, believed that women could be as competent mechanically as most men. She learned, and taught me, the proper use of various household tools. In Madison she took a course in cabinet making at the Vocational School and made for us a cherry cabinet to hold our record player and records. She was as devoted to the flower garden as Dad was. She also was fascinated by wild flowers and plants. She was delighted to find watercress and wild mint in our little stream. In our first years, she loved to go to the frequent auctions, taking Nancy and me, and acquiring all sorts of household items: old hand-carved wooden bowls for salads, beds with the original rope holes in the sides, antique sets of dishes. After I learned to drive, she and I loved to explore old dirt roads that usually winded up hills and became impassible. We had no destination in mind. We took whatever turns looked interesting. We always got lost; we always somehow found our way home.

Dad went to Hanover nearly every day to work on his research at the beautiful Baker Library at Dartmouth. But sometimes on what we called a Perfect Mountain Day, we would quickly pack a picnic lunch and take off for some medium-sized mountain in either the White Mountains in New Hampshire or the Green Mountains in Vermont. On the way up Dad would sing in his wonderful loud voice: "Just a Song at Twilight," "Clementine," and many other songs. Sometimes these trips would be planned in advance and we would be with other families.

One fine day I took off alone to climb Holt's Ledge, at the summit of which was a wide view. I took with me a sketchbook to draw wild flowers. I picked and ate lots of wild blueberries. I climbed, I rested, I walked. It was a blissful day. I took as much time as I wanted. I had no watch and no deadline, or so I thought. I had told my parents where I was going, but when I arrived home, tired and happy, I found that my parents had been terribly worried about me, fearing some drastic circumstance. They had even called the State Police. Another manifestation of my independent streak.

During the summer after I graduated from West High, my sister Nancy got engaged. We were all happy for her and hoped for the best. She had met Phil at a nearby mental hospital, where they were both working. He was short, as was Nancy, and he seemed like a nice and decent fellow.

This is all I need to say about my teen years. This phase of my life ended a week before I left for college, when our dear Brownie died of a heart attack. She had been with us since I was four years old. I took the train to Oberlin, never again to live at home. Was I sad? No. I was thinking only of the adventure that was ahead. Did I have any idea that my parents might be sad? No.

Three

OBERLIN: 1949-1955

Security, certitude, and peace do not lead to discoveries.

—Carl Jung

Suddenly thrust into the intellectual, musical, and emotional intensity of Oberlin, I entered six years of excitement, elation, depression, self-searching, and questioning. Until then my life had seemed to develop at a steady pace. Now the pace abruptly speeded up.

As I read the informational material I received in advance from Oberlin, I noticed that in the dorms for freshman women, the lights were turned out at 10:30. I wondered how I could possibly stay up that late, for I was used to going to bed around nine. The girls from New York and Chicago, on the other hand, complained bitterly about this "early" curfew. The Oberlin of that day would not be recognizable to the students there now. Freshman women had to be in by 8:30 P.M., although we could get special permission to stay out until 10:00 to study in the library or practice in the Conservatory.

Dorms were segregated by sex, but all the dining halls were in the women's dorms, where the men came to eat and hang out in the parlor before and after meals, to talk, sing around the piano, play bridge. We sat at round tables for eight and were served by waiters, male students who had work jobs. A chaplain said grace before each meal. Women were required to wear stockings and high heels at dinner, for me an extremely onerous requirement; men wore coats and ties. Liquor, cars, and fraternities and sororities were not allowed. These restrictions did not bother me; in fact I was happy that there were no fraternities or sororities. If two students got married without the permission of their parents and of the College, they were immediately expelled.

What drew me to Oberlin was the coexistence of the College of Liberal Arts and the Conservatory of Music. I wanted both. You could take five years and get two degrees, a B.A. and a B.Mus. But it took me five years to get only one degree, a B.A. with a major in music. My parents insisted that I start out in the College for at least a year. Then I spent two years in the Conservatory and two more years back in the College, graduating in 1954. My sixth year in Oberlin was spent working and taking some music education courses.

Academic life in my first year was unexciting, for I had to take remedial and required courses that were pretty much like what I had had in high school. I signed up for violin lessons but quickly dropped that because there was simply no time for practicing. I was, however, in the orchestra.

In that first year I was full of the gung-ho school spirit thing. I learned the school songs, took part in the various social activities and organized relationships offered, and I did not miss home. Far from being a bohemian, I was into my "Adapt to My Social Environment" mode. It was a chance for a new start. Maybe I would fit in better than I had in high school; maybe I would have dates. Certainly I would, for a change, be respected for being a good student. In my first year I did have a few dates, but none of them developed into the deeper relationship I so craved. After that year I had very lonely Saturday nights. I almost always had good female friends, though, and those friendships sustained me.

In the fall of my first year at Oberlin my sister and Phil were married. In January of my sophomore year Nancy gave birth to a baby boy. Phil had left her. He had epilepsy but had not told her before they were married. Nancy could not cope with being a single mother, and in the freezing weather took the baby, Jonathan, and left him on the doorstep of an academic couple in our neighborhood, friends of our parents. Mother wanted to raise the child but, probably because of her ill health and her age, the court gave custody of Jonathan to Phil's parents in Rockford, Illinois. They and Phil raised him until he was in his teens, after which a fundamentalist Christian family took him in. He had, and still has, a disability that prevents him from being able to have a regular job.

During my years at Oberlin, two events dominated the news: the Korean War, which broke out in my sophomore year, and McCarthyism. The latter affected my life tremendously. Joseph McCarthy, Senator from Wisconsin, suspected Communists under every bed. Everyone who had spoken out for peace, for the end of racial segregation, or for civil liberties, became suspect. Professors were fired. Hollywood blacklisted actors and writers. My mother went door to door, even into bars and barbershops, collecting signatures for the "Joe Must Go" campaign to recall McCarthy from the Senate.

In my sophomore year my father was invited to present a paper in Munich. It was a great chance for my mother and me to go to Germany with him—my first trip to Europe. Reservations for the boat were made. Then suddenly the State Department took away my father's passport on the grounds that he had signed the Stockholm Peace Petition, which was suspected of being Communist-inspired. That was the end of the German trip. As for the Korean War, it affected our lives very little compared to World War II, except that a very nice seventeen-year-old boy, a neighbor of ours in Lyme Center, joined the Army and was killed in Korea.

The Violin Crisis

After my freshman year, I changed to the Conservatory for two years, then back to the College for two more years, receiving my B.A. in 1954. During my two Conservatory years I always took one interesting College course, and most of the College courses I took, or audited, opened up a new world. I am forever grateful for that good education. However, the most important aspect of my Oberlin period was the search for identity, for my purpose in life. I searched, I explored, but I did not find. The search was a mere beginning.

My relationship to the violin became complicated. If I was indeed to pursue a career in music, it was a serious mistake to drop out of violin lessons right at the start. Why did I quit? I told myself it was for lack of time. But many College students managed to take private lessons on top of a full academic load. The deeper reason was that I felt threatened by the prospect of having a new teacher. I was afraid he would change the way I did things, thus challenging the validity of the teaching of my beloved Marie Endres. I did not yet understand that there are many good ways of playing the violin, and that there would be no threat in seeing what I could learn from other teachers. I did stay in the orchestra, though, and that was a priceless experience. I was placed in the fourth desk of the first violin section, next to a classmate, Dick Skerlong, who later became the principal violist of the Seattle Symphony. It was unusual for freshmen to have such a good place in the section.

In the second year, when I transferred to the Conservatory, I did have a new teacher, new for me and new to Oberlin: Nathan Gottschalk. I had two years of study with him. He did indeed want me to change many things, and he did do things differently from Marie. For example, she had told me in detail what fingerings and bowings to use, whereas Nathan encouraged me to figure these out for myself, though not hesitating to advise and guide me. He wanted to change the way I held the bow, how I did vibrato, and so on. He was an excellent musician and teacher, and a lovable man. He was good to his students, inviting groups of us to his home after one of us played in a recital. He, his wife Polly, and their two children kindly took care of my pet turtle, Small, whom he always called "Mr. Small," when I was away. But he did not give me much encouragement. Once I played first violin in a quintet by Boccherini in Elyria, a nearby town. He was there, but later said not a word about it. I asked him if he had any criticism about my playing in that performance. Was there anything I could have done better? He said no. But since I had to ask, this was small comfort.

After my first performance in a Student Recital, in which I played a Handel sonata, I received great comfort from the fact that George Trautwein, the concertmaster, knocked on the door of my practice room one day and told me my performance had been very good. I knew it was, too. It was recorded on a twelve-inch vinyl record, which I later transferred to a cassette tape. I have listened to it recently and am very pleased with my playing. I had a tremendous crush on George. When he gave me that compliment, I was very flustered and instead of saying simply, "Thank you," I felt my whole body turn to jelly, and all I could manage to say was, "Really?" George had a girlfriend and so was not available.

It was a luxury to be able to practice three hours a day on the violin and one hour on the piano, have lessons in these and in chamber music, study Theory and Music History, and get academic credit for all this. The most exciting thing, I found, was Music History, and in my third year, the study of counterpoint. I plunged into the hitherto unknown world of early music, of thinking about styles, how and why they changed from one generation to another; of new sounds, new approaches to rhythm. I fell in love with Elizabethan and Jacobean music, writing a paper for counterpoint class on William Byrd, and in an independent study I delved into English music for viols in the seventeenth century. I continued to ponder, as I had already begun to do in high school, the place of musicians in society.

But in those Conservatory years my relationship with the violin grew more and more complex. I had come to Oberlin thinking I was a terrific violin player. I had secret fantasies of being really great. Now, surrounded by violinists my own age, so many of whom played better than I, I had to confront a different reality. Why, in the Chamber Music course, was I at first assigned to play with very good players, and then more and more with less good ones? Why, when I started out in the orchestra with the glorious position of fourth desk first violin, did I get moved further back and finally to the first desk of the second violins (but not the section leader)?

The decisive shock came at the end of my junior year, when each violin major had to play before a faculty committee. My performance (I think it was the Bruch Concerto) merited only a C. How could I possibly consider a career in music, especially violin, under these circumstances?

Yet I persevered. I continued to work very hard and seriously on the violin. But all along, I also wanted to live a full life. These two desires seemed in conflict. I felt very alone in the Conservatory. I had the impression that my fellow students cared only about technical prowess on their instruments, that they had no concern, not only for the other arts, for history, for the world, but no real interest even in Music History or Theory, taking these only because they were required. There must have been some students who shared my interests, but I did not find them.

One glorious spring day, when all was beautiful, all the colors, scents, and sounds of nature making it imperative to be outdoors, I lay in the sun with some of my girlfriends and luxuriated in the warmth. Shortly after, I happened to ask my classmate Elaine Lee, who was now concertmaster of the orchestra, had she gotten out into the sun? Her reply was no, she had to practice. At that moment I knew that I did not want the violin to swallow up my life. In the summer of my third year of college, after that C, this conflict came to a head, and the independent, rebellious side of my nature took over. I had arranged to attend a music camp in Maine, to study intensively with Nathan Gottschalk in preparation for my senior recital. I was with my parents at Flint Farm when I received the welcoming material for the camp. I resented the fact that we had to have a white dress for performances, something I had no idea how to find in that rural area; and I was even more upset that attendance at chapel services was required. On top of this, I was absolutely furious that my parents, who were about to leave for a summer in England, would not let me use the car during their absence. I was twenty years old, and everyone was treating me like a child.

So as soon as my parents left, I sent a telegram to the camp saying that I could not come because of illness. At the same time I wrote to Mr. Gottschalk with the real reasons: I was discouraged about my ability to play the violin; also I yearned to spend more time on other kinds of music. I wanted to discover jazz and learn more about folk music and ethnic music. In those days a conservatory of music had nothing to do with any non-classical music. Nathan wrote me back a wonderful letter, which said, among other things, that anyone who wanted to be a violinist would have to go at it "like a bat out of hell."

I went over to Thetford, Vermont, to the home of the Hunter family, a dear family that had always been our closest friends. The father, Louis, and my father were grad students together at Harvard, and each was best man at the other's wedding. Trixie, his wife, I adored. She offered a kind of maternal acceptance of me that I never felt I had from my mother. Their daughters, Jean and Grenelle, were around my age and like cousins. I brought with me my recently purchased ten-dollar guitar from Sears, and Trixie helped me make a bag for it out of grey denim. My plan was to go down to Cambridge, where I had spent a very pleasant summer the previous year at Harvard summer school. But this time I would find a job and experience living on my own for the first time. I took the guitar with me, but not the violin.

In Cambridge I found a room with kitchen privileges, and through an employment agency, a job in the lab of the Polaroid Corporation, still run by Dr. Land, its founder. I was thrilled to be part of the working class, to surge into this plant with hordes of others at 8:00 A.M. However, after a mere two weeks, I found that I would not be able to save any money, since after deductions for income tax and payments to the employment agency, there was just enough to cover the necessities. A fellow worker suggested I go to Richard's Drive-In, where you could make good money on tips. I did that, working the six P.M. to two A.M. shift. It was one of the most miserable experiences I have ever had, but at least I did end up with some extra money.

In my spare time, I taught myself to play the guitar, enough to accompany the folk songs I already knew, and got a ten-inch record of Huddie Ledbetter, usually known as Lead Belly. This recording nourished my growing interest in the blues and early jazz.

During this summer I wrote to the dean of the Conservatory, David Robertson, who was also conductor of the orchestra, asking if I could change my major from violin to music history. No such major was offered at that time. He replied in the negative, writing that I might consider going into musicology after graduation, but for this, he thought, the best preparation would be to get a good grounding on the violin.

Not surprisingly, I had to face deeply disapproving parents when I joined them in New Hampshire.

When I got back to Oberlin, I went to see Dean Robertson and asked him why I had been "demoted" in the orchestra, and why I kept being placed with less skilled players in chamber music. I don't remember exactly what he said, but I think the gist of it was that I should not take this personally. Whatever he said, I was not satisfied. He did not tell me I was great.

After just a week or two, just in time, I switched to the College. I had far more credits in music than were allowed for a B.A. with a music major, so now I needed two years in the College and would graduate a year later than I had planned.

This conflict about the violin, and about my relationship to music, and how it all related to opposite self-evaluations as either a potentially wonderful musician or a failure, was not and could not be resolved at this time. I just lived with it. It was not until I had gone through many years in religious life that I came to be at peace about music and the violin. But that is a later part of my story.

Marty, Militant Atheist

In the Oberlin of my time, nicknames were the fashion. My classmates called me Marty, and this name stuck with me my entire six years at Oberlin. In my conformist and school-spirit mode, I did not protest.

Oberlin College was founded in 1833 by Evangelicals during the Second Great Awakening, the evangelical fervor that seized America in the early nineteenth century. The college was infused with a missionary fervor and a desire to reform society. Women and blacks were part of the student body from the beginning. Even in my time, large numbers of students were children of missionaries. Religious matters were a common topic of conversation among students. It was beyond me to understand why Oberlin had a "Religious Emphasis Week." I thought there was already too much emphasis on religion. A course in religion was among the requirements for the B.A. I chose Philosophy of Religion, taught by an atheist. I was not convinced by Aquinas' five proofs of the existence of God.

It is impossible for me now to recapture how it felt not to have faith, not to believe in God, or even in a vague Higher Power. I was shocked when, a few years ago, Helen Weaver, a former roommate, told me that I had put up a sign on my door stating: "There is no God." I had to believe it when she allowed me to read the letters I had written to her that she had saved. On one, a postcard, I saw the incriminating deed reported in my very own handwriting.

Was I truly a Militant Atheist, then, as I always tell people I was? Did I really go around arguing with believers, proudly proclaiming my unbelief? I can't remember doing so, but of course that postcard to Helen proves that I cannot trust my memory.

God had a way of reaching me through all my denial. Music was His way. As we played in the orchestra for the great choral works, Handel's *Messiah,* Bach's *Mass in B Minor,* and especially his *Saint Matthew Passion,* my disbelief was swept away, albeit temporarily: in the *Messiah,* "Surely He has borne our grief"; in the Mass, "Crucifixus" and "Resurrexit." And in the *Passion,* I remember clearly being overtaken by the words of Christ at the Last Supper:

> Da sie aber assen, nahm Jesus das Brot, dankete und brach's und gab's den Jüngern und sprach: "Nehmet, esset, das ist mein Leib."
> Und er nahm den Kelch und dankte, gab ihnen den und sprach:
> "Trinket alle daraus; da ist mein Blut des neuen Testaments, welches vergossen wird für viele zur Vergebung der Sünden. Ich sage euch: Ich werde von nun an nicht mehr von diesem Gawaechs des Weinstocks trinken bis an den Tag, da ich's neu trinken werde mit euch in meines Vaters Reich."

> But when they had eaten, Jesus took bread, gave thanks and broke it, and gave it to his disciples, saying:
> "Take, eat, this is my Body."
> And he took the cup and, giving thanks, he gave it to them, saying:
> "Drink, all of you, from this; this is my Blood of the New Testament, which has been poured out here for many in remission of their sins. I say to you: I shall from this moment forth no more drink from this the fruit of the grapevine until the day when I shall drink it anew with you in my Father's kingdom."

While these words were being sung, I believed them.

During these years I continued to consider myself a socialist, but I did not become politically active until I met Tim.

Men

Before I met Tim, my future husband, I had no serious relationships with men at Oberlin. But in Madison, at home for the Christmas vacation my freshman year, I went to a New Year's Eve party given by the University's Channing Club, the Unitarian organization for college students. There I met Bert. He was "old," twenty-three to my eighteen, and a grad student in chemistry. At some point Handel's *Messiah* was put on the record player. Side by side, lying (chastely) on the floor in the darkness, we listened to the whole thing. We then went to my home, where Bert met my parents and we had breakfast.

Back at Oberlin, Bert called me frequently. The telephone was in the hall of our dorm, so there was no privacy, and girls would gather around listening to my half of the conversation. That following summer I went to summer school at the University of Wisconsin in Madison, taking a wonderful course in Greek life and literature. I studied violin with Marie Endres at her summer cottage on the lake in Beaver Dam, going there weekly with a few other students, and practicing three hours a day.

Most of the rest of the time I spent with Bert. My parents were to be at Flint Farm for the summer. They feared that with Bert I would lapse into moral turpitude, but these fears were groundless. Bert and I had no explicit commitment to one another, and somehow I knew that he was not the one I wanted to spend my life with.

In the following year when I was home for spring vacation, one of my father's graduate students (I'll call him Max) came over for supper. In the living room after supper, I got out my guitar and played and sang, among other things, a few good old evangelical songs from my mother's (and probably *her* mother's) book, *Songs of Evangelism*: "Throw out the Lifeline," "Love Lifted Me," and others. Max knew these, too, and joined in with relish. It was a pleasant evening. Soon after, he called and invited me to a square dance at the Channing Club. The rest of that vacation, and then later when I was back in Madison for a couple of weeks before leaving for New Hampshire with my parents, Max and I spent all our time together. We talked and talked. He felt a bit strange about our relationship, since he was my father's student. He came to visit me while I was at Flint Farm with my parents. This was the summer I fled to Cambridge to find a job, and while I was in Cambridge we wrote numerous long letters to each other. We lived in the present, and I doubt that we spoke of possibly spending our lives together. But I think it was in both of our minds.

At Oberlin for my fourth year, just after the violin crisis had come to a head and I had left the Conservatory, I lived in one of the new co-op dorms, Pyle Inn. I believed strongly in the co-op ideal, and here was a chance to live it. We, the female residents and the male diners, decided everything democratically in interminable weekly house meetings. They were endless because there were Quakers, who believed everything should be decided by consensus, and Libertarians, who opposed delegating any decisions to committees or individuals. By doing all of the work ourselves, aside from a hired cook, we saved considerably on our living expenses.

I liked the social life. We did not depend on dates. We could always find company, male and female, in the living room of an evening or weekend. One day I brought down my ten-inch LP of Jelly Roll Morton, which I had purchased recently in my early attempts to discover the blues. A boy named Tim came over to listen, and told me that HE had *ten* twelve-inch LPs of Jelly Roll Morton.

Tim Wohlforth, a year younger than I, was notorious on campus, being one of the only two students with a beard. That reddish beard signaled him out right away as a rebel, and this was definitely appealing to me. I was drawn to him because of his interest in early jazz and ethnic music, as well as folk and classical music. Once I asked him if I could borrow his two-disc set of Folkways LPs, *Music of the World's Peoples*. I listened to it while I was ironing my clothes. He had built his own Hi-Fi set from a kit, a feat that I greatly admired.

Tim was a pacifist, having gone to Friends schools. He was majoring in anthropology. He disliked the "stones and bones" aspect of anthropology, but was fascinated by cultures—how people lived and thought. He had a truly brilliant mind, but was not disciplined in work habits: couldn't spell, didn't write well, couldn't type, handwriting totally illegible. He didn't bother with details like getting medical excuses when he was sick. That undisciplined part of him bothered me exceedingly, but I rationalized and minimized it.

He was gentle, though manly in his appearance. I was attracted by his good looks and his many skills: sailing, car and Hi-Fi repair. I loved that he was sensitive to poetry and music. He didn't know much about classical music, but was interested in it and wanted to learn more about it.

He knew about all the little sectarian left-wing political parties in New York City, closely following their election results. We very quickly established a close relationship. The first thing we did together was to go to Elyria with a busload of college students to hear presidential candidate Adlai Stevenson speak from the back of a train. Our first real "date" was to hop onto his motor scooter and head for Cleveland to hear Vincent Hallinan, the Progressive Party candidate for president, speak. But the scooter quickly broke down. We tried to thumb a ride, but in those days no one wanted to pick up a guy with a beard. We just spent the evening talking.

What happened to Max? Clearly in my mind, Tim had taken his place and soon had a larger place in my life than Max had ever had. I

Tim and I in front of Pyle Inn Co-op, 1952.

wrote him and told him about Tim. But he must have been devastated, for he did not answer my letter.

Soon after meeting Tim, I wrote my parents that I had met a "nice boy." My next letter to them, two weeks later, announced that Tim and I were getting married at Thanksgiving. Such naïveté, such a lack of tact and diplomacy, such insensitivity to my parents' feelings, seem incomprehensible to me now. I was twenty, Tim was nineteen. My parents were angry and upset. They insisted that we wait until June to get married, and that I come home for Christmas. I insisted that Tim come with me, to which they acquiesced. We planned to spend a week with them and then head back to Tim's parents' home in Ridgefield, Connecticut.

The visit to Madison was a total disaster. I am deeply ashamed of my behavior at that time. Tim and I were totally absorbed in ourselves, and made no effort to appease my parents. Tim argued with my father constantly. We did not cooperate in my mother's beloved Christmas customs. My mother was deeply disappointed that Tim showed no interest in some relics of my past, including a pair of ox eyes she had lovingly procured for me from the butcher. I had dissected them and preserved them in formaldehyde. Mother saw this lack of interest as a bad sign for our future, and now I see that she was right. Dad told me I'd better prepare myself for a career, because Tim would never be able to support me.

Worst of all, we decided to leave earlier for Ridgefield than planned, but prepared a secret escape, knowing that my parents would not let us go. We tied sheets together, lowered ourselves out my second-storey window, suitcases in hand, and went downtown to the bus station. Somehow Dad found out where we were and appeared just as we were about to board the bus. He was livid. I had never seen him so angry, and had never believed this kind and gentle man *could* be so angry.

A day or two later, just as we were about to leave, Mother fell on the ice outside the house. Tim, whose mother had been through psychoanalysis, was convinced that Mother fell as an unconscious attempt to keep me from leaving. I went along with Tim. We left, despite the beseeching of my father. Thank God my Swiss cousin Eugen, who was in Madison at the time, was able to help care for Mother. I felt completely self-righteous. The guilty feelings came much later.

What does this childish rebellion have to do with the main thrust of my life story, namely my religious conversion? It is an important part of my self-discovery. It shows me how totally self-centered I was, how little I attempted to understand my parents. For example, in my first summer in Cambridge, when I was at Harvard summer school, Mother had a lump removed from her neck at Massachusetts General Hospital. I rode out there every day, a long Metro ride, to see her. The day of the surgery she was naturally very groggy. Nevertheless, without a thought, I read aloud to her a paper I had written for one of my courses. Years later she had a mastectomy, and I had no clue at all as to what she must be going through. True, I was living at some distance from her; and true, no one can understand what a woman is going through with breast cancer unless she too has had that experience. Still, could I not have been more supportive of her?

It has taken decades for me to be at peace with the many ways I hurt my parents and others. This process of letting go of shame, while acknowledging my guilt, belongs much later in my story.

In this rebellion, I was at the same time conforming: I was adapting to Tim, believing that I agreed with him on all important things, wanting to please him. I was embarrassed by his repeatedly kissing me in public, yet I said nothing. In this I was not being my authentic self. Actually, I had no idea what my authentic self was. About one thing I *was* assertive: after typing one of his papers, written in his impossibly sloppy handwriting, I refused to type for him any more.

That semester, we spent all possible time together. How I managed to get my schoolwork done and maintain my four-point average, I don't know. For his part, Tim flunked out of Oberlin. He missed too many biology labs, among other things. He could have gotten a medical excuse (he had a severe pilonidal cyst at that time), but he did not bother. He failed gym, too, because he simply did not go to that class. He had to spend the

My pre-wedding photo.

second semester at the University of Bridgeport, where he redeemed himself and was allowed back into Oberlin the following year.

On June 10, 1953, about nine months after we decided to get married, our wedding took place at the Unitarian Church in Madison. Nancy came with her second husband, John Holub. They had been married not long before that. John took her to live on a decrepit farm. I don't remember how long they stuck it out, but I do remember that Nancy was unhappy and isolated and complained that John was abusive. After their divorce my parents helped her to get set up in Chicago with an apartment and a job.

Tim and I wanted to have the traditional service from the Book of Common Prayer, but without any mention of God! How the minister agreed to this, and how he pulled it off, I do not know. My mother wanted us to have a real wedding, with engraved invitations and a reception at our home. I wore a dress with a stole, made out of a beautiful silken sari that Dad had brought back for me from India. We took the train to Chicago, where we tried to hear some jazz that night, but were not accepted at the nightclub because Tim was under age. The next day, another train took us to Boulder, Colorado, where we both went to summer school, interspersed with some nice camping trips in the mountains. We lived in a trailer in Vetsville, the University's housing for veterans. Our rent for the entire summer was $55. The bathrooms and showers were in a communal building, where we also got water to carry to the trailer for cooking.

We were busy with our schoolwork, and with various odd jobs we found to augment our income. I got work cleaning houses, but after seeing a notice asking for someone to pose nude for an art class at the magnificent pay of five dollars an hour, I asked Tim what he thought of my responding to the notice. He encouraged me, saying that I had a great body and he was proud of it and did not mind others seeing it. I was scared, but I went ahead and did it. It was not as bad as I had feared, once I got over the initial hesitation. It was very professional and impersonal, and I was relieved to see that I was not recognizable in the drawings the art students had made.

In walking through Vetsville on the way to school, I noticed through some open front doors that the wives kept their quarters immaculate, and that they had lots of time to chat with each other and play golf. I thought, judgmentally, what an empty life these women seemed to have. One night we returned from a concert to find ourselves locked out of our trailer, a padlock on the door. Was this some kind of a punishment by someone who disapproved of our lifestyle, so different from that of our neighbors? At least there was one kind neighbor who cut the padlock open for us.

Through that summer in the trailer, we continued the custom of reading aloud to each other that we had begun back in Oberlin. We had sat in the lounge in the Men's Building and read *Catcher in the Rye* and the ancient Greek comedy *Lysistrata*, in which the women went on a sex strike to prevent their husbands from going off to war. The strike was successful. Reading this play was an assignment in a wonderful course we were both taking, Classical Literature in Translation, taught by Professor Charles Theophilus Murphy. These two works drew the biggest audience. In our Vetsville trailer we read *Moby Dick*, but the one who was listening often fell asleep.

We bought a 1947 Ford for six hundred dollars to make those camping trips easier. When summer school ended, we made a momentous trip down south to New Orleans, and back to Oberlin.

We loved New Orleans. We loved the architecture, the coffee with chicory in it, the French Quarter. We sought out the places important to the history of jazz. We went to Preservation Hall to hear the music. We went to clubs in the evenings, sitting at the counter, making our beer last as long as possible. Shy though we both were, we went to speak with one of the musicians, who told us that he, as a black man, was not allowed to swim in Lake Pontchartrain. We were sad and angry to hear this.

We followed a street parade for an entire day. The sun was strong, the day very hot, so at one point we went into a corner bar for a nice cold beer. One of the men there said to Tim: "We weren't sure about you. But seeing you follow this parade for hours, and seeing your beard, we decided you are okay." We were delighted at this affirmation.

We spent our two married years at Oberlin moving. In those two years we lived in four places. We were kicked out of our first apartment after just a month because the elderly landlady highly disapproved of our establishing the national headquarters of the National Student Cooperative League (NASCL), with all its files and equipment, in our living room. Tim and I were co-editors of the monthly newspaper of NASCL, and the chairman, who in the eyes of Mrs. Jolly, the landlady, was a suspicious character, was coming and going all the time. We moved into an apartment in a College house, a former dorm, for married couples. We shared the hall, kitchen, and bathroom with another couple. The wife, who worked in the office of the Dean of Women, complained about us to the dean: we washed our dog, Hound Dog, in the bathtub; we did not polish the copper bottoms of our Revere Ware pots and pans; and who knows what other intolerable misdeeds we committed. Again, we were asked to leave.

We then moved to the nearby rural town of Wellington, where we lived in a trailer park. It was a pleasant place, but we were isolated from our Oberlin friends, so for our final year at Oberlin we moved the trailer to Oberlin, to a spot in someone's back yard. That family had a teenage boy who played "Rock Round the Clock" loudly on his radio, which we enjoyed.

I had graduated, but Tim had another year to go. I worked as a salesperson in Bostwick's Store, an old-fashioned dry goods store that sold clothes, linens, fabric, and sewing notions. I envied Tim and our student friends, whom I could sometimes see walking down the street outside, or just hanging around and talking. All day I was on my feet and had to be nice to people, no matter what. In the pre-Christmas season we worked twelve hours a day, six days a week. My pay was seventy-five cents an hour. Under my breath I sang an old Wobbly song, based on "What a Friend we Have in Jesus," called "Dump the Bosses Off Your Back":

> Are you poor, forlorn and weary,
> Are there lots of things you lack?
> Is your life made up of mis'ry,
> Then dump the bosses off your back.
> Is your clothing torn and tattered,
> Are you living in a shack?
> Would you have your troubles scattered,
> Then dump the bosses off your back.

Thus it seemed most desirable and expedient for me to return to student life. I decided to take education courses for the second semester so that I could qualify for teaching strings in high school. My dear parents agreed with this and helped me financially. The ed courses were boring, but I took the greatest pleasure in my musical opportunities. I had private lessons on the cello and the string bass. My bass teacher was Jacques Poselle, first bass of the Cleveland Symphony. I loved him and loved playing the bass. Mr. Poselle told me that if I were a man, he would encourage me to aim for an orchestra position. He told me I took to the bass "like a duck to the water." What balm this was for my wounded ego! Toward the end of that one semester of study, I played bass in the Training Orchestra. This was such fun: I felt as if I were holding up, supporting, the whole orchestra!

Two young men representing the Young Socialist League came to give a lecture on campus and set us on fire. I was already a socialist, but this was a different and more exciting kind of socialism: revolutionary socialism. Tim and I were inspired to establish the Eugene V. Debs Club. Thus began our participation in the radical socialist movement, at a time when socialist organizations were at their lowest point in history, with decreasing numbers and increasing splits into more and more sectarian groups. Yet we had great hope that we could play a part in building a new and more just world.

Four

MARRIAGE, MOTHERHOOD, AND MARXISM NEW YORK 1955-1968

We should never despair even in our darkest hours. We should remember that God is always there, when outward pressure is at its worst, helping us to carry our burdens over the roughest places on our weary road.

—Father Alfred Delp, S.J.

I begin this chapter with trepidation. I am entering the darkest time in my life, though I did not see it that way at the time. It was a time of unreality, denial, falseness. Our children, Carl and Bill, were for me the reality, the truth, and the hope.

Our marriage, our whole lives, became consumed by politics. I pushed music aside for nine years. We came to New York City to be in what was then the center of the radical movement. Radical politics in the fifties consisted of three main groupings: Communism, which saw Stalinist Russia as the progressive force in the world; Democratic Socialism, whose adherents believed that society could be transformed by the democratic process; and Trotskyism, whose followers were anti-Stalinist communists, believing that only a revolution led by a Marxist revolutionary party could bring about a new world. It was this Trotskyist milieu that Tim and I entered. The ins and outs of these groups, with their factions, splits, mergers, and regroupings, are complex and not relevant to my story.[10]

What was the falseness, the denial, the unreality in these groups? First, these little parties (I exclude the Communist Party from my observations, having had no experience in it) had a very inflated sense of their own importance. They extracted high levels of commitment from their members in time, energy, and money. Thus their influence greatly exceeded their numbers. There was a tremendous sense of urgency, as if the revolution was already happening, or would happen imminently. The members were kept busy all the time: attending meetings, taking part in demonstrations and picket lines, distributing leaflets, stuffing envelopes, speaking at street meetings, studying Marxism. The illusion prevailed that WE, our little group, was the most important body of people in the world, and would lead the revolution. We had the right line, the only correct interpretation of the world. In all the socialist groups the members were very verbal. They wrote lengthy documents on all possible "questions:" the Russian Question, the Negro Question, the Woman Question, the Jewish Question, and so on. At any opportunity they would give you the party line, a detailed answer to any "question."

Another way in which the movements were unreal was that they did not respect the uniqueness of each person. We were on the margins of society, yet within those margins there was little tolerance for deviation. At times when there were severe factional struggles within the movement, it was impossible to maintain friendships with people in another faction. There was no explicit rule on the matter, but it was a reality. One could not be at ease, speak freely, with people not on "our side." One young woman, who was a musician and bought a piano, was frowned upon for this "bourgeois" activity. Anyone involved in psychotherapy was likewise castigated as being "bourgeois." Many of the members lived in slums, cold-water flats on the Lower East Side. They ridiculed anyone living more comfortably as "middle class."

The working class was extolled as *the* progressive force in the world. The youth, with their characteristic idealism and dissatisfaction with the world, were courted as potential revolutionaries. Tim and I were among these youth, and Tim, wanting to be part of the working class, shaved his beard and got work at a printing plant. We were not the hairy, scraggly young radicals of the sixties. We wanted to look neat and respectable so as not to stand out in the predominantly socially conservative working class.

We, like so many others, were longing for a place to belong, and for something beyond our ordinary daily lives. The movement gave us this place, as well as the comfort and elation of being a part of something larger than our individual selves. The movement was one of the many false, distorted, and misleading ways in which I, and so many others, sought transcendence.

But from the beginning I was upset by certain things: being required to attend a class for new members that conflicted with the group's evening of Israeli folk dancing, where I would much rather have been. I never accepted the rationale of justifying everything for the sake of the revolution, especially with the fact that Trotsky deserted his wife when he left Russia. Part of me disliked the venom with which people attacked those who disagreed with them; another part of me relished it and could dish it out to others.

Tim, despite his painful shyness, became a fiery and inspirational leader. I often held positions more radical than his, probably because I was not bound by the responsibilities of leadership. For several years Tim and I edited *The Young Socialist*, the monthly paper of the Young Socialist Alliance, and for a few years I was the organizer (chairman) of the New York City branch. I enjoyed my work on the paper, and I thought I did a decent job as the local organizer. Tim and I would talk at length about the movement, the daily minutiae and the larger picture. But Tim became so obsessed with politics that his parents, progressive-leaning suburban writers, could not find any common ground to talk about with him.

Our social lives were almost totally within the movement. We did keep up with some Oberlin friends for a couple of years, and fortunately Tim insisted on keeping Sundays for the family. We often went to Ridgefield, Connecticut to visit Tim's parents, Robert and Mildred Wohlforth. They lived in an historic colonial house with low ceilings, small rooms, and many-paned windows. Bob had for many years been an economist with the Department of Justice, but lost his job in the McCarthy period because he and Mildred moved in progressive literary circles that included Communist sympathizers, and perhaps some real Communists. When Tim would tell people that his father was an "economist in the government," they would often reply: "Oh! A Communist in the government!" Bob then joined the publishing firm Farrar, Straus and Cudahy. Mildred worked as a publicity writer for Planned Parenthood. Both were prolific writers, producing novels and many articles. Mildred had been one of the first "sob sisters," or reporters hired to present the "women's angle." Eleanor Roosevelt was one of the famous people she interviewed. She published a large number of magazine articles, most of which are hilarious, and Bob had a series in *The New Yorker*, "My Nickelodeon Childhood," about the movie theater run by his father in Spring Lake, New Jersey. Years later, when I read their articles aloud to my monastic community, we were all in stitches.

Mildred was a devoted gardener whose vegetable garden produced abundantly. She canned, froze, and cooked the bounty of her garden. Bob carved the meat (a skill he had learned in his one year at West Point) and dispensed the drinks. He put up one of those road signs saying "YIELD" over his and Mildred's double bed. They did not lack for money, but were quite thrifty. Bob was very handy, keeping the car and the woodpile in great shape, fixing things and keeping them for as long as possible. He would buy inexpensive wine at the A&P and decant it into an empty bottle of high-class French wine. Mildred would soften a chuck roast with meat tenderizer and serve it as steak. As Christmas approached, they waited until Christmas Eve to buy their tree, which they could then get for a dollar.

They were such intelligent, kind, and funny people that they were blessed with many good friends.

Since trailers were not welcome in Manhattan, we lived at first in a trailer park in Moonachie, New Jersey, and commuted to the city, Tim for work, I for music courses at Teachers College, Columbia: choral conducting, instrumental conducting, and singing in the chorus for Beethoven's *Missa Solemnis*. That was the end of my musical involvement. Since I had no professional contacts in the New York metropolitan area and no teaching experience, I could not find a job in music. Except for playing the guitar and singing folk songs, I laid music aside for several years. I thought that I didn't miss it. I found work at the Methodist Board of Missions as a typist for Dr. Wade Crawford Barclay. Dr. Barclay was a kindly man in his eighties who came downtown daily to work on his three-volume history of Methodist missions. I liked my three woman co-workers. The work was rather boring, but all in all it was a pleasant atmosphere. Neither the *Missa Solemnis* nor the history of Methodist missions made a dent in my denial of God.

A Gathering Storm

From the beginning of our relationship, Tim and I had arguments. I worried that these predicted troubles in our marriage, but Tim said not to worry, that his parents had arguments all the time and their marriage was very stable; that it was okay, even good, to express anger. I, however, had heard my parents argue only once; they generally kept their boundaries very well.

But in the very first few months of our marriage this anger erupted into a physical conflict, which I initiated. Tim must have restrained himself, because he could easily have subdued me with his greater physical strength. What caused this outbreak? I do not remember the proximate cause, but I think the underlying cause was that I was seeking a greater intensity in our relationship and did not know how to achieve this in a positive way. Such confrontations continued to occur, mostly in the form of verbal arguments, but sometimes in physical ones, for many years.

Around the middle of year that we moved East, I left Tim. I was sick and tired of living in a trailer in Moonachie, New Jersey, and more importantly, was longing for more intensity, but felt that this could not happen in our present relationship. I moved in with a former Oberlin roommate, Helen Weaver, who graciously put me up in her tiny apartment on Sullivan Street in Greenwich Village. It was just before Christmas, and Helen's family in New Milford, Connecticut, kindly took me in for the holiday. I was very lonely and had no idea what to do with my life. Tim was lonely too. We arranged to meet for lunch and decided to get back together. Tim agreed that we should sell the trailer and move to the city.

Dr. Barclay gave me a leave, and we drove down to Key West for a vacation, then to Miami, where we sold the trailer. Back in New York City, we moved to 541 East 13th St, between Avenues C and D. This was a small railroad apartment on the fifth floor, looking out onto the busy street. We lugged our belongings, and some newly acquired furniture, up those five steep flights of stairs and got settled, continuing our involvement with the socialists.

I was excited to be living in Manhattan, where I had wanted to go in the first place. The neighborhood was not as run-down as the real Lower East Side. There was a Ukrainian church, a public bath (one of the very few left), a butter and egg store, a coal and ice store, and other remnants of earlier times and other countries. From our living room windows we often saw fires in the tenements to the south of us and heard fire sirens and fireworks going off at all times of the year. On the roof we discovered new subcultures. It was easier to go up one flight than down to the street to walk Hound Dog. Other people took their dogs up there, too. I don't remember that we did anything to clean up the poop. We saw that people had built pigeon coops on other rooftops and maintained a busy community of pigeon owners. There was an active kite culture too. We tried to join it, but lost our kite almost immediately. Still, it was nice to watch the many other kites on a clear spring day.

Manhattan had its share of animal life. One day as we were eating breakfast a cat walked along the narrow ledge outside the window, carrying a fried egg in its mouth. Later, when we lived on West 95th Street, a bat flew into our living room. Besides the bats and cats, pigeons, dogs, mice, and cockroaches were ever-present. Cockroaches are indestructible. They will survive an atomic blast. They were on the Earth in the age of dinosaurs, and they will be here long after humans are all gone.

Gradually we saw less and less of our Oberlin friends, until our entire social life revolved around our fellow socialists.

I continued working with the Methodists. Tim had left his printing job and was looking for work on a magazine or newspaper. This job search took very little of his time. Most days he sat around the apartment, reading. I would come home from a day of work and find the bed unmade and the dirty dishes piled up. Though Tim had told me before our marriage that he firmly believed in the equality of women, he did not put this "belief" into practice. But after a few months he did get a job with a trade publication, *The Tobacco Jobber*. And I became pregnant.

Motherhood

I waited a long time for Carl. He must have been very content in my womb, because he was born a full six weeks after Columbus Day, the expected time. I spent most of that waiting time listening to the radio, following the Hungarian Revolution hour by hour. Finally one day I got down on my hands and knees and scrubbed the kitchen floor. We had moved from our fifth floor walkup to a tiny apartment on East 21st Street. It was on the ground floor. Dark and dusty. We painted the rooms, and even before the paint was dry, black coal dust had settled on the windowsills. You entered through a dark hallway into the kitchen. An ancient gas stove perched perilously on rickety legs. We did the dishes, washed clothes, brushed our teeth, in the kitchen sink. A small triangular corner of the kitchen had been walled off to contain a shower and toilet. The rough plaster covered old pipes and the old gas jets. Off the kitchen to the right was a small bedroom for the baby; to the left was the living room, where we slept.

On the evening of the day that I washed the kitchen floor, Tim and I trudged flight after flight of stairs to the very top seats in Carnegie Hall for a Mahalia Jackson concert. This combination of scrubbing the floor, climbing all those stairs, and the emotional impact of Mahalia's singing must have told the baby it was time to come out, for early next morning I was in labor.

It was November 19, 1956, a crisp cool bright day. As Tim and I stood on the corner waiting for a cab, I sticking way out in front and Tim carrying my overnight bag, a huge truck passed us. Its burly driver, seeing us, smiled, waved and shouted, "Good luck!"

I always find the hardest way to do things. I was in labor for fourteen hours. When I saw Carl (we had chosen names ahead of time) for the first time, he was already beautiful, and definitely six weeks old, not red and wrinkly, but nicely filled out. I wondered if he would be a socialist.

We were both politically active; at least I tried to be, but now of course we could not both go out to meetings at the same time. Tim became editor of *The Young Socialist* and I wrote articles for it under the name of Martha Wells. I also wrote an article for *The Anvil and Student Partisan* entitled "What's Wrong with Elvis the Pelvis?"[11] I liked Elvis, what I heard on the radio, but I didn't think his music was as good as the rhythm and blues that influenced his music. I thought that rock and roll was a healthy antidote to the sappy, sweet, sentimental pop songs of the 1940s. I wrote:

> The debate on the effects of music on the emotions is an old one. In ancient Greece the various musical modes were associated with different emotions and were widely believed to have beneficial or detrimental effects on the character. Some modes were thought to cause drunkenness, effeminacy and inactivity; some were considered riotous, frenzied, and orgiastic. Plato in his *Republic* permitted only two of the nine existing modes. In the Middle Ages the church repeatedly issued edicts prohibiting the use of "raucous, secular melodies" in the church. In 1667 an Englishman, Thomas Mace, wrote that the new-fangled French violin music favored by Charles II was "rather fit to make a man's ears glow, and fill his brain full of frisks, etc., than to season and sober his mind, or elevate his affection to goodness."
>
> In like vein run the arguments today: rock and roll incites young people to licentious behavior, even to riots. It has an unwholesome moral influence. A noted psychiatrist ... called rock and roll "a communicable disease—a cannibalistic and tribal form of music appealing to rebellion." *Variety* comments: "Its Svengali grip on the teenagers has produced a staggering wave of juvenile violence and mayhem." A mother in Seattle complains of her children's addiction to rock and roll: "Some of their most popular songs are open invitations to seduction." *Down Beat,* a popular music magazine, regards it as a "degenerate and neurotic music." Elston Brooks, a writer for the Fort Worth, Texas, *Morning Star-Telegram,* describes the effect on a teen-age audience of Elvis Presley (familiarly known as Elvis the Pelvis), a currently popular rock and roll singer: "Mass hysteria completely gripped the crowd. An animalistic roar split the coliseum. The girls collapsed on one another, moaning from side to side with closed eyes. They screamed. Tears ran down their faces. They swarmed toward the stage. Two girls proudly displayed scars on their arms where they had carved the word 'Elvis' with pocketknives."
>
> Undoubtedly racism and fear of sexuality played a huge part in this barrage. Many of the rock and roll singers were black. White

supremacists plainly stated their racist motives, and many newspaper editorials in the South called for the outright banning of rock and roll, even when composed and sung by white people. At the same time several individuals and newspapers in the South criticized such overt racism. The music in general, and especially the gyrations of Elvis, aroused among the attackers a fear of open sexuality. Actually, the lyrics of rock and roll were much tamer than the frank treatment of sex in the traditional blues. A third motive for all the attacks was a dislike, a non-acceptance, of adolescent rebellion. Thus the whole debate about rock and roll became an issue of civil liberties, racism, and rebellious youth. None of the motives for suppressing the music made it permissible to censor it.

Now, in my advanced years, I love that "sappy, sweet, sentimental" pop music of the nineteen-forties and fifties.

Factional struggles, writing and reading documents on both sides, and meetings occupied most of our time. In bed at night we carried on endless conversations about politics. We organized and took part in street meetings. At one, just outside Columbia, I was trying to sell *The Young Socialist* when a conservatively dressed female student answered me haughtily, "You jest!" On Saturdays we went into the housing projects to distribute leaflets. We took part in picketing the UN in protest of some policy or other: in peace demonstrations, civil rights rallies—anything that expressed resistance to injustice. In a Union Square demonstration against the requirement to take shelter during air-raid drills, I saw Dorothy Day from a distance. Little did I know how important she would become to me.[12]

Tim, Carl, and I on a visit to Bob and Mildred Wohlforth at Ridgefield.

The other side of our life was ordinary, and a welcome respite from the stress and tension of the radical movement. We visited Tim's parents in Ridgefield, and his brother and sister-in-law in Brooklyn. We had picnics. In the summers we spent time with my parents in New Hampshire. We enjoyed Carl tremendously.

We were crowded in our little ground floor apartment on East 21st Street and soon moved to a much larger place that a Party couple was vacating (by this time Tim and I had joined the Socialist Workers Party). From the Lower East Side to Upper West Side: West 90th Street between Columbus and Amsterdam. Again, five flights of stairs, but this time a wealth of rooms, strung out in a line from front to back of the building. The front room was the living room, looking out onto the busy street. A token partition opened to the bedroom, with its one window looking out onto the airshaft between our building and the next one. Following the bedroom came a hallway with built-in drawers and a window. Then came a small bedroom for Carl and later also for Billy. After this, a good-sized room that served as a dining room when we had company, and as a work room for sewing, writing, and editing *The Young Socialist*. It was into this room that you entered the apartment.

This middle room led through another hallway, past a bathroom and a large closet, which we used for a study, to the kitchen. This kitchen, at the back, was large enough to contain a long old wooden table at which we sat side by side to eat. There was a dumbwaiter to send our garbage down to nether regions.

Out the two living room windows we could see lots of life on the street. Kids played stickball; men had fights. Once we saw a shooting. Women would sit on the stoops or look out their windows to keep an eye on their children. In the sweltering summer some kind adult would turn on the fire hydrant and kids would play in the spray. Cars driving through would get doused until the cops would come and turn off the hydrant to the jeers of the kids. Then the cops would leave, someone would turn the hydrant on again, and all the spectators would cheer.

St. Gregory's Church was down the block. It was in that church that Daniel Berrigan took refuge for a while.[13] Only a few Irish Catholic families remained in the neighborhood; most had left by this time, and Puerto Ricans had replaced them.

In New York City I heard and was fascinated by words and phrases unique to the city. You didn't have to be Jewish to incorporate many Yiddish words into your vocabulary. Schlep, yenta, chutzpah, schmear ("I'll have a bagel with a schmear"), mazel tov, and other words were quite useful. One did not wait *in* line, but *on* line. A slide, in the playground, was called a "sliding pond." I've never understood that one. And if, in someone's apartment I asked, "Where is the baby?" the reply was "inside." "But we *are* inside," I'd say, confused. I finally figured out that "inside" meant *further* inside.

By now Tim was working full time for the Young Socialists in their headquarters downtown. He was paid something—maybe $75 a week, no overtime, no benefits. I felt the burdens of being poor. I lugged our laundry, Carl, and his stroller, down the five flights of stairs to the laundromat and back up again; same with the groceries. Down again to the park—Central Park was a couple of blocks away. There was a couple, rich comrades, who lived on Central Park West: the later infamous Lyndon La Rouche and his wife. She told me we should get a washer and dryer to make life easier, and to buy food in bulk. Dr. Spock advised mothers that their toddlers should have two sessions, two hours each, playing outdoors. Neither Mrs. La Rouche nor Dr. Spock knew what it was like to live with little money in a five-floor walkup.

Below us lived an elderly Irish woman, Mrs. Coyne. She was an alcoholic and had booze delivered to her door at 8:00 A.M. She would scream at us or about us at night, calling us Communists and traitors. Part of me agreed with her, and felt guilty. During the day she would pound on her ceiling with a broom when Carl was riding his hobbyhorse too vigorously for her comfort. Once Carl dropped a shoe out of our window and it landed, to my horror, on Mrs. Coyne's fire escape. I was terrified to go down and knock on her door and ask for it back. On that occasion, however, she behaved like a normal human being.

Though we had planned to have just one child and had sold our baby carriage before moving, I found that I was pregnant. In due course Billy was born. He would have waited six weeks, like Carl, but two weeks beyond the expected date I began to have weak contractions that did not get stronger. After three days of tears and total exhaustion, the doctor had me go to the hospital, and the next day at 3:30 P.M. the baby was induced. It was very strange to know ahead of time when he would be born. I had a hard time sleeping. After that, though, I slept almost all the time, despite the warnings of the nurses that I would not be able to sleep at night. When I left, they told me they had never seen anyone sleep so much.

We had named Carl after Karl Marx, and Billy after Big Bill Haywood of Wobbly fame.[14] Fortunately they could easily live with these names without embarrassment—not as if we had named them after Lenin.

We grew increasingly restless in our fifth-floor railroad flat and found a three-room apartment on West 101st Street on the first floor, above our elderly Italian landlord and his wife. The building had once been a single private house, about sixteen feet wide. The rooms were spacious and beautiful. Again we slept in the living room. The boys had the front room. By now Tim was working as editor of a trade journal, and I, for a year or two, was New York Organizer of the Young Socialists and went down to East 20th Street daily to work. We had a motherly black woman from Harlem come in daily to clean and take care of the children. I was very sad to miss seeing Billy's first steps. We discovered that Lucinda was partaking of our liquor, and one day I came home to find her, ready to leave for the day, carrying a hand-made baby blanket with a bear on it that I had used as a child. I just let it go without a word. How could I have let these things pass? I was full of guilty feelings about having a poor black woman work for us, for the tremendous disparity between us, not in income, but in education and lifestyle. I know now that it would have been more respectful of Lucinda if I had been honest with her.

In my mode of wanting to fit in, to belong, I toyed with a Jewish identity. Tim's parents helped us send the boys to nursery school. Carl went to the school at Riverside Church, where most ambitious middle-class Upper West Side parents sent their kids. But there was no room in Billy's age group, so we entered him in the Chipkin School, just a block away. I asked the director, Mrs. Rubin, if she minded that we were not Jewish, and she said no, not if we didn't mind. So Billy went, wore a yarmulke, and had a great year. During the fall festival of Succoth the school had a wonderful booth made of leafy branches, outside on the roof, where the children had their daily juice and crackers.

When kids wanted to play with each other outside of school, the mothers came too. So I made friends with several of the mothers, who all assumed I was Jewish. I never set them straight. I "passed." I was already leading a double life, not letting my neighbors know of our involvement in the radical movement. So that year I had three identities.

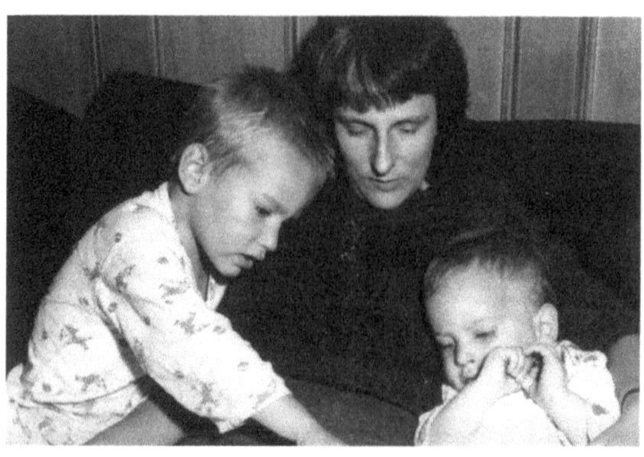

Carl, Billy and I loved to read together

Unfortunately the school closed after that year, and by then there was a place for Billy at Riverside. Bill adored his older brother, and Carl was protective of him.

The couple of years on 101st Street were turbulent and momentous. Carl, three years old, became seriously ill. The doctors took three months to arrive at their diagnosis: osteomyelitis of the left foot. After hospitalization, antibiotics, and a cast on his leg for months, Carl recovered. Had he been born before antibiotics came into use, the only available treatment would have been amputation of the leg.

I experienced deep depression. Most likely I had had depressive tendencies from childhood. I was easily upset by the smallest things, feeling that I could never live up to the expectations of my parents, afraid of my sister, feeling that I did not belong. These feelings grew more intense during high school and at Oberlin: feelings of inadequacy and loneliness; craving close relationships and compensating for the lack of them by living in a fantasy world. But now, the depression became debilitating. I found life very burdensome, overwhelming. My body felt heavy, as if something was "de-pressing," pressing down on me. The slightest frustrations would drive me to tears or rage or both. I was often paralyzed by indecision: should I take the kids out and get groceries, or stay home and clean the house? Unable to decide, not satisfied with either choice. Dissatisfied with so many things about Tim, but not facing the relationship itself.

One day in the summer of 1961, Mother was alone at Flint Farm; Dad was in Hanover working in the Dartmouth library. Going down the steep stairs, she fell, and lay at the bottom of the stairs for four hours until Dad got home. He went to the neighbors at once to call for help: we did not yet have a telephone. Mr. Godfrey, the auctioneer, came with his vehicle, which served as both ambulance and hearse, and took Mother to the Hitchcock Hospital in Hanover. From this time on her health declined. She had already been through breast cancer and a double mastectomy. Now, the cancer spread through her whole body, and back in Madison, she entered the hospital. It was just a few days after Dad's birthday, and she felt sad that she was not able to make a cake for him.

On September 21 our phone rang during a Trotskyist youth meeting we were having. We were discussing the Algerian revolution. The call was from Dad, who told me Mother had died. The Trotskyist youth continued their discussion as if nothing had happened. Acting mechanically, I asked Tim to arrange a flight for me for the following day. I would be going to Chicago and then on another plane to Madison. A plane flying from New York to Chicago had just crashed, with no survivors. I asked Tim not to get me that same flight from that same airline. But that's exactly the flight he got for me. I was terrified and sobbed all the way from our apartment to Madison.

For a long time after Mother's death, my mind returned often to the dear things she had done for me: how, when I was resting on a couch in the living room, she would quietly come and put a blanket over me. How, when I was a little girl, she would check on me every night before she went to bed, and would report to me in the morning: "You were sleeping straight as a string," or "You were all curled up like a bug in a rug." How when I was sick she would fix a tray of food for me, with something special on it—a tiny vase of flowers perhaps. How, when after reading *Bertram's Funny Animals,* I declared I wanted to have a hippopotamus, Mother immediately produced an old, patched, worn-out stuffed dog from up in a closet and called it "Hippy." How, when I was much older and she was bedridden, we would make ourselves laugh until we cried.

I did have some truly happy times in which I forgot how miserable I was. It was the children who drew me out of myself. I so loved playing with them and reading to them. I also enjoyed my friendships with other young mothers I met through the boys. But I wanted something more in life, and had not the least idea what it was. My greatest fear was that I would in my anger and frustration do harm to the children.

It was this last fear that impelled me to seek help. I applied to several clinics, and after a few rejections, found one that accepted me. I saw a psychologist weekly for one year. Then for three years I went three times a week to a psychiatrist at the New York School of Psychiatry, located on a grim island in the East River. The surroundings of the clinic looked like Gehenna, that ever-burning valley of despair. Through all this time of intense introspection, I stoutly defended my marriage. I complained about small things, never facing the central problems of our marriage. I never did come to face these problems until I was in religious life.

One good outcome of therapy was that I decided to get back into music. Except for playing and singing folk songs, I had totally neglected music for nine years. I had blocked out any awareness of the importance of music to me. I was happy with my new awareness. Planning to teach music in high school, I registered at CCNY for the ed courses I needed to get a teaching license from the city. I took the written tests at the Board of Education in Brooklyn; did some observing in classrooms; went to a remedial class to correct a lisp that I had not known I had; and finally took my practical test, a testing of my limited piano skills and sight-reading on the violin. This test took place in a busy high school in Washington Heights. When I left the music room, I was terrified by the gigantic boys running around in the hallway, and I knew right then that teaching in high school was not for me. This led to my entering the M.A. program in musicology at CCNY. But that is getting ahead of my story.

For the third time I became pregnant. I could not imagine coping with another baby. Life was already overwhelming. I decided to have an abortion; Tim had no objection. Abortions were illegal then and had to be done very surreptitiously. A young woman in the Party recommended an abortionist to me. She instructed me how to go about it. You did not call and make an appointment. You just went, bringing $600 cash with you, and sat in the waiting room until it was your turn. I was afraid. On my way up in the elevator I imagined that the elevator would keep on going, right up and out through the roof. The doctor examined me to make sure that I was really pregnant. He asked why I wanted to have an abortion, and then set up a time when he would come over to our apartment for the procedure.

The day was both Good Friday and Passover. This pleased me. I figured that the doctor must be a good atheist, as I was, for he could not be a Christian or a Jew to perform an abortion on such a sacred day. He set me up on our desk in the living room (the children must have been sent to Tim's parents in Ridgefield). To divert my attention he asked me when I had had my last period, gave me an injection, and I fell into a nescient blissful state. Next thing I knew it was over. He was very satisfied with his work, saying, "Queen Elizabeth herself could not have had a better job." He gave some brief instructions, telling Tim to go out and get me some sanitary pads, and took his leave.

Never once did it occur to me to wonder what happened to that baby. What state of development was it in? What did the doctor do with the little body? Was it in pieces? Did he flush it down the toilet? He most surely did not take it away with him. I shudder now to ask these questions.

This must have been in the afternoon. I went right to bed. Tim fixed me a delicious supper of lamb chops, and then left to see a neighbor, the husband of a good friend of mine, who wanted to interview Tim for his psychological research. Tim was gone for what seemed like forever, and I needed him. I am not sure what the official definition of a panic attack is, but I had one then, for sure. I have had three or four of these in my life, always having to do with being abandoned, but this was the worst one. Finally I called and asked him to come home. He was staying way beyond the time needed for the interview, just shooting the breeze with the psychologist. Even after my call, he stayed away considerably longer.

The previous day, I had called the local Party leader to let him know I would be out of commission for a few days. He said, "Getting rid of a kid, huh?" (He must have known what I was doing, for his sister is the one who told me about the abortionist.) This gave me a twinge of reality. But only a twinge. I had no feelings of guilt or shame that I was aware of. It was not until many years later, during my transition to Catholicism and my first years in religious life, that I faced the reality of the abortion and began to integrate it, and my baby, into my life.

The chronology of these years on 101st Street is confused in my mind. Which came first, the therapy, or the abortion? I have no memory of talking with the various therapists about the abortion, either before or after it. In any case, it was time for us to make another move. Our landlord took us to court to try to evict us, because our boys played energetically and the noise was too much for them. I understand this: the Barbinis were an elderly couple and we were right over their heads. They were also bothered by the fact that we often had gatherings of our socialist friends; these included a black woman. The court decided in our favor; but we no longer felt comfortable living there. It would be nice, too, to have a bedroom that did not also serve as a living room.

Through one of my West Side woman friends, we got a lovely apartment on West 95th Street between Columbus and Amsterdam, not far from our old 90th Street place. It was the best apartment I have ever lived in. The building actually had an elevator, a great blessing since our apartment was, for the third time, on the fifth floor. The building was so solidly built that we could have had parties or played chamber music in the middle of the night and no one would have complained. The only time we heard anyone else was when people were coming out of the elevator on our floor. We came to be friends with two families in the building, each of whom had a child about the ages of one of our boys.

Almost everything we needed was very close. Around the corner on Amsterdam was a small carpentry shop. We hired that carpenter to fix up the apartment with shelves and indirect lighting just the way we wanted it. Next to him was a little Irish grocery store where we could get Irish soda bread and Leprechaun beer. Beyond that was a pizza place where we sometimes took the kids. Diagonally across the avenue were a butcher, a candy store, a Chinese take-out food place, and a deli where you could get little roasted chickens. One block west, on Broadway, was a liquor store and the Thalia Theater, which showed the best foreign films. Two blocks west, on West End Avenue, was P.S. 75, the Emily Dickinson School, where

Carl went, and later Billy. One more block west, beyond the school, was Riverside Drive and the park. In the opposite direction, east on Columbus Avenue, was a fish store and the A&P. A block further east and we came to Central Park.

During the five years in this apartment, I grew increasingly distant from politics. The Socialist Workers Party (SWP)and the Young Socialist Alliance (the youth group the Party more or less controlled, and of which Tim was the leader) discouraged its members from psychotherapy because it led inevitably to the person's leaving the movement. Perhaps my therapy did play a part in my gradually increasing discontent with radical politics, though throughout the process I firmly stuck to the ideas of the movement.[15]

Even back on 101st Street, as Tim and I lay in bed at night, he would tell me his ideas concerning the Class Nature of the Soviet Union.[16] He was developing a new theory on the matter and was very excited about it. He was writing a long document. I listened to him, but I never read the document. I thought I ought to, but I was really bored by it.

During this time Tim and his followers, growing more and more distant from the SWP, formed an organized faction. Tim became enamored with the British Trotskyists and began to look to them as his political inspiration. Inevitably this led to a split, and Tim was expelled from the party.[17] A new group was formed. I can't remember its name, if it had one; but it ("we" at first) put out a little paper called *The Bulletin*, in imitation of the British Trotskyists' *Newsletter*. We had very limited means at first, and put out *The Bulletin* on a mimeograph machine in our study, which had, besides the machine, a single bed for guests, our two desks, bookcases, and a dining room table. I came to hate that mimeo machine. Our home was invaded by people working on the paper.

My anger at having to share our home with the movement reached a peak when we had a party to raise money for the group. Such parties were frequent in those days. You put an ad in the *Village Voice*, and people would come. I think the arrangement was that one paid a fixed amount to get in. Anyone could come; it had nothing to do with politics. Hordes of people came. Most of them were total strangers. As the level of noise and smoke rose higher and higher, so did the level of my anger. People poured into every nook and cranny of our apartment, even the bedroom. The one place that was not available to them was the boys' room. At one point a young man I had never seen before spoke to me saying, "You have such a nice apartment. How much rent do you pay?" I fled in disgust to the boys' room, climbed onto the top bunk, and watched TV with them. I felt, in a sense, raped.

After this I demanded that the mimeo machine and the collating sessions had to go. Tim acquiesced.

Around this time, in my early thirties, I entered the graduate program in musicology at the City College of New York. It was a new program, part of the City University of New York's graduate program then in formation. I was accepted as a Teaching Fellow (the college's term for a Teaching Assistant). This involved assisting professors in their courses and doing some light office work. When Prof. Jack Shapiro, who had gone to Oberlin before me, handed me a set of keys to the classrooms, office, and faculty bathroom, I nearly fainted in awe at this sign of acceptance.

Jack was my mentor, both as a graduate student in musicology and as a Teaching Fellow. He gave me increasing responsibility in teaching his course on music skills for elementary school teachers, and helped me immeasurably to become a better teacher. His graduate course, Philosophy of Music, exposed me to fascinating and varied ways people have thought about music.

As at Oberlin, I was immersed in music. I took one course at a time and did my assistant teaching. I learned a tremendous amount from my courses, my teaching, and simply from being around people whose whole life was music. Besides Jack Shapiro, who played the viola in the orchestra and in the faculty string quartet, there were Fritz Jahoda, a pianist who had been conductor of an opera company in Europe, and at City College was department chairman and conductor of the orchestra; Otto Deri, a Hungarian cellist whose specialty was twentieth-century music; Felix Galimir, violinist; Ruth Rowan, musicologist; Dabney Gettel, theory. They were huge sources of knowledge, experience, and inspiration. I began playing the violin again, playing it, and later the viola, in the orchestra. I enjoyed getting back to the violin. I no longer wanted to be a great violinist, as I had in high school and at Oberlin. As a teaching fellow I was a quasi-faculty member. I did not feel competitive or threatened by the students in the orchestra, but I certainly recognized that I was nowhere near in the same league as the string players on the faculty.

I was far from believing in God, but through my courses I began to be interested in religion. In a Bach and Handel course we explored the history of Passion music, and I read the four Gospel accounts of the Passion of Christ, the first Bible reading I had done since I was eight years old. The closest I had previously come to believing in God was when I played in the orchestra of Bach's *Saint Matthew Passion* at Oberlin. As part of our study of twentieth-century music, Otto Deri had us study Stravinsky's *Threni,* a setting for chorus and orchestra of the *Lamentations of Jeremiah.* The music was strange enough; but the text was stranger still. Was it referring to real events in history, or was it made up? Curious to find out what all this was about, I read a book called *Understanding the Old Testament.* But the significance of the Lamentations in the liturgy, and other things I had heard about in music history, such as the Elevation of the Host, were simply blanks in my understanding.

As my immersion in music was giving me a new life, a life of my own, the bonds between Tim and me were growing thinner. Yet we had some good times, too. I took the boys and spent the summers at Flint Farm, sometimes alone and sometimes with my father. Tim came up on weekends. In the city we did things with the kids: biking in Central Park, going to a museum or a movie, driving out of the city for a picnic or a hike. Sometimes Bob and Mildred Wohlforth, both of whom still worked part-time in the city, would take us out to a fancy dinner or a show. My father had to come to New York for a meeting once a month and would take Tim or me, in turns, to plays.

The dark depression was dormant, lying in wait for new opportunities to attack. I did have a lot of resentment of Tim in many small ways that I could have handled with him in a positive way, but instead I just complained and bitched and felt sorry for myself. Was this a case of passive-aggressiveness on my part? Had I heard of such a thing then, I might have recognized it in myself.

Part of me saw the signs of a decaying marriage; mostly I closed my eyes to them. Tim was becoming involved with Deborah, a young girl in the movement who had a huge crush on him. She wore ultra-short miniskirts even in the coldest of weather. She was married but her husband was out on the West Coast. She had had a baby when she was only thirteen with an older, married, man. She became the full-time secretary or office manager or whatever it was, of the movement. She called up every morning to ask if Tim would be coming down to the office. She snapped photo after photo of him as he was giving a public talk. One day he brought her home with him—I cannot remember why—and she slept overnight on our couch in the study, in a scanty nightgown with sheets and blankets only half covering her, hoping, I imagine, that Tim would come into the room and be instantly overwhelmed by her body. Once when we were driving home from a visit with the Wohlforths in

Ridgefield, Tim told me that her favorite song was "Tell It Like it Is, Baby." How could I not have seen?

All during my marriage I was continually strongly attracted to other, unattainable men, and fantasized about them.

One evening in March 1967, I was lying on the living room couch listening to Bach's *Saint Matthew Passion*. Tim was out at a meeting. When he came home he was moody. He lay down on the couch where I had been. I went over to him and tried to cuddle with him, but he would not let me touch him. I went out to Broadway to get him a gift of travel slippers, for he was to leave for London the next morning. Back at home, I began my onslaught. I did all I could to get him to admit that he had had sex with Deborah. I cried. I pleaded. I went into the bathroom intending to take an overdose of pills in an attempt to get him to touch me, but he would not. At last in the middle of the night he confessed.

Next morning, after doing the breakfast dishes, he left in his three-piece Brooks Brothers suit (a gift from his father). He said that he would not be coming back; he was going to live with Deborah. His last words, unbelievably, were: "Take my suit [another one, of course] to the cleaners, and my shirt to the Chinese laundry." I said nothing. He left.

I kept the kids out of school that day. It was March 16, early spring, a cold damp day. We went out onto the slushy streets to get boots for the boys. I cried all day. But I immediately wanted Tim's stuff out of the house. I called Danny Freeman, a friend of ours in the movement whom I was fond of—he was a real friend—and asked him to come over that evening and pick up Tim's stuff. I took all his clothes (including the suit and the shirt), his Marxist books, a lot of his jazz records and our tape reel of *The Magic Flute*, which we had recently seen together, and anything else I could find, dragged the pile into the elevator, and took it all down to the lobby for Danny to pick up.

This was a Wednesday. The following Sunday was Easter. I took the boys to the movies—*The Greatest Show on Earth*—and cried the entire time. Everywhere I saw couples with their children. I was the only single mother in the world, evidently. At least I did not see any others.

The next weeks were a horror to live through. I wanted to die, or rather to kill Tim and Deborah. It was worse than losing your husband through death, for my very life, my very body, had been totally and decisively rejected. I do not wish to re-live this time, or to resuscitate the way I felt then. I do not need to recount the nasty things we did to one another. I did try not to speak ill of Tim before the children. But I wanted to tell the world about how terrible I felt: I wanted to write a book with every detail of how I had been mistreated. I was living a soap opera.

Carl and Billy were devastated, of course. It was my crying that upset them the most. If I, on whom they depended, could not handle things, what were they to do? One time at supper, Billy said poignantly, "There used to be four people at this table."

Yet somehow I got through it. From somewhere I received the strength to go on. Part of me missed Tim dreadfully. We had shared life together for fifteen years. He had a nice soft body, very comforting to hold. And just the mechanics of living, of taking on the things he had done, of being a single parent, seemed overwhelming. I had been dependent on him in so many ways. If I was driving us up to Ridgefield, I got so tired that I would ask him to take over the driving. Two years later I was not only driving the boys up to Lyme and back alone, but drove, alone, all the way out to Kentucky and back.

I would often hear Tim's key in the door; hear his voice; talk to him in my mind. But now our double bed was all mine. I felt a new freedom. I moved our bed into the dining room-study, and gave each of the boys a separate room. I lay in the bed diagonally, taking up as much room as possible. I could sit up in bed and read as long as I wanted. I read voraciously, dropping the sections of the Sunday *Times* onto the floor one by one. I read depressing novels like *The Lord of the Flies*. I could have quiet mornings without having to listen to jazz on the radio.

I wrote a letter of resignation to the Socialist Workers Party, simply a formalization of an existing fact. I left for personal reasons only. I still thought I agreed with the politics. I kept our picture of Lenin up in our dining room-study-bedroom.

I had to finish my Masters' thesis[18] so that I could receive my degree and become a lecturer full time at CCNY. It was a mercy I had this deadline or I might have given up the whole thing. I was beginning to form an identity of my own. I had always "belonged" to some male or other: I was Merle Curti's daughter, Tim's wife, Carl and Bill's mother. I was beginning to become simply myself. The process took years, even decades; but it had begun.

This year 1967 saw more than the end of our marriage. In the fall I began teaching full-time. At the very beginning of the school year Carl, now eleven, had to have open-heart surgery. He was born with an unknown defect in his heart, and now he needed a cath test to determine the cause. This test involved being hospitalized, and was almost as traumatic as the later surgery. It revealed that Carl had aortic stenosis and would need major surgery.

I paid a substitute to teach my first two weeks of classes, arranged for Billy to stay with neighbors, and off we went to University Hospital. Carl had a roommate, an eight-year-old boy who was very good company for him. I left them playing cards together and went home. As soon as I walked into the apartment, the phone rang—it was early evening—and a nurse from the hospital asked me to come down again, as Carl was scared. I went back at once and sat with Carl all night. I was so grateful for that. He was whisked off to surgery earlier in the morning than we had expected, and I would not have seen him at all. There were hours of waiting, of not knowing if Carl would live through this. At last I was led into the recovery room and at once broke down, though I held myself together. Carl was awake, but he had tubes sticking out all over his body. As I left, Tim was coming in, and for a brief moment we laid aside all the bad stuff and held each other.

Years later Carl wrote about his experience. It wrenched my own heart to read that when he woke up from the surgery he looked up and saw Tim and me, together. He thought he had died and gone to heaven, a heaven he had never believed in.

In the hospital I read aloud to Carl, and then at home to both boys, *The Borrowers* by Mary Norton. The book was a great comfort to the three of us. Carl was sent to a special public school for kids with heart problems for the rest of the school year. My teaching got off to a shaky start since I had missed the first two weeks of classes, but I got through that. I taught at CCNY for another year and a half, did what I could do to reach out socially, and began to build a new life.

I realized that I needed to get a PhD if I was to continue to be a professor; and indeed what else could I do? I loved being a scholar and sharing my enthusiasm for music with others. I applied to the doctoral programs at Columbia, Berkeley, and the University of Kentucky. Columbia offered me a four-year full tuition scholarship. Berkeley turned me down entirely on the grounds that I, at thirty-five, was "too old." I chose Kentucky. They offered me a good scholarship, and I wanted to get the boys and myself out of New York City. I was planning to focus on Baroque music with Franklin B. Zimmerman, the noted Purcell scholar who had taught at Dartmouth and was the husband of a friend of mine. Just as I was on my way out to Lexington to see the University and the city, Frank called me and said he would not be at UK after all (after just one year there). He had accepted a position elsewhere, but in his place would be George J. Buelow, another Baroque specialist. The boys did not want to go. Against their wills I made them get their hair cut (it was the Beatles mania then), explaining that they would be teased mercilessly out there if they had long hair.

So began a new adventure.

Five

A FOREIGN CULTURE KENTUCKY 1968-1969

This life is too much trouble, far too strange, to arrive at the end of it and have to answer "Scientific Humanism". That won't do. A poor show. Life is a mystery, love is a delight. Therefore I take it as axiomatic that one should settle for nothing less than the infinite mystery and the infinite delight, i.e. God. In fact, I demand it. I refuse to settle for anything less.

—Walker Percy

I had made a visit to Lexington in April 1968 to see the University and meet my professors. Visually, I was going back to the fifties. The girls and women had teased bouffant or beehive hairdos, or slept with curlers in their hair. They wore cotton shirtwaist dresses, plaid, striped, or flowered, with sleeves, collars, buttons, belted waists; or full skirts and neat, tucked-in blouses.

In the heat of summer I left New York for good with Sammy, our dog. Bob and Mildred Wohlforth were to send the boys later after I had found a place for us to live. A friend on the fringe of the Movement, Jimmy, helped me load up our old VW Beetle. We stuffed the insides and tied things to the roof. At the last minute I realized I wanted the broom and the mop, so we attached them to the roof too. I drove for two days. As I neared Lexington, I had a strong sense of destiny: I would meet my future husband there. The destiny part turned out to be correct; the husband part was not.

When I got there, I found a house to rent in a recently built subdivision called Blueberry Hill. When I unpacked, I found that my violin, which I had unwisely packed in the trunk of the car, had come totally unglued. It was a beautiful two hundred-year-old violin that I had had since the eighth grade. To repair it required serious surgery. Perhaps the violin came unglued because I myself had become unglued with the end of the marriage.

Our house had two large pin oak trees in the front yard, a large back yard, and a basement garage big enough for not only a train set, but also a ping-pong table. I was pleased to hear the sound of cows nearby, but not pleased when I discovered that they came not from a farm but from a slaughterhouse.

On my arrival, before the boys came, my neighbors invited me over for a meal. They had two little boys, Zane and Zachary, who asked me repeatedly where the boys' Daddy was, a poignant reminder. It was hard for them to understand that he lived far away.

We were definitely "strangers in a strange land." I can't speak about the culture of Kentucky in general, but in Lexington I discerned among white people two distinct groups: the Rich White People of the old South, genteel, often cultured, some in academia, some horse breeders living on the beautifully manicured horse farms in the area, some undoubtedly prosperous businessmen. I lived among the other group. My neighbors were mostly from the hills of Eastern Kentucky and spoke a different language from that of the Rich White People. Bill became "Beal"; pill became "peel." The school kids used the word "sweet" as a derogatory term. Perhaps it meant a sissy, but not gay; the teachers and guidance counselor in Carl's school were not sure what it meant.

A boy from the neighborhood came over to play with Carl. When I asked him if he'd like a cookie, he answered, "I don't care." That sounded rude to me. I figured if he didn't care, why should I give him one? I found out later that he was being polite. In stores, a cashier or saleslady would say something to me, and I'd have to ask her to repeat it. And a second time. And a third time, after which I gave up trying to understand what she was saying.

At school, one of my professors, Donald Nugent, kept talking about "par." It took me a long time to figure out from the context that what he meant was "power." The same with "are" and "hour."

As for black people, I simply did not see them. They must have been there. The days of segregation were supposed to be over by then, but there were no black people in my neighborhood, in my classes, in the stores and restaurants and gas stations we went to.

At least, there was a family from India who lived across the street from us. The father was a professor; they had a couple of children one of whom was a boy about Bill's age. Theirs was a Catholic family. Once when I was taking Bill and the boy, Steve, somewhere in the car, I asked Steve what he wanted to be when he grew up. "A saint," he replied. I have often wondered how his life has developed.

I was so grateful that I had made the boys get haircuts. They had enough to deal with in school. Bill was asked a question by his teacher and answered, "Yes." She said, "Yes what?" He did not know what she meant. Thus he learned he was supposed to say "Yes, Ma'am." Another time he announced to his class that he did not believe in God. Of course this caused general consternation. But in general the boys did okay. Bill joined a Cub Scout den and took piano lessons. Carl joined a coin club. And though he was only eleven, the girl across the street invited him to a dance. She called and spoke with me, for Carl was at his coin club at the time. I told her I doubted if he would come, but I would certainly let him know. He surprised me; he did want to go! The girl told me that Carl would need to get her a corsage and I would need to provide the transportation. I drove them and picked them up; they had evidently had a good time. When we got back to her house, I had to tell Carl that he should get out of the car and accompany the girl to her front door.

I loved school. I have always loved studying and libraries and learning new things. I could easily have been a student all my life. Two things were a special delight. The University's music department owned some viols, so I was able to learn to play the treble viol (viola da gamba). I took lessons from Professor Gordon Kinney, and when I had learned enough I played regularly with a new faculty member, Frank Traficante, and a couple of students. This was the realization of a long-held dream: in junior high when I first read about early musical instruments, I fantasized that I could go into museums and get permission to play their viols, vielles, kits and rebecs.[19] At that time the boom in early music had not yet begun, and I had no idea you could find someone who made these instruments and one could buy them. Now, at last I was able to play the music I had already learned to love. Frank and I ambitiously played two-part pieces from Bach's *The Art of Fugue* in public; and with two others we played a program of Renaissance music.

The second special delight was that I was able to take non-music courses, Renaissance History (first semester) and Reformation History (second semester). These were first-level graduate courses, and since I had taken no history at Oberlin, I went to see Professor Donald Nugent, the teacher of these courses. He told me that he emphasized religion. I was happy about that. My curiosity about religion had been aroused by my studies at CCNY. Mr. Nugent thought it would be okay for me to sign up. These courses opened up a new world for me: a world of people—Saint Thomas More, Henry VIII, King Francis I of France, Ann Boleyn, Saint Ignatius, Saint Francis, and so many more—a world of new ideas, places, events. Prof. Nugent was an amazing teacher. I was fascinated that he could do three things at once: lecture fluently with his back to the class, erase the blackboard with his right hand, and with his left fill up that space with new writing.

I heard from other students that he was Catholic, and that he lived simply and gave a lot to charities. He was very familiar with art, music and literature, as well as philosophy and religion. All this greatly enriched my understanding of music.

But far more than that: he changed my life. His faith, and the way it enlivened his whole being, made religion seem the most exciting thing in the world, and this excitement spread to me. One day I was in the library studying, as it happened, for one of his exams. He walked by and stopped, and we had our first conversation. He told me that he was a "radical Catholic." I had no idea what this meant, but I was very intrigued by it. We had a few other good conversations as the year passed, and after the academic year was over we became friends.

In New York City, if you were a Christian you did not advertise it. In fact, except for two of my colleagues, people just did not talk about religion. But in Lexington, religion was in the air. People spoke freely about their faith. By this time I was seeking for God, for religious experience. I didn't believe in God yet, but I wanted to. I began going to the Unitarian Church on Sundays. At first I took the boys with me to Sunday school, but they did not respond to it, so I went alone. I felt truly happy and peaceful to be going to church. I joined the choir for the Christmas program. The services did not answer my longing for God, but it was a beginning.

In addition to Don Nugent's courses, I took the seminars of Dr. George Buelow.[20] These two courses, and the work on the viol, were all I could handle. The first semester had to do with Baroque music, mostly involving the realization of figured basses. The second semester was Wagner. I had never liked Wagner. My only exposure to his music was playing some of it in orchestras, and seeing *Tristan and Isolde* when I was at Oberlin. The Met presented the opera in Cleveland, the first opera I had ever seen. My seat was an entire city block away from the stage, and for four hours I watched two people on the stage doing nothing but singing; no apparent action. I was bored to death. Five minutes of Wagner was about all I could take. My boredom was inevitable: I had made no preparation for the opera. I did not know that it's a waste of time and money to go to an opera you know nothing about. You need at least to read the libretto, especially if the opera is in a foreign language, and familiarize yourself with the plot and the characters. But now,

Dr. Buelow introduced his students to the richness and beauty of Wagner's works, especially the *Ring* and *Tristan and Isolde*. I learned about the music, the man, the social context, Wagner's revolutionary place in the history of music, and his place, with Marx, Darwin and Freud, as a dominant figure of the nineteenth century who changed the shape of the world.

I loved the *Ring*—its roots in Norse mythology, its rich symbolism, the fact that it could be interpreted in so many ways—Marxist, Christian, Jungian—and above all the beauty of the music, its wealth of tone colors, its brilliant illumination of the text. But it was *Tristan* that got to the depths of my being. My yearning for a love relationship that would be all-consuming, overwhelming, the total immersion of myself into another, the complete union of two souls—*Tristan* spoke to this, and in fact made my longing even stronger.

One day as I entered the music building I saw a fellow grad student, John Arnn, a young man twelve years my junior. To my routine "How are you?" he replied, "I'm depressed." So we talked, and thus began a close friendship that lasted for many years until he died of AIDS at the age of fifty.

One fine day in April, John and I each received an invitation from Dr. Buelow to go to his house at seven P.M. We were mystified, curious. We, and as far as we knew, no other students, had ever been to his home. We wondered if this invitation was for supper or not. We prepared for either possibility by eating a small amount before setting out. Dr. Buelow's mother, with whom he lived, served us a huge dessert of ice cream and cake. Dr. Buelow then informed us that he had accepted an invitation to be Director of Graduate Studies in Musicology at Rutgers, and he hoped that we, of all his students, would transfer to the PhD program there. For the second year in a row, the University of Kentucky had to search for a new musicologist who specialized in the Baroque period.

We had little trouble deciding to go. For John, who was young and single and had grown up not far away in Louisville, this was an adventure. But what an upset this meant for me! After all the trouble of moving from Manhattan, getting Carl and Bill established in new schools, meeting a new culture and a whole new set of people, the boys and I had to face it all over again.

Six

TURMOIL AND TRANSITION NEW JERSEY 1969-1978

I fled Him, down the nights and down the days;
I fled Him, down the arches of the years;
I fled Him, down the labyrinthian ways
Of my own mind.

—Francis Thompson

As we drove east from Kentucky and approached New Brunswick, New Jersey, the boys and I were happy to see pizza places and bagel shops and other familiar signs of the East. We went straight to our new home in New Brunswick, which I had rented sight unseen for $150 a month—a small house on Drift Street, a tiny street just one block long. The first floor had a small kitchen, a small living room, and a room that I used as a combined bedroom, study, and dining room if we had guests. Upstairs was a wide hallway, which the boys could use as a play space, and two tiny bedrooms. My bed downstairs was against the front window, right next to the sidewalk, since there was no front yard. Directly across the street was a fire station, from which fire trucks rolled out in the middle of every night, sirens screeching. After a few days I did not even notice this sound. And the firemen were very helpful in letting me know if they saw the kids doing anything dangerous, like climbing out onto the roof.

We lived in a working-class neighborhood, with Ted's Diner conveniently located at the end of the block. My father-in-law, Robert Wohlforth, offered to pay for the boys to go to Rutgers Prep School. Overcoming my reservations about private schools, I took Carl and Billy to Rutgers Prep for an interview. Carl was admitted to the eighth grade, but the elementary school did not have an opening for Billy, so we enrolled him in our neighborhood public school. Both boys made friends and seemed to adjust fairly quickly to their new surroundings. They went to New York City every other weekend to see their father. Tim was working in the city and living with the second woman he had after me. He took the boys to Party picnics (he had rejoined the SWP) and to a big peace march in Washington, D.C.

After our year on Drift Street in New Brunswick, we moved across the river to Highland Park, where we rented a two-bedroom apartment on Donaldson Street. These apartments were fairly new and in good condition. Bill had to change schools again—four schools in as many years—to the middle school in Highland Park. Despite the uprooting the boys had experienced, they made friends with boys in our apartment complex. A few of these friendships have lasted through the years.

At Rutgers I was completing my course work for the PhD, then moving into my dissertation, which took so long to complete (five years) that when the boys were asked, "What does your mother do?" they would reply, "She's doing her dissertation." In my first year at Rutgers, I worked part time in the music library. Thereafter I taught at Livingston College, a brand-new college of Rutgers. My first year was as a Teaching Assistant, teaching forty kids beginning Music Theory—a nightmare. As a student, and at CCNY, there were never more than ten students in a theory class, and I had no notion of how to deal with forty. I was miserable. The college had, it seemed to me, two contradictory missions: one was to help underprivileged kids, mostly black and Hispanic, who were aiming to move up in society; the other was to serve well-off middle-class white kids who wanted an experimental college and wanted to escape from their bourgeois backgrounds. These disparate groups really needed different methods of teaching. The college had not found its identity, nor had I. It made for quite a mess.

At Livingston, I was the sole representative of "classical" music. This had its positive and negative sides. I felt isolated, as if I were pushing something that hardly anyone was interested in. The other side was exhilarating. I had three colleagues who, while trained and quite knowledgeable in "classical" music, were primarily devoted to other areas. It was these three people who made Livingston tolerable. All three were composers. Daniel Goode, who had actually been a student at Oberlin in my time, was in charge of developing an electronic music program for the college. He loved birds and Scottish fiddle music and incorporated these into his compositions. Barbara Benary was an ethnomusicologist, especially interested in gamelan music.[21] She built a gamelan and taught people to use it. Philip Corner, a pianist and calligrapher as well as a composer, designed the theory program. All three formed an ongoing gamelan group and wrote pieces based on gamelan procedures. They became good friends, and my association with them did wonders in opening me up to entirely new ways of playing, teaching, and thinking about music.

There were also several excellent, well-known jazz musicians on the faculty. But much as I had loved early New Orleans jazz, I did not understand and could not relate to the kind of jazz they were involved in. I felt guilty about this: I thought I *ought* to learn about it, since I would then appreciate more what my colleagues were involved in. But my life was too full of obligations already. Had I been more settled in my life and my identity, I could have learned much from these fine musicians, but I missed that opportunity. Perhaps that's why, at one stormy department meeting, one of them called me a "white middle-class racist." I could not deny that I was white and middle class, but I did not think I was a racist.

One of my courses was a seminar with Dr. Buelow on the music of Bach. I was very excited to learn about Bach's use of rhetorical figures and number symbolism in his music. I loved searching for order in music, for connections conscious or unconscious. In Bach's music I found a transcendence, a reaching for something higher than I. Once again, Bach's music led me to Scripture. I was writing a paper on his Cantata No.70, *Wachet, Betet, Seid Bereit (Watch, Pray, Be Ready)*. It was composed for the final Sunday of the liturgical year, just before the beginning of Advent. The Lutheran Church, like its parent the Catholic Church, emphasizes death and the end times throughout these last weeks of the liturgical year. The text of the cantata and the expressiveness and symbolism of the music instilled in me a great awe. It was late November, with short dark days, the very time of year for which Bach wrote the cantata. The somber reminders of the end—the trumpets announcing it—with the words "Heaven and earth will pass away, but My Word will not pass away" brought me great comfort and reassurance.

While I was working on this paper, I wanted to attend a Lutheran service to get some idea of the context of Bach's cantatas. On the Sunday after Christmas I walked from Drift Street to a Lutheran church, just two or three blocks away. The sidewalks were solid ice. I was impressed by the reverence and dignity of the service. It was the Feast of the Holy Innocents. The music was tasteful, and to my amazement the congregation knew by heart and sang in harmony the many sung responses. At the Kiss of Peace[22] a growing discomfort seized me, for I had no idea what I was supposed to say or do. I was definitely not in familiar territory. As we went out of the church, the pastor was standing in the entryway greeting the people. Because of my shyness, I tried to hide behind the crowd and slip out unnoticed, but his penetrating eyes found me out.

During this decade of the 1970s I experienced my mid-life crisis. I questioned: Where am heading? In my days at City College I had a curiosity about religion and a growing interest in it. In Kentucky I was consciously searching for God. Now, in New Jersey, I believed in God as a First Principle, the entity that got things started in the first place. But this abstract idea of God had no real impact on my life: it did not demand anything of me.

I tried on different personae. I dipped my feet into various waters: radical feminism, yoga, health food, academia. I shunned politics, but I did always vote, at least for the president. I was attracted to the New Age movements without getting directly involved in them. Returning home from a day at school, I would sit in a comfortable chair, have a beer and a whole piece of matzo spread with sweet butter, and read the *East-West Journal*. I read a book about Findhorn, the famous New Age community in northern Scotland, and another about the various communes and New Age communities springing up all over the country. I wondered if I might fit in with one of them. I developed an interest in wild edible plants, medicinal herbs, alternative medicine. I stopped coloring my prematurely gray hair and let it grow long.

Around 1970 I made my first trip to Europe: to visit my Curti relatives in Switzerland, to attend the *Ring* cycle at Bayreuth, and to revel in the medieval remnants to be found in the old town of Zürich and the German town of Rothenberg ob der Tauber. The following summer, while Carl and Bill were at camp, I spent six weeks in London doing research for my dissertation and searching for remnants of the seventeenth century. I spent the other summers at Flint Farm with the boys and my father and my stepmother Frances. (My mother had died in 1961, and Dad married again in 1970.) I thought I wanted to be a musicologist, get my PhD, teach in a university, play early music, maybe get a book or two published, maybe make a bit of a name in the field.

My involvement in early music gave me great pleasure. Thanks to my father's help, I bought a treble viol, which I sent for from Germany. A year later I bought a matching bass viol[23] from the same maker and begin to study with Judith Davidoff. I had heard Judith play at concerts of the New York Pro Musica, and got to meet her at Pinewoods Camp in Plymouth, Massachusetts, which I attended for two summers. I went weekly or every other week to New York City by bus, lugging my bass, taking the subway up to her apartment on West End Avenue, and treasured every minute of my lesson. I met others who played historical instruments, both for fun and to do some concerts.

All this sounds like a good life. But I was really miserable. You could say that emotionally, psychologically, and physically, I was living on a dunghill. My propensity to initiate relationships that inevitably end in rejection came to a head. The pattern: I would become deeply attracted to, deeply emotionally involved, with men who reason would tell me are incapable of a relationship. I would fantasize, as if I were still in my teens. I would take ordinary gestures of friendliness to be signs that the man was attracted to me. But nothing would happen. The tension would mount, and at last I would take the initiative and declare my love. This always provoked a huge rejection and I would be totally devastated, wallowing in tears, jealousy, and self-pity, seeking counseling, unable to sleep at night, feeling that I was worthless. This rejection was inevitable because my need was too great. I did this once before in a big way while I was still a Trotskyist. But now I did it again, not once, not twice, not three times, but four times. At last I prayed to God: I ask that I could accept His will.

I cannot and do not wish to retrieve the depths of that phase of my life. There is no way I can describe it. But that does not matter. If you have experienced long periods of chronic depression, you will understand. If not, be thankful. Now, I can see that what I was enduring was truly hell, a hell of my own making. In *The Great Divorce,* C.S. Lewis defines hell as attaching oneself to a person or thing that is unreal. I was attaching myself to mirages of my own imagination, not to real people. I thought this was love, having no idea what love really is.

I found my teaching situation exceedingly stressful. The stress came both from my own weak identity and from objective circumstances. I was a single mother of preteen boys, with limited financial resources. I often felt that I couldn't handle things. If, for example, I was frustrated by some dead end on the telephone, I would give up and cry, or get so angry I hit myself, hard.

My body responded to these stresses. For years I had what I called a Mysterious Disease: a slight temperature, or a feverish feeling without anything showing on the thermometer, not enough to elicit any medical concern; aches all over, especially in the muscles of my face, often so severe I simply had to go to bed. I had this Mysterious Disease at least half the time.

During my summer of research in London, a new friend, Carol, invited me to go with her to a retreat place in the country, an old and grand estate. By "retreat" I do not mean anything organized. The guests could spend their time as they wished. They were apparently rather well off, and practiced yoga or other forms of meditation. Carol was a regular practitioner of yoga. An American teenager was working there. I heard that he was recovering from drug addiction. He made beautiful jewelry, and I bought a pair of silver earrings he had made. Carol and I returned to London together and she, a native Londoner, took me to the Charing Cross neighborhood. We wandered aimlessly and peacefully along small labyrinthine streets, looking into used bookshops.

All at once I noticed that one of my new earrings was missing. I was very sad to lose it, not only because it was new and beautiful, but also because it was made by that nice young man who was getting his life straightened out. We could not possibly retrace our steps to search for it: we had been walking around randomly with no attention to where we were going. Carol suggested that we continue walking aimlessly, peacefully, trustingly, this time not talking, but thinking meditatively about finding things. We crossed a busy main street, heavy with traffic. Reaching the far side of the street, I looked down and saw—my earring! It was in the gutter just a few inches away from one of those grates that leads to the sewers below. It was all scratched up from having trucks and busses and cars run over it.

To me this was an absolute miracle. Had we been trying rationally to find that earring, to retrace our steps, we would never have found it. That it was there, that it had not been knocked into that sewer, that no one had picked it up—and that I had noticed it—was indeed miraculous.

For the first time in my life I felt the hand of God, not as an abstract First Cause but as a personal God who knew me and was guiding me. I was happy beyond imagination. I was content. I did not feel I had to jump to any sort of decisions, I did not say to myself, "Now I am a Christian" or some such thing. I simply lived in the wonder of what had happened.

New Perspectives: Yoga

Back in New Jersey, back teaching at Livingston, back with the boys, back with my dissertation, and boy, was that back of mine ever hurting. I had been intrigued by my initial exposure to yoga in London, so I signed up for a class at the Y in Princeton. I liked the teacher, and wished to get more deeply into yoga. She suggested that I contact her teacher, Shyam Bhatnagar, who ran a center in Princeton for yoga studies and practices. I called, and the young man who answered the phone said that by working with Shyam I would get more "in tune with Nature." This sounded good to me. I went down once a week for "therapy." The sessions began with my telling Shyam how the week had gone and what my concerns and questions were. Shyam would give advice and prescribe various asanas (yoga postures) and other practices. Then I lay face down on a hollow wooden bed and received a massage of the spine as a sound system playing Indian music surrounded me, through the air and from speakers in the bed. The sounds were played by a tambura, a wonderfully resonant and beautiful instrument.

Following his advice I became an instant vegetarian. At first my protein was simply dairy products and eggs. Then I discovered *Diet for a Small Planet*[24] and later on, the Hare Krishna cookbook, which had delicious and easy recipes along with lots of indoctrination. I enjoyed learning to make ghee and wonderful combinations of spices. For Carl and Billy I continued to cook meat.

I began seeing Shyam in October 1973. At this time I began a journal that I have kept off and on ever since. The first notebook consists entirely of information and instructions for my yoga practice. There is scarcely any mention of teaching, and only one reference to my dissertation. I learned that most of the time we breathe more clearly through one nostril than the other. To some extent we can control this temporarily. I copied lists of which activities were best done when the left nostril was dominant, and which with the right. I kept a daily record of which side I was breathing on when waking up. I wrote down the colors that went best with each day of the week (Saturday—black for Saturn, etc.). I recorded my experiences with meditation, or attempts to meditate; I wrote the symbol for "Om" at the beginning of each entry.

The ultimate goal of yoga is union with God. "Yoga" is Sanskrit for "yoke." If you work hard enough on your yoga practice, you can ultimately reach this goal. The practices vary with each individual according to her or his needs and state in life. Meditation is the means by which we can arrive at union with God. At first it was physical and emotional pain that drew me to yoga, but it did not take me long to realize that union with God was what I wanted, that the total union with another human being that I thought I desired is not only impossible, but actually destructive. However, the idea of God that Shyam presented was very different from that of the monotheistic religions. Was that what I wanted? I could not yet know.

The vegetarian diet, the exercises, and the many other changes in lifestyle were meant to prepare the body and mind for meditation. Since all energy ultimately comes from the sun, we can receive that energy best if we are all ready for meditation by the time the sun rises. By that time we should have taken a shower and done our asanas. Then we sit, preferably in lotus position (which I was far from able to do), looking at a candle flame in front of us—preferably a ceramic lamp with a wick and with ghee as fuel—and focus on our breathing, and notice our fleeting thoughts without judgment. There were many days when I had to shorten the morning routine. If I did everything I was supposed to do, it took an hour and a half.

After most of the sessions with Shyam I was on a high; the car drove itself home automatically, effortlessly. After five weeks of this new regime I noted that I felt better in many ways, though all my problems persisted. The darkness remained: the depression, the feelings of helplessness, jealousy, paranoia, inadequacy, feeling left out. The constant preoccupation with what kind of an impression I was making on others continued. The Mysterious Disease—insomnia, headaches, digestive problems, frequent colds—consumed a lot of my attention. I was hooked on yoga, but I realized that it could take me only so far. I recognized that for me, at that time, it was an important catalyst to my spiritual search. Yoga, the boys, my health, and my relationships were my main concerns.

I agonized a lot over one of my colleagues at school, R., with whom I had fallen into my usual self-destructive pattern. I tried very hard to handle this in a more mature way, and evidently I succeeded, for until I reread my journals recently, I had totally forgotten that I had had this attachment. As for Carl and Bill, I worried a lot about them: they were teenagers, they were finding their way; they were often cranky or incommunicative; they left messes all over the place. They played their music so loudly that even after I required them to use headphones I could hear the sounds from the other end of the apartment. They did not come home when expected, without calling me. We fought over the use of the car. In other words, they were quite normal boys, but I worried that I was not a good mother.

I was diligent about teaching. Preparing for each class took a lot of time. I kept on struggling with my dissertation, but though the subject had fascinated me initially, by now my heart was not in it. For years I questioned the professional path I had set upon. Was I doing this—getting a PhD and aiming to spend my life as a professor—to please my parents? To fulfill some desire of theirs for continuity, a desire that my sister could not possibly fulfill? Or was I doing it for myself? I truly loved music, but it was becoming clear that performing was not to be my medium. Every time I took part in a concert, especially one I had to organize, the stress for weeks ahead was almost unbearable. I truly loved scholarship; I still do. I loved working in libraries, doing detective work, finding things out. I loved the quietness of it, the lack of deadlines, not having to deal with many people.

Still, I was desperately lonely. I felt that I had no close friends. I longed to get married again. I missed having someone to share my life with, to discuss the events of our days at night, to hold and be held by.

But there were many joys, too. Often the boys and I would have remarkable conversations; sometimes one or the other would come forth with words of surprising wisdom and perceptiveness. Carl had a gift that gave me much comfort. Sometimes I would be feeling miserable and would be very bitchy. Carl could cut through all that, put his arms around me and say, "I love you, Mom," and my heart would melt.

Music, playing it alone and with others, also comforted me, as did good moments with friends, colleagues, and students; and teaching a good class with responsive students; and "good" meditations. As I had always done since at least the eighth grade, I evaluated each day: terrific, terrible, and degrees in between. I thought that by my own diligent and persistent efforts I could control my life.

But then I read Thomas Merton, from whom I learned that the happiness and peace we all want does not come from outside us, from external happenings; it comes from within. It is a gift from God.

Yes. In that fall of 1973 I was beginning to pray, to thank God and to ask Him to help me. I was keenly aware that I was in a period of deep transformation; that all the attention I was giving to myself, to all aspects of my life, was a necessary part of this process.

That following spring I was having very severe pain in my face. I correctly suspected that it was at its worst when I had to do something I did not want to do. There were times I wanted to escape from everything: from saddhana,[25] teaching, music, the children, the house. *"I just want to quit. Can't FACE it."* I considered leaving yoga. Shyam said that would just make everything worse.

Every fortnight, at the full moon or the new moon, I was supposed to stay up all night, mostly being quiet and meditating or doing some mild exercises; and to fast from food and from talking the following day. Trying to do this was a great struggle. Sometimes I managed pretty well and recognized some benefits from the experience. More often, I got headaches or even nausea, ran into conflicts with the boys, and felt generally terrible. More important, more destructive, was the anxiety I had for the two years or more that I tried these sleep-food-speech fasts.

In my journal, I expressed terrible worry about a coming concert with Anita Randolfi, my recorder friend from New York City. About Livingston, I wrote:

November 18, 1973

I hate Livingston: it makes me depressed or sick every time I go there. I can't take a lot of stress—need quiet, not too many people.

In other ways a lot of things seem to be falling into place. I finished The Hobbit a few days ago. At the end they discover that the way they had planned to go, which they couldn't take because of various misfortunes, had been rendered impossible to use. They could not have gone any other way than the way they did go. This idea is vastly important to me. Wherever I am now—that is the right place for me to be. Wherever I have ever been—I had to be there in order to be where I am now. ... Peace. I am happy.

December 5, 1973 (Wednesday)

Dream: I am looking (thru a telescope or binoculars?) at a forest, thinking it ended at a certain place, & gradually discovering that it went on and on. The vistas of the spiritual path lying before me?

December 9, 1973 (Sunday)

Yesterday also a very bad day. I was depressed. Called R. He said he was glad I did, we talked, but there was no Great Rapport or Closeness. Took B. and a friend shopping, with few results. Carl not around at all—the two minutes I did see him he was in a bad mood. B. didn't want to have supper at home. By this time I was in a bad depression—the old "It's Saturday. night & nobody loves me" thing. BUT I got out of it—and how? God did it via Thomas Merton. So many things rang a bell (his chapter on bells is beautiful). What I had been doing was looking outside myself & therefore away from God for salvation. To the children—to the little "successes" of events in one's life. I can see I am becoming attached to R. If I am in love, if I do fall in love, please God let me not let it be the center of my life. Let You always be the center of my life.

I pray today will be a good day. I pray that You will help me to be the kind of person that can create a good environment for the children to be in.

New ideas, new expressions were entering my life: things like "It's not meant to be;" "Live in the moment;" male and female energy; influences of moon cycles on us.

But I was full of confusion about yoga: the attitudes toward women, and what seemed to me to be magical doings. There was a mimeographed booklet called "Live Wise" that provided detailed information and directions about yoga "according to Shyam." I was disturbed by its clear bias against women; they did not seem to exist. Personal pronouns were always the masculine ones. Directions were given for how to handle various ailments; but there were no references whatever to women's health concerns. What bothered me even more was, you should not look at a "cripple" in the morning before meditation. Jesus would say, that's exactly whom you *should* be looking at. It seemed so heartless to deliberately avoid a fellow human being in order to keep oneself "pure." Another thing that bothered me was a spiritual competitiveness among the followers of yoga: people compared themselves to others, and spoke of so-and-so being "higher" than another so-and-so. At one of the group meditations, a scruffy young fellow was there, and two women whom I was friendly with spoke disparagingly of him as someone, like the "cripple," to avoid. But I will say for Shyam, that as he passed by the young man (whom he seemed to know) he reached down and gave him a friendly pat on the back.

November 24, 1973

But I am sure of one thing: I believe in God. I question whether any one human being has a monopoly on the truth. Every human being has limitations—of being human, of being in a particular time, place, and culture.

November 25, 1973

Whatever obstacles, doubts, etc. I encounter on the Woman Question, I'll always remember one thing: God does not put women down, though people may. And when they do, they usually do not know what they are doing. Don [Nugent, my Kentucky friend,] *sent me Fellowship* [the journal of the Fellowship of Reconciliation, a peace organization]. It was *devoted to simple living—religious communities—beautiful article by Merton—the whole thing opens up perspectives not only for my life but ideology and commitment: puts vegetarianism etc. in a political context. ... Have fantasized for two days about living in a Christian community where all is shared in common.*

Toward the end of that school year came a major landmark in my journey toward the Church. One Sunday I decided to go to church at the campus Episcopal Church, St. Michael's. I had been there before, to play a concert, and again to take my sister, who was visiting, to Midnight Mass. But this time was special. As I entered the church, my friend Dan Uhl was playing Bach's Passacaglia in C Minor on the organ. I was overwhelmed by its beauty and majesty. Then during the service I heard words from Scripture that hit home: "the peace that passeth all understanding." I also heard: "In Him we live, and move, and have our being" (*Acts 17:28*). The music and the words reached the core of my being. They still do. To think that we are *in* God—that He is all around us, like the air!

After the service I spoke with Father Thomas Carr, the priest. I asked him some questions: Wasn't the Eucharist[26] something like cannibalism? What about the image that the Episcopal Church has of being upper class? Father's answers seemed honest and sensible to me. He himself wondered about whether the Eucharist was something like cannibalism. He also admitted that the Episcopal Church did have the reputation of elitism, but that the Church was working on correcting this reputation. I was impressed by his honesty and humility.

Soon after, I went to the Episcopal Church in Highland Park, just a couple of blocks from our apartment, on a weekday morning. Besides me, there was only an older couple. The priest asked me afterwards why I had not received Communion. "Because I have not been baptized," I said. He showed me the sacristy, with its very wide drawers where vestments were kept, and said something about Henry VIII. I have very positive feelings about the Episcopal Church, the church of my father's boyhood, his mother, his sister my Aunt Jean, and my sister Nancy. But I did not jump to join it.

I did, however, call Father Carr and asked if his church had a prayer group or Bible study group I could join. He said no, and anyway there was nothing over the summer; but, he said, the campus Catholic Church had such a group, and he suggested that next fall I call their priest.

Which I almost did.

That summer, at Flint Farm alone or with the boys, I encountered Jesus consciously for the first time. First thing in the morning I would sit on the flat stone step outside the kitchen door, warmed by the rising sun over Smarts Mountain, reading the New Testament. The love that Jesus had, His unfailing response to the needs of those around him, His high intelligence, manifested in the arguments He had with the Pharisees and others, deeply impressed me. Most of all, He made me think. He was constantly throwing out challenges, things that seem not to make sense to our ordinary ways of thinking. If you would save your life, lose it. Be perfect even as your Father in heaven is perfect. Love your enemy. Bless those who persecute you. The Mary and Martha story, a challenge for most women. The cursing of the fig tree, even though it was not the season for it to produce fruit.[27] And more, much, much more.

> Now it came to pass, as they went, that he [Jesus] entered into a certain village: and a certain woman named Martha received him into her house. And she had a sister called Mary, who sat at Jesus' feet, and heard his word. But Martha was burdened about much serving, and said, "Lord, dost thou not care that my sister has left me to serve alone? Bid her therefore to come and help me." And Jesus answered and said unto her: "Martha, Martha, thou art worried and troubled about many things: But only one thing is necessary. Mary has chosen the better part, which shall not be taken away from her."

Falling in Love: fall 1974-spring 1975

One of the students in the theory class I was teaching was a woman in her thirties, married with two children. Somehow I found out that she was Catholic, and asked her about the prayer group that Father Carr had told me about. She said yes, it met on Wednesday evenings, and it was an "experimental liturgy." She invited me to come. The "experimental" part appealed to my radical side.

Actually, it was an expanded Compline service,[28] though I did not know that then. I remember it clearly. The chapel was dark, lit with candles. We sang three psalms, which much later I found out were the three traditional psalms of Compline. There were readings, and many prayers offered spontaneously by anyone who wanted to contribute a prayer. We knelt and sang, in English, the "Salve Regina." It was not familiar to me at all, but everything that evening made such an impression on me that I remembered later which psalms there were, and the words and music to the "Salve Regina." All this would have won me over, but then there was *folk dancing*! It was beautiful, done by a group that had practiced it; most of us watched. That sealed the deal. My student, Jeanine, took me to meet the priest, whom everyone called just "Seb." I asked him at once, "What do I need to do to get baptized?" From then on I met with Seb, Father Sebastian Muccilli, every month.

After this, Jeanine and her husband David (who had been a priest) took me to the home of a graduate student couple where a few people from the service were gathering. We talked about prayer. At home, I went to bed, but could not sleep. It was exactly like suddenly falling in love. I was afraid. I knew my entire life would be changed, and I did not know how. I just knew I wanted to be in the Church: the Church as I then knew it, which was limited to what I had read and what I had just experienced. I disagreed with the Church about three important things: I thought abortion was perfectly okay; I thought that priests should be able to get married; and I thought that women should be able to be priests. I just didn't care about these disagreements, and I never spoke about them with anyone. It was simply the process of living in the Church that gradually changed my mind.

I began going to Mass weekly. Father Seb arranged for Marge Goetz, a woman in the congregation who lived nearby, to bring me to Mass each week. Marge was a mentor to me in the traditions and customs of the Church, and we soon became good friends.

Now that I had come to believe in God, now that I had decided to be a Christian and a Catholic, my life was devoted for several months to preparing for Baptism, that essential sacrament that would take away all my sins up to that point. First I was accepted as a catechumen. I was overwhelmed by this ceremony, part of which involved kneeling and receiving the sign of the Cross on my forehead from every single member of the congregation. From that point on, I was not to attend the second part of the Mass. After the Liturgy of the Word (the readings from Scripture and their responses, the homily, the Prayers of the Faithful), I was dismissed with a special blessing.

This reception into the catechumenate took place in January 1975, on the feast of the Baptism of the Lord. I was to be baptized at the Easter Vigil at the end of March. Since October I had been reading and studying about the faith, meeting monthly with Father Seb and attending the weekly prayer services. After entering the catechumenate, all this intensified, and I went through the various steps and ceremonies that the Church prescribes in preparation for Baptism. I continued to live my life: teaching, working on my dissertation, being with my sons.

Carl and Bill accepted my decision easily. It was probably no crazier to them than my involvement with yoga. But when Dad came to visit and

I told him I was preparing to become a Catholic, he said: "Well, if you decide to become a nun, I hope it will be in a teaching order." He was way ahead of me. Being a nun was not in my vision yet.

I was extremely naïve about the Church. In November I attended the annual meeting of the American Musicological Society, held that year in Washington, D.C. At the hotel where the AMS was meeting, the U.S. Bishops were also meeting. The nearest church was Saint Matthew Cathedral. I went to Mass there one weekday morning, and was deeply impressed by the large numbers of people there, including many bishops and many musicologists. Only later did I learn that the big crowd was there because it was November first, the solemn Feast of All Saints, and a Holy Day of Obligation (meaning that all Catholics are obligated to go to Mass on that day).

These were the external, visible preparations for Baptism. My inner life was complex and mostly painful. The best way to convey this period is to quote excerpts from my journal. On Ash Wednesday I wrote down the following Lenten resolutions:

February 12, 1975

I shall pray daily, in preparation for my Baptism, that the Lord help me:

—to be free from envy, which puts a distance between me and God, me and others, and prevents me from being thankful;

—to trust You, to submit to Your will, to have faith that You will guide me in Your own time and in Your own way;

—to have confidence in Your mercy, Your love for me; to remember always that Your grace is greater than my sin;

—to try to love generously and selflessly, without expectations, without thought of reward, in Your service;

—to thank You for all the blessings You have bestowed on me; to keep my life in perspective by remembering the misery of others.

All this is fine. But how was I actually living? During the time from my first service at the Catholic Campus Ministry in September, 1974, to my Baptism, Confirmation, and First Communion at the Easter Vigil on March 30, 1975, I questioned many things about the Catholic faith. I had frequent and almost violent swings between being happy and being miserable. I was sometimes terrified, and at all times wondering what my life would turn out to be. I was still struggling with depression, anger, physical pain, and exhaustion, and with strong but unrealistic attachments to a man. I was still seeing Shyam, alternating between appreciation and distrust. Both were justified: he did give me some wonderful insights, but also was not happy about my becoming Catholic, and predicted that one day I would leave my faith and the Church. Instead, in time, I gave up saddhana.

I read voraciously: Merton, Lanza del Vasto (*Return to the Source* and *Make Straight the Way of the Lord)*, the Catechism, Clement of Jerusalem's lectures on the rites of Christian initiation. I prayed and read Scripture morning and night.

Around this time I went to the city to see Julie Winter, the wife of my colleague Phil Corner and an astrologer. I knew nothing about astrology, but I was curious to see what I could learn about myself from it. I was with Julie for about an hour and a half, and in that time, even though we had never talked together before, she came to know and understand me amazingly well, and in a way that gave a strong confirmation to my spiritual side. Almost all of what she saw in my chart corresponded with my own experience. Something about the Moon at the time of my birth meant that I would have a low level of energy; something else meant that I was very ambitious. She said it was like trying to drive with the brakes on. I found out I am a very strong Capricorn, with the Sun, the Moon, Saturn, and Mars in Capricorn. So, a serious person, strongly committed to duties and obligations, not comfortable in the limelight (Elvis and President Nixon obviously did not share that trait with me!), not much concerned about money, very aware of authority persons, but preferring to be helpful to authorities rather then to be in authority myself.

Above all, Capricorn the goat would choose the most difficult way to the other side of the mountain: he would go straight up and over it, whereas most people would find an easier way, going around it. How true that is about me! I remember how my colleague Barbara Benary had her baby after two and a half hours of labor, and I after fourteen. Her PhD dissertation was a little over 200 pages and she did it in a year, while mine was 612 pages and took seven years. Joining a line in the supermarket or the ferry landing, I am drawn inevitably to the slowest-moving line. It may look shorter, but always there is someone ahead of me who has a big problem and holds everything up.

But the most exciting thing of all was that Julie observed, first, that I was in the midst of a profound transformation, and second, that I have a strong spiritual side. She was really amazed to discover this, and said, "You may have been a monk in a previous life." I shouted silently, "How about THIS life?" I did tell Julie that I was soon to be baptized as a Catholic.

I floated out of her apartment, floated down Broadway, and floated up to keep an appointment with Martha Bixler (a musician specializing in recorder and harpsichord, whom I had met in Northampton when we were both babies), to play Mozart sonatas. I could not have been happier. A side of me that was most precious to me, but was not much noticed by anyone else, had been strongly confirmed. I felt understood for who I really was.

But that high point, that elation, could not last. The demon of depression refuses to be dormant for long.

January 19, 1975

Another pd of depression! I'm learning how helpless I am, how buffeted by desires, how in need of ego reinforcement. How I sank in mire of desire! What does present state come from? It's clear that I've been more irritable and really angry than I've been for ages—it is the same old alienation, lack of ability to love. What causes this lack, this distance? Reacting, rebounding, against fierce and irrational desires, fantasies, expectations, that surfaced for two weeks. I must wait and pray for faith, and for the experience of God's love for me, and if I'm not always in that state of awareness, maintain faith. Today in morning prayer I became aware of how faithless I was, relying on good feelings. Let me take advice I so freely give to others: Don't ask what people can't give. Be grateful for what they do give, unasked. But <u>expect nothing.</u> Let me learn not to lose the center of myself, which is in God.

January 26, 1975

Re: vocation. The stumbling block to my freedom and my growth right now is NOT the PhD, NOT the academic life. How can I consider big changes in my life when I can't work on the little challenges, which really are the big ones? For at present, the challenge of attachment, of selfish "love," of desire, is the biggest. This is the one I accept NOW. One day it may be right for me to revamp my vocation. Now, I'm doing ok at it; I get enjoyment; I am of some help to people, I hope, in that I try to relate to them humanly; I am supporting myself and my boys. Let this be.

My basic problem: I don't trust God—I don't surrender to His will—I don't really believe that He will make me any happier. I think, more than a mystical experience, what I want is to live for the rest of my life with more happiness and joy than I've had up to now. To live without getting depressed and sick every winter. I can't help being envious and resentful of others who have more than I, or have fewer burdens than I.

February 7, 1975, Friday (A list of discontents)

I feel angry and rejected and depressed because every morning when I get up the kids have left a mess in the kitchen. Also because I fear I don't have the stamina to do my job, or what is expected. Also because I'm not at all sure I'm in the right profession, but don't know what else to do. Also because all the mechanics of living—errands to be run, things to be fixed, bug the hell out of me. DAMN! I'M MAD! Why and at whom? Also because I feel inadequate as a teacher—in grasp of subject and in ability to put it across.

February 20, 1975 (Thursday)

Today, thank God, I think the cloud has lifted. Of course, it's a non-teaching day, and a beautiful warm sunny day. I see buds on the cherry tree. I've heard my favorite funny bird (a cardinal) a few times lately. I sit here and can hear the birds and can see both windows, filled with trees, stretching out into farther and farther distances. The moon was beautiful last night.

February 21, 1975 (Friday)

How ironic that I write this the very next day. I am as depressed as I ever have been. I don't understand why my life has been so tough and so unhappy. I'd give up my abilities, intelligence, "good background," and all other advantages in a minute if I could just have one thing—to feel good about myself.

I was so naive to think that "having a religion" would give one peace and joy.

Dan just called about Music Craft [Livingston's theory courses] *& I told him the story of how all seven people in* [my sight-singing] *class thot they hadn't learned anything and that the class was a waste of time.*

I do not and have not felt very penitential since beginning of Lent. I've been doing penance all my life What I need rather is to lighten my load. "His yoke is easy, and his burden is light."

February 28, 1975 (Friday)

Still another week of suffering. Crying a lot. Am I being punished, and for what? Should I accept the suffering? Maybe God is giving me this so I can fully experience the symbolic (or is it real) death and resurrection of Baptism? Time will tell.

March 1, 1975 (Monday)

Very very depressed again last night. Cried uncontrollably in bed. If a man is intended for me at all, I won't have to try to find him. He will just appear. Please let me learn. Why do I, like Sammy [our dog] *and the porcupines and skunks, keep getting into the same mess over and over again? I often wonder if I have a mental illness that comes and goes.*

I wish for an intimate friend with whom I cd share these thots.

My eyes are puffed and swollen. I am brought very low and the Lord is my only refuge: in these times it is simply an intellectual thing, a knowing that his light will shine on me again.

I realized that I had great impatience and frustration with the congregation at the Campus Ministry. At the same time I knew that I was accountable only for myself; that outside troubles are really inside. I didn't see people turning their lives around, trying to live like Jesus. I knew they did it, somewhere, but I didn't know them. I read of many congregational efforts to share with the hungry, to become hungry, but not here. I saw comfortable little cliques, people hanging out with people they liked. My friend Marge was a godsend. She shared many of my concerns.

The 2nd exorcism was yesterday; it was a very solemn experience. But for me, the devils are there in greater force than ever.[29]

March 2, 1975 (Maundy Thursday)

I'm receiving so many blessings. All kinds of people are thinking of me, praying for me, writing to me. Christians are without a doubt the most responsive people I've ever met. For good reason! I only wish Carl and Bill could have some inkling of what this means to me—as my Dad surely does—but how could they? So I feel distant and impatient w/ them. Forgive me, and help me to be patient. And to live in the present, love unselfishly, keep You in mind more, be more faithful. If I go through the exorcism, receive all the love and care that this community is giving me, and still feel miserable, does this throw Baptism into question? Or is it not necessarily supposed to make me happy?

At last, the long-awaited day of the Easter Vigil came: March 30, 1975. The Church was only a few years past the cataclysm of Vatican II. The Campus Ministry, like so many other faith communities, was heady with the possibilities that had opened up, with all sorts of innovations in the liturgy. I will describe it as I experienced it then, that is, with no previous experience of Holy Week or Easter in the Church. The Vigil was an all-night happening that combined all the important days of Holy Week: Holy Thursday, Good Friday, Holy Saturday, and Easter itself. All this was new to me. The Vigil began with a dramatic reading from the *Lamentations* (of Jeremiah) in the chapel. At some point we were all directed into a large room where a supper was served, in the middle of which the priest came and washed the feet of one person at each of the tables. At the end of this meal the liturgist, a musician and a former Benedictine monk, sang the song of Moses, "Give praise to the Lord for He is good, for His mercy endures forever." We all repeated this refrain after each verse of the psalm, which describes the crossing of the Red Sea and the liberation of the Israelites from the oppression they had endured in Egypt.

We returned to the chapel for the Gospel and the homily.

Then we proceeded to another room for the Liturgy of Baptism. There was one other person being baptized—a baby. It was now past midnight. We all held lighted candles; we sang a newly composed Litany, which included Dorothy Day, Daniel Berrigan, Mother Teresa, and other contemporary people, along with several familiar saints. There was the blessing of the holy water. Then the baby and I were baptized, and I was given a white robe (an alb) to wear. On our return to the main chapel, the Liturgy of the Eucharist followed and I received Communion for the first time. Then I received the Sacrament of Confirmation and was given a beautiful Jerusalem Cross from the Holy Land.

All of these proceedings lasted until about six in the morning. I think we had started about 10 P.M. I had invited a few people from church over for breakfast. I made blueberry pancakes with maple syrup.

I was tired, of course, but elated, floating in the air. Thus began my life as a member of the Body of Christ.

Seven

NEW LIFE

I leave the past behind, and with hands outstretched
I go for the goal.

—Philippians 4:13

My sister Nancy had always been a tremendous challenge to me. I was afraid of her unpredictable attacks, verbal or physical. She couldn't stand it when I swallowed my saliva, which we all do all the time and never notice in ourselves and others. One time my parents, Nancy, and I were driving from New Hampshire to Oberlin. Nancy became more and more tense, and kept saying to me, "You distended your throat." I became more and more tense myself, more and more self-conscious about swallowing, so that I could not control it. Suddenly Nancy erupted with a violent physical attack. Dad, who was driving, pulled over (we were in a residential area) and, livid but controlled, told Nancy that we would leave her behind if she did not calm down.

I was ashamed of Nancy. She usually appeared sloppy and unkempt, her slip showing, or a bra strap hanging out, or lipstick smudged. Her table manners were nauseating. She often kept her mouth open with her tongue sticking out. She behaved in strange ways. She said terrible things to people. To a Jew: "I wish Hitler would kill all the Jews in the world." To an older woman: "Mrs. —-, why don't you have any children?" To a still older woman, "When are you going to die?"

Once in high school, we were all at dinner when Roger, a boy from school who sometimes walked part way home with me, a boy who was not at all popular, a bit slovenly himself, who loved opera, called and asked if I'd like to come with him and his father to a lecture by the Red Priest. (The Red Priest was Anglican, English, and a radical. I do not remember his name.) "Sure, I'd love to," said I.

Nancy disappeared from the dinner table, later returning with no explanation.

Roger did not come at the appointed time. I waited. The time of the lecture passed. Still no Roger. At last I called his home, and his mother told me that Nancy had called them and said I could not go after all, because I had to study my Latin.

What pain! I went out in the night, walked on and on around the streets of our neighborhood for an hour or two, angry, sorry for myself and for Roger. Next day I told Roger how badly I felt, and tried to explain about Nancy. But I know he was very hurt, and we did not walk together any more.

So I could not love my sister. Decades later, she became an important part of my spiritual growth. After my Baptism I was hungry for more spiritual food. I wanted to take advantage of all the Church had to offer. On the weekend of Pentecost, 1975, I made a retreat at the Cenacle. For years I had driven almost daily past the Cenacle retreat house on River Road on my way to and from Livingston. The Cenacle Sisters are a religious order of women living Jesuit spirituality. Their primary mission is to offer retreats and spiritual direction. The retreat I had signed up for was to be a silent retreat for women.

The Cenacle house was huge, immaculate, and tasteful, with spacious grounds neatly landscaped. The weather that weekend was gloriously sunny and clear. At the retreat we listened to conferences given by a priest, Father Denis Krausnik. At other times we could pray and reflect in our room or outside. I did both. The priest was available for Confession, called after Vatican II the Sacrament of Reconciliation. The Sisters were available for spiritual counseling. I had not yet made a confession, and it was time to make a general confession encompassing my whole life. I asked Sister Barbara's help in preparing for this confession.

Non-Catholics often look upon Confession with envy. I and my high school friends thought that Catholics could just go to Confession, be forgiven, and then go out and do whatever they wanted to do. Actually, although Jesus, acting through the priest, forgives us and absolves us from the sins we have confessed, we must promise to reform. Jesus rescues the woman accused of adultery from death by stoning, and forgives her, but he does tell her, "Go, and sin no more." Confession is one of the greatest gifts the Church offers us. We can encounter Christ on an intimate level, and experience the relief and the freedom that comes with His mercy and forgiveness.

May 15, 1975 (Saturday)

3:30 P.M. after seeing Fr. Denis

It is a gift to be thankful for, that I have enough faith to perceive my sins as I do. Let me be humble enough to accept this gift.

Re: my sister (and this can be applied to all people who seem to be burdens):

Don't accept responsibilities out of obligation. Have the courage to say no. Accept my limitations. Pray that I will be able to love from the heart.

I can accept my gifts if I always remember that they come from God. I need not then feel guilty about having more than others may have. For example, I am intelligent, more intelligent than many. But not for one moment can I be proud of that, or take credit for it. So please God, let me humbly accept whatever talents I have as gifts from You, and may I use them in Your service. Amen.

Thus I could cease to feel guilty that while Nancy had so many problems, I had relatively so few. I could cease to blame myself for not being able, really, to help her. The way was opened for me to learn to love her at last.

5:40 after seeing Fr. Denis again.

A tremendous burden was lifted. I felt like embracing the universe. So my sins of the past have been torn out of this book—and the sins of the present—and thrown into the wastebasket. I can live in the present. I am to offer the Mass tonight to pray that I will be strengthened in the knowledge that Jesus loves me as I am and that I can therefore forgive myself.

9:30 P.M. after Mass and penitential rite with water.

I am beginning to realize how beneficial and how important to me is the sacramental & symbolic life of the Church, and how rich this life is. For I am aware on an experience level of God's love and forgiveness. How could I not have seen it before? How clear it is now! But there are no new words that I didn't know before:

"God so loved the world that He gave His only-begotten son."

(to Judas): "My friend, why have you come?"

"Father, forgive them, for they know not what they do." And so much more.

If this kind of love and forgiveness exists and has happened, how can I presume to think it would not include me?

Amazing Grace–I know now what that is! Thanks be to God.

An important practical result of this Pentecost retreat was that I began seeing Sister Barbara regularly for spiritual direction. She helped me greatly in my struggles with depression and attachments. She introduced me to the Ignatian-inspired Examination of Consciousness, in which we spend time each evening recalling how God was speaking to us today, what He is asking of us, how we have responded. She gave me what I very much needed: a place where I could be guided in my reading of Scripture, and where I could ask my endless questions about it and about Catholic doctrine.

Another conversion

In grad school I had often wondered: why was I doing this? Why was I suffering the conflicts of teaching at Livingston? Was I undertaking the PhD not for myself, but to fulfill the dreams and longings of my parents? As I entered more deeply into the spiritual life, I felt a growing conflict between that life and my academic work. If I devoted the requisite time to teaching and the dissertation, I could not devote adequate time to prayer, spiritual reading and yoga (which remained important in my life for quite a while even after Baptism). I resented the time that the dissertation took. My heart was not in it.

I had been very excited about the dissertation in the beginning. I was looking at seventeenth-century English sources in the Music Division of the New York Public Library, thinking I would choose a dissertation topic in the field that I had been drawn to ever since Oberlin. I came upon a little book, duodecimo size,[30] called *Apollo's Banquet,* published in London by John Playford in 1670. This book was intended for the newly emerging amateur violin players such as Samuel Pepys. The violin, which had always been considered fit only for dancing, was just beginning to be accepted in gentlemanly circles.

Apollo's Banquet gives a few pages of instruction for playing the violin, but consists mostly of 212 unaccompanied tunes of all sorts, from the theater, dance music, and so on, and several French dances. I naïvely thought this would be a nice contained, well-defined topic: one book. Not too difficult. I was intrigued by the curious titles of many of the tunes: "La Madam Moysella," "She Would if She Could," "Mrs. Abigall's Jigg," "Love in a Tub," "Sir Martin Marall's J[ig]," "Gray's Inn Jig," "Fleece Tavern Rant," and so many others. Considering all the diligent work I did in studying this book, I am now amazed that it never entered my head to look up Restoration plays to see if, and how, these pieces fitted in, and equally amazed that my mentor never suggested this either.

In the preface to the dissertation I listed all the personal and musical interests that drew me to this work:

> The investigation of English seventeenth-century instrumental music at Oberlin and a Master's thesis on Orlando Gibbons' chamber music; a lifetime of playing the violin and several years of playing the viol; a long interest in folk music, especially from the Appalachians; and an introduction to the grace and subtle beauty of English country dances. In addition, the study of this

> work afforded me an opportunity to indulge what is the love of most historians: the physical, material contact with old books; searching through them, and through museums, city streets, country roads and villages, and wherever else one might deepen one's acquaintance with life in one's past. For history concerns not simply the lives of other, distant people; it also involves an important dimension of ourselves, without which we cannot hope to be complete.[31]

I was surprised and excited that Dr. Buelow, my dissertation mentor, approved my choice of this humble book. I began my research eagerly.

But that was before religion became my primary interest. The dissertation had by now become a grim duty, an impediment to my spiritual life and growth. What I had thought would be a well-defined topic became at least an octopus, if not a millipus—extending in all directions. Where did the tunes of each genre—courante, bourree, sarabande, jig, rant, Canaries, et al, [32]—stand in relation to the history of each genre? Who played these tunes, in what social settings? What was life like in seventeenth-century London, and where did composers and musicians fit in? What did all those strange titles mean? What could we learn from the implied harmony of the tunes? Most challenging of all, where did these tunes come from? Were they new or did they come from existing sources? I found many to be attributable to known composers. Who were these composers?

Above all, what did all this have to do with God? With the deepest desires of my heart?

It was Shyam who helped me on this. He said: "We have to go to the basement and clean it. But that does not mean we have to *live* there." Once I came to understand that getting the PhD was actually a spiritual task—that I would not be able to progress in the spiritual life until I got it done—then at last my motivation was clear and I could zoom ahead, as fast as scholarly work in musicology ever zooms. It was clear now that the Lord was really calling me to do the dissertation, whether or not I ended up remaining in academia.

July 14, 1975

I still have trouble accepting my profession as being worthy in the eyes of God. I have trouble accepting gifts. Is this why I have romantic notions about living a Catholic Worker life? I doubt that I'm cut out for that. Let me humbly accept my gifts and use them. It is important that some people who teach in college be concerned with the whole selves of their colleagues and students. Important too that music be a dimension in people's lives. And good that I'm teaching at a place where most of the students have very narrow backgrounds. And good that I had the experience of the bad music history class to learn to practice what I preach and reach the students where they are.

But I don't need to talk myself into this. I need to work on accepting God's gifts and His forgiveness, separate sin from guilt, do now what is my job now, let the future worry about itself.

July 20, 1975

Dr. B likes my chapter on French Dances. It reflects my confidence. The state of one's mind does affect the quality of one's work. My work before, tho I spent much time on it, communicated the impression that I didn't care.

I'm grateful that the Holy Spirit is praying within me all the time (Rom.8:26-27), and that "we may be growing most strongly at a time when our minds seem dark and dull" [source unknown by me]. *For I am in a state that writers refer to as "dryness."*

Whatever my resolve, there is no way I could have written my dissertation without the help of my father. Nor could I have survived the period when as a single mother of two boys I was also attempting to get a PhD and teach. His generous financial support, and more important, his emotional support, were endless. During our summers together at Flint Farm he helped me to combat the devil of procrastination, which plagues me (as it did my dear mother). After breakfast he would say, "Now go upstairs directly and work on your dissertation. I'll do the dishes." Otherwise I would have spent the best hours of the day puttering around with household tasks.

Yoga, still

It is amazing to me now that I was still hooked on Yoga According to Shyam. My journal still has many pages recording which side my breath is on; lists of exercises (asanas) to do; attempts to do days of fasting and silence; foods to eat, etc. One week I was upset because I had forgotten to feed the ants on the previous Saturday. Shyam had added the ant-feeding to my list of yoga practices. Was it to teach me compassion for the little beasts? Was it because Saturday is ruled by Saturn, black is Saturn's color, and ants are black?

It was time to have a Water Purification. Shyam said this would help clear away a lot of first chakra problems and bad effects of having eaten meat. I was always game for a new spiritual experience. This Water Purification achieves the same results as a preparation for a colonoscopy, but the means are gentler. Under the guidance of one of Shyam's assistants, Laura, who attended me all of one day and overnight, I was given lukewarm salted water, sipped slowly, in huge amounts; did various gentle exercises to stimulate the digestive system; listened to music that evoked water; and sat on the toilet every now and then, until what came out was as clear as water.

The result was a clear complexion, a relaxed body, an increased sensitivity to sounds and to any strong stimuli. I was to follow a very strict diet. At first, just very simple kichari—mung beans, white rice, and butter cooked to a stewy consistency. No salt, of course. Over a period of several weeks specific foods were gradually added. I put the ingredients for the kichari into a thermos bottle at breakfast time and filled it with boiling water, and by lunchtime it was perfectly cooked. That way I could eat properly even when at school.

August 11, 1975

Sometimes it's only taking a walk that I can think or feel straight—or at all. Let me ask for nothing—only live in the present and be open to it. Becoming aware of many insecurities:

1) diss.—realize I'm goal-oriented—disappointed at not getting it done.

2) feeling split between saddhana and the Christian life—knowing it's in my mind; I do need roots and a commitment. At this point I still feel no need to understand how to integrate the areas of my life.

But the spiritual quality of my life, and the discipline, has deteriorated since 1) stopped being able to sit [meditate] at sunrise, 2) made resolve on diss.

Summer rapidly going. Thoughts on teaching already. Good that I've tried to live day by day on diss. and not set heart on finishing, which is nowhere near. Last 2 weeks recovering from water purif. (2 wks ago today). Physically weak and can't (or don't wish to) explain this to people; fortunately Carl is here and I can talk w/ him about most things. Work has slacked off. It was good and simple to eat nothing but rice, mung beans, butter, and drink only water, for a week. Gradual additions, but simple diet for 6 weeks, no raw vegs, etc. Interesting to see how I function as I am, w/o stimulus of coffee, tea, snacks, etc.

As physical shit came out, now emotional shit. For a week or so felt very insecure re: faith. Fearful that a terrible test wd come. Fearful of Shyam's prediction that community (or was it the Church per se?) wd cause me great pain. Teilhard's piece about God depriving us of things we're attached to is most helpful.

Other shit comes out in dreams. Long forgotten things. Come out so I can confront you all and let you go. Shit—really and truly—tasted—terrible shame of a proper lady coming onto the scene—is this the hospital when I was 3-4? (I was hospitalized for an ear infection, and have always remembered playing with my feces, dabbing bits over the bedspread, and actually tasting it.)

Playing the ukulele for people and not really knowing how. (At Oberlin I did play and sing folk songs with the ukulele.)

Sex w/Tim and total inability to communicate what my needs, feelings, desires were.

Others I've forgotten. I pray, come out and be gone! Interesting to watch. O yes—most attractive and famous man, not really my type, interested in me and "looking me over," listing my bad and good points as one evaluates a horse or dog.

Am very impressed w/ total instability of life, of feelings and states. The more I am aware of this instability, the more I will desire the Permanent. Let it happen. Before seeing Shyam Fri. tried to think of how I felt. Couldn't—not in touch w/ feelings at all. Sensed something big lurking under surface—whether to be feared or welcomed—how can I know till it surfaces. Undoubtedly both.

Family

Becoming Catholic meant a real break with my family, though my sons were tolerant. They wanted me to do what would make me happy. Dad's initial reaction to my conversion was mild. His real struggle came later, when he learned that I was to become a nun.

So it was not a total break, as it had been for anyone who became Christian in the early days of the Church under persecution.[33] It was simply that what had become most important to me, my relationship with Christ and the Church, my seeking God, was outside my family's realm. They had no way to relate to it. They could not share or comprehend my joy at my Baptism, for example. They were not present, and if they had been, they would not, could not possibly, have understood.

Thus our lives went on, together and from a distance, much as before, except that they could not share that which was the center of my life. That was the real break.

Nancy, my sister, was the only family member who could fathom what my entering the Church might mean. She had always believed in God, and was a member of the Church of the Ascension, high Episcopal, near where she now lived in Chicago. She was happy that the church had real nuns, the Sisters of Saint Anne, who wore traditional habits and had rosaries hanging from their belts; that there were votive candles (she lit one for me now and then), and incense.

Nancy and I in Chicago.

She had for several years a period of relative stability. After her second marriage ended, she went to Chicago, took some courses in word processing, and found a job at the Railroad Retirement Board. I went out to visit her once. She found me a room at the YWCA, near her. The curtainless window looked out on a busy street, with traffic, and lights sweeping back and forth, all night. Nancy had a little apartment, one room with a kitchenette and a bathroom, where she lived with the thirteen cats she had picked up at a shelter. The cats each had a name, and were companions for her. She would write me letters as from her cats. The apartment stank, from the cats and from Nancy's very poor housekeeping habits. As I remember this visit, it seems that we had no huge fights or upsets. That is really unusual, perhaps unique in our relationship.

July 2, 1975 (Friday)

Hard to sleep last nite—had coffee at supper so could type in eve.—STUPID—cough, sore throat, fever, all worse yesterday and today. PAIN today and a bit depressed. Nancy called yesterday, was evicted, felt like dying rather than live without her cats.

I feel pressed and worried again. Must learn to leave things in God's hands. GOD HELP ME!

July 3, 1975 (Saturday)

Things getting better. Still some fever but still I think cold is better. God gave me a good sleep last nite. Nancy is better, prob. will not have to move. Called her and Aunt Jean today, who wishes she had my faith. Alas—I told her she really does, but doesn't realize it.

It's interesting that Nancy led the way in so many areas in my life. She is the one who got me into violin lessons. She got acquainted with the Catholic Worker in Chicago, and when visiting me and Tim on East 21st Street, she took me down to the CW house on Christie Street. We went there for their lunch for street people, and I may well have seen Dorothy Day from a distance. Amazingly, Nancy also went to meetings of the Socialist Workers Party in Chicago well before I joined it myself.

As for Dad, he had found new support. One summer when I was with him at Flint Farm, an old friend dropped by to visit. She was Frances Becker, the widow of a good friend and colleague of my father. In fact the Becker and Curti families had been friends not only in Madison, but way back in the Northampton days. Frances was a wonderful woman and turned out to be very good for my father. Dad had always had a terrible time making decisions (one of the signs of depression), and Mother had always helped him to weigh the pros and cons and come to a conclusion. Frances refused to do this, thus helping Dad to grow, even in his seventies.

Though I liked Frances, and knew she was good for Dad, I had the normal reaction to her as an intruder. On that first visit, she picked some cattails and arranged them in a copper pot by the fireplace. A fine thing in itself, but a sign to me that when they were married, she would be re-arranging the house and making it her own. And so she did. I had to let go. I had to let go of my father a bit, too.

The Real Church?

I had been going to Mass at the campus ministry for less than a year and had been baptized for only two or three months. The Church in the mid-1970s was still absorbing the changes of Vatican II. Since I had had no experience of the "old" Church, and hardly any experience of the Church outside the campus ministry, I did not know yet that the campus ministry was not exactly representative of the Church as a whole. But almost from the beginning I had been seriously disturbed by some things there. The first sign of this disturbance occurred when I and a few students were talking with Barry, the liturgist and a former Benedictine monk. He showed us a cartoon that obscenely poked fun at a notice that had been posted outside a local church. I had stopped outside that church, seen that notice, and admired it. It said that following the example of Christ's obedience to the Father, would the women please have their heads covered at Mass.

I grew increasingly uneasy at the Kiss of Peace. People milled around as if at a cocktail party. I was furious when one man asked me, *at the Kiss of Peace*, "How is your dissertation coming?" Another cause of my discontent was that many of the students and adults were disdainful of parish churches. People would ask: "How sad that Seb (the Campus Ministry priest) will be away over the summer! What will we do about Mass?" My dear friend Marge Goetz, who became a mentor and guide for me from the day that Seb asked her to take me to my first Mass at the campus, would answer this question with, "Go to your parish church!" She was secretary of St. Peter's, the parish church near the Rutgers campus.

When I was away I would go to "regular" Catholic churches: in White River Junction, Vermont, or Orford, New Hampshire, or Washington, D.C. I went once to a Hungarian Catholic Church in New Brunswick, and occasionally to the church in Highland Park where I lived. I made my second Confession at the Shrine of Our Lady of La Salette in Vermont. So I was beginning to experience the larger Church. And the Campus Ministry was not a monolithic entity. Father Seb certainly did not agree with Barry the liturgist on the matter of silence and contemplative prayer. But he did go along with some outlandish ideas: one time the consecrated bread, not unleavened as the Church prescribes, was just passed around among the congregation in a basket from which we helped ourselves. (I like to think that Seb was just as surprised as I was by this, for it did not happen again.) And Barry had wanted me to wear a bathing suit at my Baptism! Thank God for ordinary Catholics like Marge, and for the many other fine and well-meaning people I knew from the Campus Ministry.

By the summer after my Baptism, Mr. Liturgist made things quite clear:

August 24, 1975

Sunday. Barry gives "homily" (Seb being away) and splits community wide open. Main issue: Is the Eucharist <u>nothing but</u> a communal celebration? A party? Is silence legitimate? What is the role of priesthood? Of liturgy? I suspect strongly *that radical liturgy is a copout from radically changing ourselves and the world. Evening, Mr. Liturgist comes over [to my apartment] quite rigid and unyielding, even more anti-clerical and anti-silence than I thought.*

The period between my entry into the Church and my entry into the Abbey of Regina Laudis was an agonizing one. Why did it take so long for me to discern where my life was going? True to my Capricorn nature, I could not easily see the light. All this time, that Light was indeed leading me, but I did not know it. I needed time to sort out the major conflicts I was living with. Was my vocation to teaching and music, or to life in a Christian community? How could I resolve the tension within myself between the Church and my yoga practice? What should I do about the factionalism within the campus Catholic community? Could I ever learn to love people in a constructive way? Balance my desire to be open to others with the need for solitude? Could I ever resolve the conflict between wanting to do the will of God, accepting events and people as they were, and wanting things to happen my way? Between acceptance and trying to be in control?

August 23, 1975

I don't want to live in community. I want to live <u>alone</u>. And I can be peaceful if life is as externally quiet as this summer. What I haven't learned yet is how to be still in the midst of heavy responsibility and activity and involvement w/ others. At Livingston I thot I can't take this life. Am not made for it. But I realize much of my tension this week came from <u>not accepting change</u>, which is God's will. Nothing is permanent except Himself.

Despite my desire and need for solitude, my feeling of being drained by people, I spent a lot of time with others. My journal reflects constant unannounced visits from colleagues, church people, friends, even my students. Within one week Dan came for supper on Wednesday and stayed till 11:30; Phil dropped in on Thursday afternoon; Friday I drove to Maplewood to have supper with a couple from church; and Anita, my musician friend from New York, came to visit Sunday to Monday.

I worried a lot about Carl and Bill. At the same time I enjoyed them, admired them, respected them, was proud of them and full of love for them. There were times, too, when my complaints about people were turned into their opposites:

September 15, 1975

Yesterday at Mass—the readings for the day and the homily had to do with the Cross—I felt full of love for all there; I looked at people I didn't know and had never seen, and others I did know, and saw Christ in all of them. The Communion psalm response said, 'When will I see You face to face?' and I feel that I was seeing Him then. I am beginning to see or to know the fact that we love only by His love flowing thru us.

September 17, 1975

I feel still a sort of reverence for people since Sunday and since school has begun I have really loved my students, all of them.

September 28, 1975

I thank God for this semi-quiet day: for a productive day on the diss; for insights, for moments of peace—which, I realize, are the best on walks in Highland Park, sitting in my room, or at Mass.

I see that I've been trying to play the role of missionary to community. Trying to convert it to My Way: life style, Catholic Worker, Catholic Peace Fellowship, Fellowship of Reconciliation, etc.—all of course to no avail. I don't relate to other places this way. Why the difference? Because Christ holds out such possibilities! But I'm arrogant, and think I'm better than anyone else, and think there's no one in community who can help me spiritually. And yet here I am. What to do? Wish I cd worship and pray and work and live w/ people who desired as I do <u>*contemplation.*</u>

Though the Campus Ministry actually called itself a community, it was not a community. It was simply a way of referring to all the people who came to Mass there. I was confused in my thinking, in expecting this gathering of the faithful to be a community in the sense of a commitment to one another, in shared values such as a contemplative life, nonviolence, sharing the life of the poor. We, and all Catholics around the world, were and are united on a higher level, that of the Eucharistic sharing of the Body and Blood of Christ. The Catholic Church is truly catholic in its inclusion of so many types of spirituality, expressed by the various religious orders and lay communities.

Reading gave me invaluable help. In this same month of September 1975, Dorothy Day wrote about her own struggles with depression in *The Catholic Worker*:

"Often I am tempted to depression, thinking that I have scarcely begun to live a spiritual life, even to live the life we all profess to, that of voluntary poverty and manual labor. ... 'The worst malady of all is sadness, caused by lack of trust in the Lord and the desire to impose our own will on Him.' Pope John wrote this in one of his letters to his family."

I also found a good piece of advice in *The Catholic Agitator* (a local West Coast Catholic Worker-inspired publication):

"Radical Christians needn't put down people who are wealthy, wasteful, extravagant, or stingy, as long as we don't follow their ways. God is their judge, and ours. We ought rather to put our energy into being examples of a better way, just as Jesus Christ is ours. Each person must live his own life as God leads him."

October 4,1975

That is, GOD RUNS THINGS. All is done by him. I can't radicalize anyone, including myself. LET HIM RUN THE SHOW; LET ME ACCEPT YOUR WILL, NOT SET MINE AGAINST IT. I am looking for humility? Obedience? Here is where they are.

October 13, 1975

Most frustrated and confused not only about Shyam personally but by Eastern religion in general. After all this time I still revel in attachment to pain, drawn to it like a magnet: I do not want to let go. How do I learn detachment? By saddhana, I guess. But with all the doubts? I feel the need for guidance, desperately.

But I still went to see Shyam. He suggested I come each week for a pressure point massage ($10). I did not do this; but I did write down his detailed suggestions on diet and exercise. He gave me a new mantra, to a five-headed goddess. I had tried to be diligent concerning all the things he had asked me to do, but this was too much.

This year of 1975-76 seemed for a while to be going better at Livingston. I realized that I was too easily affected by the responses of my students. I had become somewhat better at accepting that sometimes a class will be great, sometimes terrible, usually in between. My evaluations from the students were more positive. I was also more accepting of the need to finish my dissertation.

I realized that wallowing in self-pity and depression is pride—overestimating my own importance, expecting perfection of myself. I prayed that I might grow in humility—attribute *all* successes to God—recognize *all* as a gift.

Life went on in this way, veering from times of relative peace, contentment, appreciation of life and of other people, to times of despair: feeling miserable physically, incapable of dealing with the mechanics of living—teaching, the household and the boys—fearful and impatient with living into an unknown future. Some of my classes, especially the one that dealt with early music performance, were nightmares, with everything going wrong. One set of student evaluations was very unfavorable and cast me down. As I look back on this period now, I conclude that I was really not a very good teacher. I had a lot of potential, but the turmoil in my personal life got in the way of teaching. My insecurity and ambivalence about an academic career were highly detrimental to my teaching and relationships with the students. And, looking over the occasional detailed logs of how I spent my time, I realize that I did not even put in a whole lot of time on teaching: less than thirty hours a week including class time.

After one particularly unpleasant early music class, I wanted to give up. Only one student was there at the appointed time. Two came ten minutes later. Two others were very late. One student had dropped the class without telling me; another had dropped out the previous week. Only one or two had their music with them. The apathy, the confusion, the passivity, dragged me down. At home, I cried. I had always thought I wanted to teach a group to perform early music, but now I felt that maybe I should accept the fact that I'm not cut out to do this sort of thing.

February 13, 1976

5:30 A.M. - wish I cd escape this whole thing. Wish some very wise person wd really understand what I shd do. Wish I cd get rid of all responsibility for a while. Why don't the demons just leave? I can't cope with my life. This year might as well not be happening. I don't see any use in it. The Lord makes us pick ourselves up from falls. But I wish He or someone wd do it for me. I want to give up; it's too much of a struggle. I'd like a life where I can be useful, can help to add to the peace and happiness and love and fun of life. But I seem to be detracting from it, for myself and for others.

7:45 A.M. Finished, thank God, w/ another long spell of crying. I think definitely this is a sickness. No one has ever understood this side of me and no one ever will, and it probably always will be a part of me. Today I see Julie [the astrologer I had seen once before]—*Hope and dread. We'll see what the day brings.*

February 14, 1976

No one ever helped me so much with my life and had such insights into it as Julie. I am mystified by how she does it, but I trust her. The process confirmed the direction I've been thinking about: contemplation, community, creativity. A synthesis of traditional and radical.

Insights on why Shyam is not good for me: I hate detail. The compulsive attention to detail supports the Capricorn side of me which threatens the space that I'm needing more and more of.

On the level of rationality, obviously the only sensible thing for me to do to is to remain in the academic life. The choice of any other path can be understood only on an entirely different plane. The question of my life's direction will take its proper time. I must trust and respect that process, must trust that <u>it will resolve itself</u> at the right time, that I can't control, push, or force it.

Seeing Julie was a very high experience, lasting all the rest of the day and in fact still lasting—despite having had only 4 hrs. of sleep, being in a pit of depression, and looking like a ghost beforehand, afterwards I looked visibly different; and the city and the people looked much better too, and the world was benevolent.

A dream just four days later confirmed this new strength.

February 18, 1976

A dream about Brownie, cocker spaniel, lifelong companion of my childhood from age 3 to 17. Old, somewhat fat, not what one would think adventurous. A house, upstairs, wide space of a spiral staircase as in a very rich person's house (certainly no house I've ever lived in). You can look all the way down to the bottom, down several storeys. Brownie, probably of a late weekend morning, wants to be let out. I don't want to take her, am debating whether I can hold off for a while. Aghast, I see her slip thru the railing and fall down past all those flights of stairs—she will die—but she lands without jarring on all fours, having fallen sedately upright all the way. She heads for a place in the basement where she can get out.

I too wish to take a rash step, surprising those who don't really know me—a leap—to get out of the restrictions confining me—to be free—don't need anyone's permission this time.

I didn't remember the dream till I sat down to pray. But while getting dressed I was daydreaming of rash actions. ... My public image will change.

Around this time I began to think seriously about visiting the Abbey of Regina Laudis to make a retreat and ask if I might spend a year there. I had read in *The National Catholic Reporter* that the nuns there sing Gregorian chant. I already realized that what I wanted to do musically was to form a Gregorian chant group.

February 23, 1976

Luke: Mary and Martha. This made me cry today. Martha is such a Capricorn. So burdened with things most of which are not necessary. It always touches me that Jesus says my name twice—a tenderness and caring there. Why cry? Sorry for myself? Why didn't Jesus say Martha could join Mary? But Martha obviously didn't comprehend what Mary was doing. Martha is my Capricorn nature: service, obligations, worrying, envious, appealing to authority, wanting something for herself but not able to reach for it directly. Can these 2 natures be in one person? I think in me, they must be. Mary is silent. I have not identified w/ her in this story

One day I was driving with Carl and Bill down Route 27. On a sudden impulse, no premeditation whatever, I pulled into an A&W Root Beer place and ordered a hot dog, Coke, and French fries. I relished their taste. There went vegetarianism and saddhana, all at once. I felt free and elated.

I thought about living in community, and actually drew up a list of things I thought my ideal community should have.

March 4, 1976

[I envisioned] *a living-working small community, in the country or at least with some land and fairly quiet. Democratic; decisions by consensus. A common devotion to silence, meditation. Getting up early and going to bed early. Either no TV and radio, or at least people who can take it or leave it. People desiring above all to live as fully as possible in harmony with God; not necessarily Catholic, but a strong Catholic component. With garden and strong interest in growing and preparing at home as much of the food as possible; locally grown; minimum dependence on commercial food. All income earned by individuals to be turned over to community and distributed on basis of need.*[34]

The community would have both women and men, married or with celibacy outside of marriage. I myself wanted to keep my income under $2400 a year so that I would not have to pay any income taxes, so much of which go to support our nation's wars.

As for my musical life within the community, I wanted the opportunity for contact and work with musicians interested in early music, chant, new music, ethnomusicology. I wanted to teach music both inside and outside the community, to adults who wanted to learn: doing what I liked, no grades, exams, or degrees. I wanted to have people to sing with.

The democratic, decisions-by-consensus idea harked back to those interminable house meetings at the co-op dorm in Oberlin.

My dreams told me a lot about my developing spirituality. I paid serious attention to them, writing them down and analyzing them. Cars were a major theme, struggling up a far too steep hill, or perching on the edge of a cliff or going up around hairpin curves on a mountain road and meeting another car going down. Sometimes a car would fall over the cliff, sometimes it would be miraculously saved. The car represented my spiritual life.

April 4, 1976

Last nite dreamed all night. Was driving (with someone else, I don't know who) up a very steep mountain road—not to be believed. I was very frightened. A car or truck came down—we pulled over for it, then realized we cdn't make it—the other person turned our car around in a very narrow space, front wheels extending over the edge of the road where a sheer drop was, scaring me to death. I don't remember the process of getting down. Then I was told that that road is the steepest in all of Europe (!). Then I saw the same mountain from a distance, from below. A car hurtled off the edge, out into an arc, falling on a beach amidst people—huge explosion, flames, people rolling over on the ground to put out flames burning themselves. Wondering if people in the car were killed—how not?

April 5, 1976

The dream is clearer now. It was working in me all day, making me sad—I let the sadness be, not trying to figure out why it was there. Several days ago as I sat down to pray, the word "time" came to me. I didn't know whether this meant to give more time to prayer, or to respect God's time for things. That day after the word had come to me, the reading in John was where the disciples leave for Jerusalem. Jesus says he isn't going, for his time has not come yet.

That's what the dream means. If you go too fast, too steeply, toward the mystical life, you get scared for your very life; you fall and hurt yourself and others. It was God himself who was driving the car and brought me back to solid ordinary ground, where wounds need to be healed and clogged toilets cleaned out. He saved me from great danger. I am spiritually ambitious. I want to push ahead faster than possible. That, however, is against my nature and God's will. Let me accept cleaning the toilets and bandaging the wounds.

Easter Sunday, March 19, a year after my Baptism, I got up early, took my prayer book, walked to a nearby park and sat and reveled in the peace and beauty of the Risen Christ. At the previous night's Easter Vigil I had been deeply upset *"by the gimmickry of the liturgy and the crappy music badly played and sung."* But that could not spoil the joy of Easter morning, a gift of God.

I was at the beginning of an important new phase, one that would shape the rest of my life. But I did not know it.

Eight

REGINA LAUDIS

The monastery is a dynamic challenge. It requires that you do something to change, to become more pliable so that you can take on Christ in a new way. This is a lifetime process. Either it works, or it doesn't.

—Lady Abbess Benedict Duss

I drive toward Bethlehem, Connecticut, with growing anxiety. I pass a fiddlehead fern-shaped sign on my left, "Saint Gregory's." This must be it—but no, it is an old New England house. A bit farther on, another fiddlehead sign. This time: "Abbey of Regina Laudis." I turn in, see a large building on my right, park the car, and see a door, next to which a sign beckons me to "Ring and Enter." I come into a small room with a two-person bench, some book-laden shelves, an arched doorway, and an interior window with a crosshatched wooden grille and a curtain behind it. Soon a nun opens the curtain and says "Benedicamus Domino!" with a big smile. I introduce myself. The nun responds, "Oh, you are the one who wrote us your life story!" I discover she is Mother Mary Aline. She tells me the guests are at supper, indicates where I should go, and I join them. A Franciscan sister, Mother Josina, presides at the table and tells me that this is a typical monastic supper: soup, bread, salad, and fruit; and that it is permissible to drink my soup directly from the bowl.

I had been thinking for years about living in community, about monasteries, but this was the first monastery I had ever visited. I had heard about Regina Laudis[35] from three sources. Ellen Weaver, a former Grey Nun and now in the congregation of the Rutgers Catholic Campus Ministry, told me that Regina Laudis was a community of nuns, many of whom had been professional women, and that they had just elected an Abbess. In *The National Catholic Reporter* I read the report of someone who had visited there and heard the nuns singing Gregorian chant behind a high grille. In *The Catholic Worker* I read that Helene Iswolsky, a Russian emigrée and a long-time friend of Dorothy Day, had died, and as an Oblate of Portsmouth Abbey was buried in a Benedictine habit. Shortly before her death, the article reported, two nuns from Regina Laudis had visited her.

"What should I say when I write to a monastery asking if I can visit?" I asked Father Seb. He advised, "Just say that you would like to experience monastic life as it is being lived today." I wrote, saying exactly that and no more. On February 26, 1976, I received an answer from Regina Laudis, signed by Mother Mary Aline. She wanted to know more about me and how I had heard of them. The letter gave me the identical bodily feelings that one has when one is first in love, at the beginning of a relationship. I didn't trust this feeling—it had never failed to cause me pain and tears.

Obediently, I wrote a two-page single-spaced typewritten letter in which I identified myself as a musicologist and a new Catholic who wanted to hear Gregorian chant in its monastic setting. I said that I thought chant was the *future* music of the Church. I said also that I was seeking silence and solitude to consider the course of my life.

The replying letter was discouraging about the silence and solitude. It said that the Abbey wants its guests to experience community and that the interaction between the guests is important. I replied that that was fine with me.

I came Sunday, March 21, at suppertime. The next morning I already had thousands of questions, the usual questions that most guests ask: How do I find my way in the *Monastic Diurnal* (the book used for the daily prayers of the Divine Office)? What is the difference between Sisters and Mothers? Between black and white veils? Do the nuns eat meat and eggs? When do they get time to learn the chant? How do they keep together in choir without a conductor? Where do the community members come from?

Most people, even Catholics, think that in religious life "Mother" means the superior of a community. For contemplative Benedictines, this is not the case. The title "Mother" is given to a nun at the time she makes her Perpetual Vows. It becomes an integral part of her name. "Sister" is the title given to a woman, not when she first enters the community, but after several months, when she becomes a novice.

March 23, 1976 (Tuesday)

Am improving slightly in finding the texts of the offices. But it wd take at least a year to get the hang of it. Lauds & Prime, today at least, all chanted on one note. Gloria Patri, w/ deep bow, marks each Psalm. At Mass, the Tract ... was haunting—w/ descending diminished triad as in Easter Gradual, "Haec dies."

I'm not entirely in touch w/ how I feel. Am simply trying to get used to being here, which maybe I never will. On the one hand, so many aspects of the life agree with me. The food is almost entirely home grown, and is vegetarian! Milk, butter, bread, cheese, honey, nuts, all kinds of fruit including currants, produced here. None of the white macaroni & cheese stuff. All excellent & simple. The land is beautiful & lovingly cared for, just as I'd wish to see Flint Farm taken care of. The guest house, St. Gregory's, is old, wide squeaking floorboards, iron latches, beams in ceiling. Everything is, as in all Catholic places I've experienced, ultra-clean.

The stars at night have seemed very close, virtually leaping out of the sky at one. This is where one can get the awe, the fear of God, without which one can't begin to pray. The birds, the sky, trees, all of nature are conducive to this awe-filled worshipful state. The way of life: the Hours, the chant, the early rising, the relative purity of life, are likewise conducive to worship.

Some of the nuns are a joy to behold; it lifts my heart simply to be in their presence. I love the sisters whom I've seen on their way to do physical work, in longish blue denim skirts.

On the other hand, I feel like such a stranger, as I am. Have met no one w/whom I feel comfortable or "en rapport." Of course it takes time; but some people one can feel drawn to right away. Not that I have trouble getting along w/ anyone.

The Psalms are so beautiful in Latin.

I was keenly aware that chanting the Psalms in Latin puts us in touch with all the people throughout the centuries who chanted these very same words.

PRAYER TIMES AT REGINA LAUDIS

The Catholic Church has two major types of communal liturgy: Mass, which centers on the Eucharist, and the Divine Office, which consists of prayers at various times day and night. Benedictine monasteries follow the scheme of the Divine Office as recommended by St. Benedict in the fifth century. The times set apart for the Divine Office (also called *Opus Dei*, or Work of God), can vary according to the needs and customs of each monastery, but in all cases they provide a framework that encloses each part of the day in prayer.

1:40 A.M. Matins
6:15 A.M. Lauds and Prime
8:000 Terce followed by Mass
12:00 Sext
2:00 P.M. None
5:00 P.M. Vespers
7:30 P.M. Compline

The major prayer times are Matins, Lauds, Vespers, and Compline. Prime, Terce, Sext and None, each lasting about ten minutes, are called the "Little Hours."

March 24, 1976 (Wednesday)

Vespers & Compline for the Feast of the Annunciation tomorrow. Music–esp. the 4 Vespers antiphons & "Ave Regina caelorum" (Hail, queen of the Heavens) incomparably beautiful. The Liturgy will bring me closer to the Blessed Mother.

Had a very good "parlor" with M. Mary Magdalen[36] *today. She tells me to look for a confessor & suggests I come back here to study the Commandments. I know I will.*

Yesterday had the joy of conversing & working w/ M. Prisca, who is in charge of the herbs. I helped her to pick twiggy stems out of dried celery leaves. Today have job of stripping lavender.

Today a jumble because I don't have my glasses, purse having bn left somewhere. Also because I can't assimilate this experience while here. There's not enough time & too many people to relate to. Two nice young women here today but they never stop talking & ultimately this wears me down. Sr. Grace who teaches & administers at Edgewood College in Madison, Wis! And Nobuko, my roommate. I need time away! Or just time! And more silence!

March 26, 1976 (Friday, at home).

The trip home yesterday was effortless. The car drove itself home. It was good to see Bill again & have him read his paper on the Middle Ages to me. He calls himself "Sir Wohlforth."

There is no need to think about whether that life is for me or not. Whatever is the right life for me, the right place, will present itself, or I'll be drawn to it, effortlessly.

I already had some new insights as a result of this first visit to Regina Laudis. I realized that the very fact of centering one's life on the Hours is a means for solitude and silence, within community. If the words were just spoken, it would be in the head only. It is the fact of chanting that makes the difference. The work has the same function: it is very Buddhist—work *is* (or can be, depending how you do it) meditation & centering. This was to me a completely new way of viewing things.

I found that most aspects of my Utopia were present at the Abbey. It became clear that I was not meant to go in the activist, Catholic Worker direction, despite the strong attraction that life had for me: a powerful and compelling "should." My radicalism, my support of the activists, would be in another direction, but I did not know what that would be.

March 30, 1976 (exactly a year from my Baptism)

I see more & more clearly that Livingston is bad for me—my health & well-being. I feel so distant from everyone. Who can know how I feel? I MUST leave & yet don't know where I should be. Surely not in another college. Like Abraham—I must have the faith to leave, not knowing where the Lord is taking me.

I must live a quiet life, seeing few people, going out seldom, close to nature. This is not at all the life of the performing-teaching musician.

It is mid-Lent now, and I worry that I am not doing enough, not making enough sacrifices. I resolve to eat no more desserts. The very next day I break this resolve.

We must die to be reborn: every Eucharist & every Lent-Easter. That is why fasting before Eucharist: not some ascetic discipline aimed at self-enlightenment; a giving of self. I have not given, only talked. Forgive me & give me the strength & will to give for the rest of Lent, at least. The best area for me is food—a difficult problem area & one in which I have not felt in my heart enough contrition at my greed & others' suffering, despite what I've said & written.

So I set up a modified fast for myself on Wednesdays and Fridays. But soon enough I give up this attempt. Sister Barbara, the Cenacle Sister with whom I meet for spiritual direction, tells me that

penance is a gift. We can't set it up for ourselves. That is vying with the Lord's will. My penance is [already] given: to accept need to work hard on dissertation despite weak body, and to come to learn how dependent I am on God. Without Him I am nothing. Yet "should" we not make a sacrifice externally?

April 4, 1976 (the day before Low Sunday)

For 2 weeks I've been singing all the chants of the Mass of Easter day. The ones repeated—"Haec dies" & "Victimae paschali" grow so deeply in one—I wish I cd hear them at R.L.

In these months of my first visits to Regina Laudis, my life went on much as before. The boys were growing. Bill, totally disgusted with the middle school in Highland Park, was now going to Universal High School, an alternative cooperative school run by the teachers and parents. Without my knowing it, he had skipped most of his classes at Highland Park Middle School, going only to the shop classes: small appliance repair, auto maintenance, TV repair. His ambition was to live self-sufficiently as a hermit in the woods. At Universal, he had a teacher of English, Hilda Barr Dixon, who amazingly was the same woman who had been the principal of Rutgers Prep Elementary School and who had interviewed us and told us that there was no room for Bill at that time. Hilda Barr lived near us and drove Bill and another student to school each day, since Universal had no bus service. She became a mentor and friend to Bill, inspiring him and restoring his love of learning.

He and I never had to fight over use of the car. Not wishing to repeat the fierce arguments I had had with Carl concerning his use of the car, I decided that if Bill was going to have a car to use, he would have to earn the money for it and for the insurance. He complained bitterly about the injustice of this plan, but I think it was one of the best decisions I have ever made. Bill did earn the money, bought an old car for $600, fixed it up, and hung out with his greaser friends in Highland Park. I was proud of him. We had some wonderful conversations and good times together, which I sadly knew could not happen easily if I were to live in a community. One day (February 3, 1976)

Had a nice, funny, warm talk w/Bill. He observed that I cdn't sleep because I loved the Abbey, & then said, there were 3 things in my life that made me really happy: 1) going to the Abbey, 2) going to Mass, and 3) playing the viol. Then he added, there are other things, too, of course, like cooking weirdo food that ruins my life! He really knows me. What a character he is!

Carl, after graduating from Rutgers Prep, went to Cook College, the ag school of Rutgers, the State University. After two years there he quit and worked at a large print shop where he met the young woman who was to become his first wife. He was now living with other guys in a rented house. He finished college at Livingston, starting there while I was still teaching. It was strange to encounter him on the campus now and then.

I treasured my relationship with him, too. We had our differences, as I also had with Bill, but we could always talk. Though he no longer lived with me, he came over a lot, often bringing friends. He was so loving and giving to Bill and to me, coming to the rescue of each of us in times of need. I felt that I could talk more with him about my real self than with anyone else.

Teaching and an occasional dreaded concert, over which I would be in a state of terrible anxiety ahead of time, but which always turned out well, still took most of my time. My work on the dissertation went on. I would finish one chapter after another, and even finished the extensive bibliography. I was living two entirely different lives at once: the academic and musical, and the spiritual.

After a couple of months I made my second visit to the Abbey. This time I brought my friend Marge with me. I was exhausted from work, and undoubtedly nervous, too, so I spent two hours lost in Edison, New Jersey, trying to find Marge's house.

May 14, 1976 (Friday, at Regina Laudis)

I can't thank God enough for being here. A sense of peace & quiet enveloped me as I neared Bethlehem in the car.

The moment of arrival in the parking lot, the bells seizing me deeply, bring tears. Immediately into the chapel; the middle of Vespers; tears here too. Feeling at once that nothing had changed, yet I had. Feeling unbelievable happiness.

Am I in love with this place? Do I trust that feeling? Am I scared of it? Can I meet the challenge to let it be fully itself, not trying to possess it, not having expectations?

Visit w/ Mother Mary Magdalen right after supper. Again tomorrow! She is radiant & beautiful. I'm able to feel a bit more comfortable & open. Poverty, sin, confession, salvation. Tomorrow: prayer for others. I change my family, present, past, & future. My mother, & all. Bring them all back home!

In the chapel at Compline: the natural light, just two candles, the deepening dusk, the hypnotic repetition of psalms, the smells: wood, & flowers; the warmth & peace & tangible silence.

Then seeing M. Prisca and M. Josina [the Franciscan who was living at the guest house]. Deo gratias.

May 15, 1976 (Saturday)

Utterly sleepless night. Don't know why. Day was too strenuous & I pushed myself too hard till I got here. Enjoyed digging in M. Prisca's herb garden in A.M. Hard, sweaty. Now a part of me is in this place. In aft. talked w/her about an hour. She knew Peter Maurin[37] *& knows Dorothy Day.*

May 16, 1976 (Sunday)

A few things remembered from Mother Mary Magdalen on Friday: Poverty, according to St. Benedict, is detachment, is treating everything in its integrity & sacredness, letting it be what it is. For example, food: a gift of God, & to sustain our bodies, & every meal a sacred occasion, prefiguring the Eucharist. So the environment for the meal, the conversation, etc. becomes the setting for this sacredness. The integrity of every thing. Every material thing to be treated as a sacred vessel of the altar. So, there are saintly birds flying around, as they are fully expressing their nature as birds. I see this outlook—the relatedness of everything, the integrity & sacredness of every thing & person, manifested here in thousands of ways.

May 18, 1976 (at home)

And there are times there [at Regina Laudis], too, where my prayer life is nowhere because I am just not "together," or am exhausted, or have gas in the stomach, or whatever. It is good that this weekend was "ordinary" spiritually, for right away, soon in the game, I am shown that the monastery is not a panacea, an idol. I can't worship it. It is a part of the world, a very special part.

My third visit to the Abbey, for a full ten days in July, was a decisive one. Amidst emotional highs and lows, bliss and anxiety, I gathered up the courage to tell Mother Mary Magdalen how I felt about the Abbey; how I was strongly drawn to it and felt I might be called to spend my life there. I also wanted to write to Lady Abbess to ask if I could see her, and ask if I could come to the Abbey for a year to learn about chant in its natural setting. Mother Mary Magdalen's response was not encouraging. "Everyone is in love with Regina Laudis. That does not mean one enters." One had to be in one of their lay communities first. Besides, the fact that I had been married was problematic. The Abbey had one previously married woman—Mother Jerome, a widow; but the Archbishop had stated that there would be no more. Mother Mary Magdalen summed up the situation: I do definitely have a call. But I don't know what it is, and the Community does not know. We can work together on finding out. The odds are against being able to enter because of my divorce.

This seems now to be wise and sensible. But then, I was devastated. I was also very bothered by the other guests, who all seemed to come to the Abbey for the purpose of talking. A bit of a conversion began to take place, though. One particular guest reminded me a lot of my sister: very large, but unlike Nancy, not very intelligent. At first I did not like her at all. But by the end of my visit I actually came to appreciate her more than any of the other guests. This movement from hostility to hospitality was to happen many times in the years to come.

I fretted, worried and anguished, wondering how Lady Abbess was going to respond to my letter. As more days passed, the more anxious I became. By the last day of my visit I had somehow arrived at a happy, peaceful state, accepting with equanimity that I might or might not see Lady Abbess. At the last minute, she sent for me and we spoke for ten or fifteen minutes. When I asked her if I could spend a year at the Abbey studying chant, she told me that they did not receive guests for such a long time. She suggested that I contact Dr. Gwynn McPeek, a professor of music at the University of Michigan in Ann Arbor. He was a medieval scholar, Catholic, and closely related to the Abbey. That would prepare me academically for a shorter stay at the Abbey.

I found this brief meeting very disappointing. Lady Abbess was reserved, business-like, right to the point. There was no warmth in this meeting. Even worse, it seemed that the Abbess was asking me to go even more deeply into the academic world that I so much wanted to leave. I wanted so badly a year of a whole different life.

But then—a day or two after I was home—I had a dream. I recalled the first part vaguely. It was on a theme frequent for me: I was living with a couple of people in an apartment, with too much to do and too little time, and there were arguments about the division of chores.

July 18, 1976

Then I was alone, in what was lower Manhattan, but transformed, unrecognizable. Much reconstruction & new bldg going on; in a filled-in dock area, some kind of Catholic center for the performing arts, many fascinating-looking bldgs; a church toward the edge I was on, traditional ladies w/ lace head coverings coming out, I realizing they wdn't understand what my kind of prayer was. Looking for a Tudor-like apt. complex on W. 17th St., described in a guidebook I had. But the street signs all had unfamiliar names, letters & numbers but not in the usual system, so I didn't know if I was above or below 14th St; in fact I didn't have any bearings at all.

Many old houses being restored; city radiant & sparkling; many sides of lofts, where one cd see where the floors of the torn-down buildings had been; on these all sorts of revolutionary (good) slogans painted in letters one storey high. At one point stepped into modern place, all glass & narrow escalator that cd take one in 4 directions to a lower level w/ various shopping areas, like a dept store, but much prettier. I couldn't figure it out so left.

Once I was nearly blocked by a very large crowd of workmen, prob. at an outdoor union mtg; I sensed they wd be hostile to me & somehow managed to fly over them, which they were aware of. All this time I was conscious of being inadequately dressed, for I had on the nightgown & ancient striped cotton duster that I had at R.L., & slippers. I did see several interesting-looking apt complexes; & a block of garish Victorian bldgs, much decoration, barn-red. Had to cross a very wide street, sort of like Astor Place, but many cars from L to R, among them a long caravan of squashed up VWs, each painted w bright colors & designs, had apparently been in a demolition derby, going very fast, refusing to stop for a light.

A Bowery bum confidently took my arm & got me safely across; safety in numbers as many people all decided to cross at once. Then went on his way with his wife.

Part 3: Shortly after, I came into an area just off the street, an arcade, but lined, instead of stores, by rich ornate wooden carving on all sides. On the left was an entrance to a chapel. It was called "Faith Chapel," transported bodily from 17th c. England. In real life, Faith Chapel was in the crypt of St Paul's Cathedral. Named after St. Faith, one of those shadowy figures whose existence scholars are not sure of. Built on top of the ruins of the old St Paul's, it was where the Stationers were buried & one of the 2 places where John Playford[38] wished to be buried. I doubt that I ever saw it. In dream, read a placard explaining the place. It had a date in the 1670s. By the entrance was a nun, standing and praying to herself, and a Rich Lady standing opposite her.

It is impossible to capture in writing the radiance, the sparkling quality, the attraction, of this city. Even the construction sites were interesting, and the tenements. A lonely journey; not a word spoken with anyone. The guidebook I carried did not relate to what I saw before me. Old signposts were gone; new ones meaningless. There were so many places I wanted to stop and explore, but went on.

This long dream came back to me in fragments throughout the following day. On reflection, it seemed as if this dream told the story of my life. The early part, in the apartment, was my life with Tim, in which there was much hecticness and argument over division of labor. The Catholic school of the performing arts—God knows—the past, an Oberlin transformed—or the future? The union meeting, which scared me and over which I flew, was the years of political life. The place with the escalators was the hesitation before the bourgeois material existence, the temptation of the expected and the ordinary. Yet it was of a much higher quality than the ordinary: say, Lord & Taylor's compared with Woolworth's five and ten.

The Bowery bum, of course, was the pull of the Catholic Worker in my life, and it *did get me across the street.* Immediately followed by Faith Chapel, representing the work on my dissertation. All of this except the unexplained school was in the correct chronological order of my life. I now stood at the chapel door; *I had not gone in.* Yet I *was* in, surrounded by the wooden carving. Were the nun and the Rich Lady guarding it, to keep me out? But they were silent. I was free to go in, or not to.

The Rich Lady: I had noticed with discomfort at Regina Laudis the deference with which a very rich lady was treated. Christ somewhere severely criticizes the host who offers a rich man the best seat at the banquet and makes the poor man sit in the back. Yet I did not know the circumstances. Did she ever have to face any trouble in her life, I wonder?

Father Seb's homily Sunday helped me with the Rich Lady. We have no idea what God has planned for her, what function she has in His plan for salvation, what suffering she may endure, either now or later. And it is not our business.

Now I had to deal with this dream, with my plans for the year off, with carrying out what Lady Abbess had asked me to do. After procrastinating for at least a month, I gathered up courage to write to Dr. McPeek. He replied with a seven-page letter, and after that we carried on a lively and intense correspondence until, the following January, I went to Ann Arbor for a weekend to meet him.

That weekend was stuffed every minute. Dr. McPeek showed me around the Music Department, took me to one or two concerts there, and showed me the University's beautiful gamelan from Indonesia. Mainly, Dr. McPeek and I talked and talked in his office, he serving me cups of the strongest coffee one could imagine, black. From all this talking—about chant, the Church, the Abbey, his life, my life—came ideas for my chant year. These plans were solidified when, shortly after our talks, I visited the Abbey and had a parlor with Lady Abbess. This was longer, more relaxed and pleasant than my first meeting with her.

The plan for the year 1977-8 was this: I would spend the first semester at Ann Arbor as a visiting scholar, which would give me library privileges and permission to audit any classes I wished. This would prepare me for further research and experience in chant. Then I would go to France for several weeks, work at the Bibliothèque Nationale in Paris, then visit the Abbey of St-Pierre de Solesmes[39] for a couple of weeks, and THEN, at last, come to the Abbey for the rest of the academic year.

I had a semester's sabbatical coming to me from Livingston, and I applied for a few grants, none of which came through. My dear father would support me and the boys for the second semester.

Meanwhile, life at home was full. My journals throughout the 1970s give the impression that I spent most of my time crying. That is a little misleading, since the purpose of the journals was to figure out my problems and worries. Now that I was getting acquainted with Dr. McPeek through the mail, and in my letters told him about events in my life, the journals are heavier than ever with inner and outer struggles and problems. Many good and amazing things happened in this academic year of

1976-77. I actually finished the first draft of my dissertation, which Dr. Buelow really liked. On Ash Wednesday, 1977, he unknowingly gave me my Lenten penance: to finish the dissertation entirely by Easter. This I did, much relieved at seeing the conclusion of this burden. The response of the faculty committee at my defense was very positive.

One day in August my Kentucky friend Don Nugent called, asking if I would like to go with him to the Eucharistic Congress in Philadelphia the very next day. We drove down and back in one day. We got to hear Dorothy Day and Mother Teresa of Calcutta both speak in the same session. Their presence, their simplicity, humility and holiness were more than I could have hoped for. But I was shocked at the lack of respect for the Eucharist in this Eucharistic Congress, in that dozens of cameras flashed and clicked just as the priest was raising the Host at the Consecration.

At home, I read Thomas Merton's *Zen and the Birds of Appetite*, in which I found a very useful passage that clarified the rift in the Campus Ministry that had been brewing since before my Baptism and had developed into a bitter factional situation. Merton wrote that the "progressive" trend in the post-Vatican II Church was anti-mystical, fostering the notion that one who thinks contemplation is important is undermining "community." This fit our liturgist, Barry, and those of like mind, to a T. Small wonder that Father Seb was discouraged, and I also.

The weeks after those decisive visits with Dr. McPeek and Lady Abbess were full of stress, anxiety, depression, even panic. I was paranoid. I feared that these promising relationships and plans would somehow come to naught, that I would be abandoned by those I had come to depend on. I had opened myself to Dr. McPeek and Lady Abbess, I had been very vulnerable, and now, not having heard from them since our meetings, I felt that I was being punished for my openness.

March 8, 1977

It's a sunny, clear, beautiful day. But I'm in depths of depression, as I have been for 3 weeks. The confidence, joy, hope, I had, is <u>gone</u>. All areas of life seem to be equally insecure. The dissertation is the most predictable thing. Somehow, it will get done. But then? Am I still to be going to Ann Arbor, & how about the rest of the plans for next year? And mainly: I make $15,000 a year. Where does it go & why do I have none? I have no car; if someone gave me one outright, I'd still have no money for insurance. After depositing my paycheck, keeping cash for the week ($50), and paying the rent, my account had $14 in it. And I owe hundreds *of dollars. And am I to pack up everything in this apt. and move? What an immense job, right on top of finishing a diss. And then I will have no home and Bill, as he leaves home for the first time [to Goddard College], will have no home; the very home will be no more. That's not good.*

No small wonder it was such a stressful time. Everything was up in the air. Everything was changing. My sons were growing up and leaving home, I myself was leaving my home, my job, my way of earning a living, my familiar friends, and I was at a climactic point in a long and deep personal transition.

One night I had a series of four dreams that reflected the depth of my fears. One involved being in an airplane when the entire front part of the plane fell off and I was about to fall thousands of feet down into the water. Another involved two VWs, one red and one blue, crashing into each other. A third had to do with Tim's leaving our marriage suddenly without warning. The last and most important concerned a baby. That one I will consider in a later chapter.

Thank God for the stability of Mass, prayer, the psalms. Thank God for the happy times with Carl and Bill, which far outweighed the tensions between us. We had many great conversations, and a couple of memorable camping trips.

Somehow things worked out. I did hear from Dr. McPeek and Lady Abbess. On a visit to the Abbey in June, Lady Abbess was both kind and severe with me. She helped me to see that in my distress I was feeling as though the world should be centered on me, and thus being oblivious to the fact that others had lives to live apart from me, that I was just a small part in their lives. I was humbled, but helped. Lady Abbess appreciated my openness, honesty, and clarity. But she told me that the Abbey and those whom it appoints to work with me cannot be manipulated; they refuse to play the parent, they will not play along with any wallowing in self-pity; they will not coddle me; they expect me to grow up. I need not always live in this pain.

I realized that I was being greatly humbled through my connection with the Abbey. With what sense of self-importance and arrogance did I first come! I had now exposed myself to Lady Abbess in all my childishness. Relating to the Abbey was the opposite of my position in the rest of my life, where I was almost always in authority, teaching, and giving advice to almost everyone. At the Abbey, I was a little child with nothing to give and everything to learn.

Thus I left for Ann Arbor and a year that changed my life forever.

Nine

SABBATICAL YEAR
ANN ARBOR AND FRANCE 1977-78

If any one among you thinks that he is wise in this age,
Let him become a fool, that he may become wise.
For the wisdom of this world is folly with God.

—Saint Paul

I have always loved scholarship. I could easily have been a student, a scholar, for my whole life—if I hadn't needed to make a living. If I had no deadlines to meet. If I could wander off on any paths that looked inviting. Many a New Hampshire summer, I spent contented hours in the stacks of Baker Library at Dartmouth. That very building, in a clean Colonial style, spacious, quiet, invited me to come in and do research. I could go freely into the stacks, where there were carrels to pile up the books I pulled out to look at. In the stacks, I made discoveries that I would never have found in the card catalog.

So now I had my chance. I had a whole year in which to study and learn. Where would it lead me? This gluttonous desire for learning could be a path to my true vocation, or it could lead me away from it.

I drove to Ann Arbor alone. Carl was almost married; Bill was now a student at Goddard College in Vermont. A rich array of tempting choices challenged me. I wanted to do it all. I audited Dr. McPeek's class on medieval music, which focused almost entirely on chant. Dr. McPeek gave me hours of his time. I would go to his office in the morning. He would make for himself and me his unbearably strong, black instant coffee, and my compliant, anxious-to-please self never told him that I really didn't like it that strong and would have liked to have some milk or cream in it. He was preparing me to do research on chant in France, but he was also preparing me for the Abbey. He knew Regina Laudis as well as one probably can without being inside it. He spoke at length about the Abbey, its spirituality, its customs, its people. He venerated Lady Abbess, saying he would not want to live in a world she was not part of.

Besides this, I began attending a seminar on ethnomusicology, which Dr. McPeek thought would be most helpful to my chant studies.

I loved it, but soon realized I could not handle the work it entailed in the time I had. I went to one gamelan session: the University owned a beautiful and very valuable Javanese gamelan.[40] I was thrilled by the one session I attended, taught by Professor Judith Becker, but again I realized it would take me away from my chant studies. Then there was a Sacred Harp group.[41] I had no experience with the tradition of Sacred Harp singing; I had only become aware of it in an academic context. I loved the music, but again I realized that getting involved in this group, which was like immersing oneself in a foreign culture, would pull me away from the main purpose of my being there. Years later, I fell in love with that culture.

The one thing I did stick with was that one evening a week, or maybe every two weeks, I brought my bass viola da gamba to join a few people to play viol music. We always met in the same house, where lived a woman who not only played the viol, but also made the best cookies I have ever had. Both the music and the food refreshed my soul.

Amazingly, within that brief three months, I also did a lot of traveling. I went to Madison to see my father. I drove to Notre Dame and its sister college, Saint Mary's, to visit a couple whom I had known at the Rutgers Campus Ministry. I made two visits to the Sisters of Mercy in Alma, Michigan, the first one for Thanksgiving weekend. The Sisters were most welcoming, inviting me to present my views on chant to them. I spoke about how Gregorian chant is beneficial for the body, and how it is supportive of the contemplative life. I went to Northwestern University to the annual meetings of the American Musicological Society, where I spoke with a recruiter from the Dearborn branch of the University of Michigan. Was I serious about looking for another academic position? In any case, I was subsequently invited to come to Dearborn for an interview, which I did.

A few weeks before my time at Ann Arbor was up, I registered for a course in French conversation at the Y. This proved to be very helpful in refreshing my memory of the two years of French I had taken in high school.

All these things, even the ones that I tried just once or twice, were enriching and never a waste of time. It's not surprising that the introspective side of my life almost shriveled up and dried, with all this activity. I'm sure this was a relief from the decades of intense self-examination that I had gone through. I had no close friends except Dr. McPeek, who was more of a mentor than a friend. Having dropped into a place where I knew no one, I met many people whom I liked. But I was not there long enough to develop any lasting friendships. I was lonely in a way, but had little time to think about that. The hardest thing I experienced was not being able, for the first time, to be with Bill on his birthday, to make a cake for him, to celebrate with him.

All those morning meetings with Dr. McPeek, and all the reading I was doing on chant, led me to settle on a topic for research in France. McPeek, in his lectures and in our meetings, had mentioned that the rhythm of chant was a "hot topic" for research, but he never specifically mentioned the new work on semiology at Solesmes. Semiology is the study of the ancient notation of chant before the development in the twelfth century of the square notation, which is still used. However he did stir up my interest in the quilisma. That is a wavy character in both the ancient neumes[42] and the square notation. It is now interpreted as a "weak" note—that is, one not emphasized, that fills in an interval, most commonly a third. Usually the first note of this group of three is lengthened slightly. The quilisma occurs most often in relation to half-steps—that is, on B or E. Dr. McPeek mentioned several guesses scholars had made about the quilisma: it might have signified a quavering of the voice, or a microtone,[43] a chromatic note or any note outside the diatonic hexachord. It might have pointed to or reflected earlier pentatonic melodies.

In retrospect, this seems to me a very strange topic to choose. I was a total beginner in the scholarly pursuit of chant. I really had no idea what I was doing. Why did I not gravitate toward a more humanistic, or historical, or aesthetic, or sociological, investigation of chant? These broader areas are much more consistent with my personality than the study of one neume. For example, I would have been more capable of undertaking the study of "Women Composers of Chant in Monastery x." This would surely have been far more likely to get a grant than my vague statement, in grant applications for the sabbatical, that I simply wanted to study chant in general.

The great deficiency of this semester was that it was all words. I had no living experience of the chant, either singing or hearing it. This, however, would be remedied somewhat in France and then intensively at Regina Laudis.

France: January 9-February 21, 1978

In Paris, I hardly ever saw the sun. On the few clear days, the sun did not appear until about 9:30 A.M. because of the tall buildings in its way. It was cold all the time, and *I* was cold, and I *had* a cold. There were two sides to my life: either I was thrilled and fascinated and in love with what I was seeing and discovering, or I was overwhelmed with loneliness, discomfort, self-pity. My journal became my best and only friend, the only place where I could freely express myself. [N.B. In this section on France, some of the journal entries are undated.]

I established myself in a pension on the Rue du Four (Street of the Oven), a narrow street on land formerly owned by the Benedictine Abbaye St-Germain. In medieval times people came there to a communal oven to bake their bread.

The pension must have 50 or so people—two sittings for a meal—and most of them are young American females studying at l'Alliance Française—a very selfish & discourteous lot—just like most people in that generation—not bad people, just selfish. The noise here, indoors & out, is unbelievable. Room: small, corner w/sink, wardrobe, little table, small fireplace (used to be functional) w marble mantelpiece on which I have put my favorite Christmas greetings & snap of Carl & Bill & me; orange, yellow, brown flowered wallpaper, dingy fine mesh curtains at the window w/ small holes in one; metal shutters, iron railing outside (one cd sit there on a cushion in good weather), bare floor, wood, clean; 2 folding chairs. Outside, very narrow street (I can't see the sky unless my head is at floor level), view of blank wall, many people passing by in the street, Brasserie across, very popular, & another nice looking less pop restaurant. Food: potage, poulet au pois, pain (pas de beurre), & tangerine, & water. Simple, not bad; I will not get fat on it!

I had come to France with three goals: to look at ancient chant manuscripts and to hear, in churches, as much chant as possible; to discover traces of the Middle Ages; and to improve my French. On my first day, then, I applied for a reader's card at the Bibliothèque Nationale, registered for a course at l'Alliance Française, and walked. At once I noticed the layers of history in evidence.

Medieval: names of streets, & their shapes—names of saints everywhere; traces of the organization of the city by occupations. 17th and 18th c. buildings: small ones with 5-6 storeys; large palatial ones like the gov't bldgs on the rue Grenelle, w/ huge beautiful enticing courtyards. The 18th, 19th, and 20th centuries manifest in another way, by the wide boulevards and huge monuments: the "official" city, which, as in London, doesn't attract me much. How much of the past in the most incredible bread store I noticed today? And other stores & their strange contents, one full of nothing but jars of jam! Then the present, with people just living & doing their things & most of the time taking all this history for granted. Sidewalks often in the old parts of the city, about 2 ft wide & parked cars often preempt them so you have to walk in the street. The Bibliothèque Nationale neighborhood is great: 17th c: Lully, Moliére, Richelieu, Mazarin, all in evidence. In the Salle des Manuscrites—IT IS COLD IN THERE.

It seemed to be the same temperature as the outdoors: 40 or 50F. I learned to dress as for winter in Wisconsin, yet my hands were so cold it was hard to write. The French did not appear to be bothered at all by the cold.

I was thrilled to be holding in my hands manuscripts that were a thousand years old or more. I was amazed that I was allowed to do this, for they will not last forever. These books, used in the liturgy, were copied by monks, set up on lecterns and sung from by a whole schola, a group of maybe five or six monks. I loved finding little whimsical drawings in the margins, or seeing a hole in the parchment—maybe where a lamb's little leg had been—carefully outlined in red. I did take time with the manuscripts that had Graduals[44] in them; I did make lists and thematic indices of Mode V Graduals. How much better it would have been if I had been looking at these Graduals with the background I have now—of singing them over and over again at Masses throughout the years. I was merely dipping my toes into the edge of a vast ocean of work already done by others. To do any meaningful research with the meager background I had was impossible. The whole point of choosing a research topic like mine, "The Quilisma in Fifth-Mode Graduals," was simply to give me an entrance point into that vast world.

I sometimes enjoyed the challenges of functioning in France, which was like Survival in the Wilderness. I found the French people, with a few notable exceptions, very patient with my attempts at speaking their language. But more often than not, I was discouraged by these challenges.

At the pension: Things are difficult in certain ways. A sign in the dining room says, no washing of clothes in one's room; if any are found, one will be fined 5F for each garment to cover the cost of gas & water. And no electrical appliances—they will be confiscated if found. I had thought of getting a little light, for I can't read in bed. O well. Last night noise inside & out was frightful. The 13th c. night life of what I pretended was the Latin Quarter continues in the Boucherie—steak house. They sing, pound the tables, shout, jump up & down, till 1 A.M. closing time.

One morning I woke up with the aches and fever that indicate flu. But I went out anyway. I went to Mass at Saint-Severin. Though France was reputed to be a secular country, I found all the Masses well attended, and people praying at other times, too. This day I lit a votive candle for the first time in my life. It was for Nancy, who was still living in Chicago with her thirteen cats. It was probably the only thing I could do for her. May she, who was one of the least, now be sharing in God's kingdom.

Following this, I went to the Cluny Museum. It was fantastic, but too much for me in my physical state. I did at least look thru all the rooms. Aesthetically, the most pleasing were the Unicorn Tapestries, & the best of them the first (Sight), because the Unicorn is laying his head in the Lady's lap. The Chapel was the best room, in that even after all the hundred years and other uses, I could feel a great difference here—the energy of prayer. Those abbots of Cluny must have spent a lot of time praying when they were at their Paris mansion. After this, I liked: a statue about 2 ft high of Saint Barbara. On her right, with her leaning on it, was a tower about her height, with a real opening so that if you were 2" high you cd go in & up a circular staircase; the stained glass, but I was too tired by then to look at details; the choir stalls which had carvings under the seats, of things secular and almost pagan: a man killing an animal, 3 bears dancing, imaginary beasts playing musical instruments, etc. Are they there to amuse the nuns & monks when they are bored? Anyway, a fine example of the mixture of sacred & secular typical of the Middle Ages.

Then, all the objects of daily life: belts & buckles; jewelry; miniature things for children, found in the Seine: games, utensils, etc. Little box for traveling! And multitudes of religious objects: chalices & patens, monstrances, crosses. Earlier things tend to be simpler. 14th c. & later tend to be complicated: a monstrance can be an entire building in miniature; the foot of a cross, a whole city. Also, a Book of Hours, which you could see every page of. And writing implements from 12-13 c. & pages from 9th c.

I was well aware of my naïveté in these matters: *To get the most out of museums, I should have: 1) a guide book; 2) a French dictionary; 3) opera glasses; 4) Jim Pierce*[45] *dictionary, or another, explaining Christian iconography, attributes of Saints, etc.*

As for the music being sung or played at Mass in the several churches I visited, I was very disappointed. Probably the best music I heard in the Parisian churches I attended was at Notre-Dame de Paris, the first cathedral Mass I had ever attended. But compared to any Mass at Regina Laudis, it was disappointing.

January 15, 1978 (Sunday)

Mass at Notre-Dame de Paris! This time, I belonged there as a worshiper. Throngs of people. A good 10 priests in the entrance procession, w/ candles & incense. All-male choir. The promised "Latin Mass" was not exactly what I'd expected. Mostly in French.

The Kyrie was sung with an alternation of three textures: the choir, in chant, the people, and the choir in polyphony. Spoken words were inserted between the sections. The Gloria in Latin, alternating between choir and people. A lot of people sang, tho no texts or music were given out. It must have been Gloria VIII for I noticed it began w/ the "theme" of the disgusting Peloquin Gloria. The Credo was perhaps III—I was lost. And they took up the collection during it!! Totally wrong—the collection shd be part of the Offertory. The readings (in French) appeared to be the same as I heard at the Abbey a week ago (the Baptism of the Lord). The "Gradual" was a responsorial psalm in French. The sermon was about Baptism. There was a great procession before the Gospel: the Book was carried & all the 10 or so clergy accompanied it to the lectern. The "Offertory" was an organ piece based on "Wie schön leuchtet der Morgenstern" ["How Brightly Shines the Morning Star," a traditional German chorale for Advent]. *The Pater Noster was in Latin. It was great to sing it there with all those people. The Kiss of Peace was done only by the clergy. The vast majority of people received Communion in the hand. After Communion the choir sang a polyphonic setting of "Sicut Cervus" very beautifully. To go back: the "Agnus Dei" was completely choir polyphony. ALL THE CHANT WAS ACCOMPANIED BY THE ORGAN!!*[46]

Several days later I went again to Mass at Notre-Dame. It was in Latin, with the inevitable organ accompaniment. It was followed by an Office chanted *recto tono* and without the organ. It sounded good; was more compelling—something powerful about men's voices and the lengthy reiteration of one pitch.

On one occasion I went to Mass at Saint-Sulpice. Lugubrious French organ music—I hated it, and disliked the church visually. But it was Mass, and I could understand a lot of the readings and the homily.

Soon after my arrival in Paris I visited the church of Saint-Germain, just two blocks from my pension. It is the oldest church in Paris. Originally it was a Benedictine abbey, signs of which are all around. Entering the church, I was surprised to see a man in back reading a newspaper the whole time I was there. A Spanish Mass started, during which something was sung to Bob Dylan's "Blowing in the Wind."

I could not go to daily Mass there, because it was at the same time as breakfast in the pension, but I visited there each morning before setting out for the library.

Outside the church is fascinating—park, garden, monks' burial ground—whole neighborhood up to rue St Benoît. On the other side, an old, quiet, expensive neighborhood, rue du Cardinal, rue de l'abbaye, rue de petite Boucherie–galleries, modern art, very fancy. Inside again, was quite amazed to find that Mabillon (17th c. Benedictine), & Descartes, are buried there.

Saint-Germain became my spiritual home. There I poured out to the Lord my worries, my hopes, my desires. I discovered that one of the side altars was devoted to Saint Benedict. There, I prayed fervently for his intercession, that I might be able to live under his Rule.

I am learning about myself. I thought I was the kind of person who can adapt to other cultures, who is not chauvinistic or complaining. I wanted to live while here as much as possible with local materials, food, etc. But I must confess the toilets are the smelliest, most unpleasant, as bad as any of the worst gas-station ones in the U.S.—many w/o either toilet paper or towel. It often smells bad on the Metro, too. The roller towel in the Bibliothèque Nationale is never changed & it's a wonder there's no epidemic.

January 18, 1978

At noon was overcharged at lunch & tho I know the words to say, I was confused & just couldn't cope with the situation, & was so upset & so lonely & angry that I cried on the street & in the Metro. <u>Will not</u> go into such cafés again. In Paris there seems to be no time for courtesy or kindness. The landlady here is very dour, probably sick but certainly self-pitying; the students are very selfish or discourteous or whatever it is. They simply make no attempt at meals to introduce themselves to others or to engender a general conversation. If I had no assertiveness I'd sit there meal after meal in total isolation.

This week two Parisiennes have seen me standing & pondering a map or piece of paper & have offered their help.

Have I described the Alliance Française yet? An incredible place; crowded, filthy, with a decent stand-up "bar" with drinks (beer the only alcoholic) & snacks; the smelliest john I've ever experienced; and in Paris men, janitors etc., walk into johns all the time, and some public places are totally co-ed which is very disconcerting. Today at Alliance was terrified to discover I had been locked in from the outside! Screamed & banged on the door, at last was rescued, they thot it was a big joke. Students from all countries, all classes & ages & occupations,

French the only common language. Classrooms dingy, & long benches w/ attached writing surfaces, rigid and immovable. What must this do to children? People wander in & out of class freely all during the 2-hr class. I was terrified the 1st day; the prof talks at regular Parisian speed a lot & I understand nothing; I do understand when he explains grammar. The 1st day I was convinced it had been a mistake for me to do this. But I must realize: No matter what happens, there is no possibility I will not accomplish my main tasks, one of which is to improve my French.

After a few days, I did drop this class and entered two classes, taught by two different women, in French conversation. These proved to be more manageable and more what I needed. The classes at Alliance were in the afternoons. Toward the end of my time in Paris, I discovered that one could arrange for private lessons in French pronunciation in their language lab. I found this very helpful. I liked the conversation classes, too. They were smaller and more informal, and we had a chance to get acquainted with each other. I was the only American, and was surprised to discover that my classmates were very interested in my country. Madame Piquet's class all went out to lunch together on the last day of class. It was such a pleasure to be in a restaurant with others for a change.

Can walk thru Luxembourg Gardens on way back from l'Alliance. My only chance to see any trees or birds. It's very large, vast stretches of mud, sidewalks, a bit of grass, & all the trees are planted in straight rows. A cold, lonely city, especially if you are isolated by language. I am really sustained by the prayer of others & by being able to go to St-Germain before going to the BN each morning.

Excursion One: Chartres (January 21-23)

Two days at Chartres, one day at Jouarre.[47] Both followed the same emotional pattern that characterized my entire stay in France: darkness, bad experiences, self-pity, isolation, and discouragement, contrasted with their opposites. The Cross and the Resurrection on a tiny scale: that's what our lives are all about.

I was reading Henry Adams on Chartres, and wondered why he never became Catholic. How could he be so full of wonder, admiration, and reverence at the beauty of Chartres and of Our Lady, and not fall in love with the Church itself? I have never found the answer to that question.

I was so happy to get out of the city and see once again woods, canals and rivers, fields. I feared I would not know when to get off the train. At last the Cathedral loomed up across the fields. I looked for a place to stay, wanting quiet, a view of the Cathedral, and a medieval house. I found them all, and other things besides:

This hotel—unbelievable—scares me. I was too hasty when I looked at the room and simply did not see the dirt. I saw that it was shabby—wallpaper, plaster, & floor covering (2 kinds of linoleum) cracked and peeling. Bedspread quite dirty; bed linen very coarse, & bottom sheet has several machine-stitched seams in central places; but linens apparently clean. WC on a whole nother floor & no t-p in it & it has a wet floor.

I was scared to find my way in the middle of the night through the dark hallway, up the narrow dark stairs, to this bathroom.

In room, 2 electric lights, a radiator, a lavatory, under which is a sort of portable bidet. Wonder if anyone else is staying here? It's someone's house, about 500 years old with little having been done to it in that time. It is quiet, so far. Street is 2-3 blocks from the Cathedral, about 6 feet wide & a block long. All old streets here are very narrow. This is a pleasant surprise—more the air of old sections of towns in Germany—some literally 3 ft wide, virtually a gutter. One can get a beautiful view of the Cathedral thru a slit 2 blocks away to the south, by La Vielle Maison Restaurant (which was mentioned in a National Geographic article & which looked great, but I didn't dare go into it alone).

My room smelled of urine. Floor unthinkable to step on w/ bare feet. DIRTY. Cup unusable. This room can teach me: 1) Don't covet those little narrow medieval streets any more. They may look tempting and romantic; but I am more fastidious than adventurous. 2) Don't be so stingy with myself. 3) I really have quite middle-class tastes & habits.4) I hate like hell going to restaurants alone; and I probably ought not to travel w/o a companion who knows the language and the country.

I had arrived at Chartres on a Saturday afternoon, January 21, 1978. After finding my room, I entered another world in a Cathedral itself. God meant me to come today. It's been the 1st beautiful day since I've been in France. The thing inside that I kept returning to was the glass windows on the West; for the sun was shining directly thru them. There was such a luminous quality throughout the whole nave. I tried to be rational and tell myself this isn't the Deity, it is a perfectly natural phenomenon, sun shining thru colored glass. But my body and soul contradicted this. I think those artists must have been very conscious of the effect of colors on the harmony of the person, just as the musicians were conscious (I assume) of the effects of sound.

Mass at six P.M. in French, terrible organ music, the sung music exactly like the fake music in the U.S., unleavened by Protestant hymns.

I came here as a pilgrim, to pray for a special intention (that I become a monastic). I found it difficult to pray in the big cathedrals. Too many people wandering about; too many distractions. Maybe I'll be able to pray tomorrow.

I wrote copious comments on the art inside and outside the Cathedral. There is no point reproducing most of this here; Henry Adams and so many others have written incomparably about these things. Just a couple of notes:

My favorite sculptures are the South Door of the Royal Portal: the shepherds & sheep, Annunciation & Nativity, and all; and the Zodiac & especially Mary shown as a master of all learning. All the world of creation, the cosmos and Man's creation, here given central meaning. South Porch: I really liked this, as much as I got to see while suffering from the cold. We need masculine strength & energy & theological clarity & we need the Last Judgment and Christ trampling underfoot the Dragon of Evil. We cannot pretend that Evil doesn't exist. … I looked from simply an intuitive emotional view. There just isn't time or energy to take in so much detail.

Sunday morning was dreary, bleak, dark, terribly cold. The wind swept through my inadequate clothing. I fled my "hotel," surprising the man in charge by refusing their breakfast. I tramped the streets in the neighborhood of the Cathedral, looking in vain for coffee at least. I looked wistfully into the windows of La Vielle Maison.

I was fascinated by the streets: so narrow the street lights are suspended from above on chains fastened to the buildings on each side, no room for poles; and on one street, houses kept from caving toward each other by metal rod—sort of jacks—across the street.

Became very depressed. I am tired of people laughing at me, or being impatient, or angry even; and I can't stand for long this isolation. I forgot to mention that the hotel room smelled very bad, the must & mold of 500 years, and dampness permeating everything. It's beyond me how I did such a thing. I don't want to forget it because people actually live in such surroundings every day of their lives.

Cold and hungry, I walked around the Cathedral to see the thousands of sculptures around the doors. I went in to hear the last half of the "Latin" Mass at 9:30. No recognizable Gregorian at all. This Mass and the one at 11:00 were identical to the 6 P.M. Mass of the previous day, & I had the same reaction. Never have I seen so much beauty in one place. Would that the music could be worthy of its surroundings. Maybe once it was. Maybe, some day, it will be again.

Finally accepting my middle-class reality, I went to the touristy part of the town and had a lovely noon dinner at a restaurant that actually had a cloth tablecloth and napkins, real wine glasses, good service, quiet, no music, no pinball machine. I felt much better. In the afternoon I returned for a final visit to the Cathedral.

I thought I couldn't pray here, tho today was quieter and more respectful. I did kneel for a while in front of the Virgin, the most venerated shrine: lit w/ many candles & lights above; the place glows w/ warmth. I did pray, I guess, though certainly not in words, as usual.

One last look at all the main windows in the 4 directions. Peace shattered by breaking glass & the uniformed guard chasing a man, yelling at him, striking him. My heart stopped I think. I went to where the glass was, terrified at violence to the stained glass; it was a wine bottle, & the man a Bowery type wino. I don't blame the guard at all. So Real Life, Evil, Poverty, Violence, cannot be kept even from this sanctuary. Didn't know how this whole Cathedral struck me till I walked out that door, knowing I might never see it again. I felt exactly as if leaving a lover. Cried.

One last look from the square, the wino standing in the doorway cursing the world in general, a French woman speaking to me not knowing I wouldn't understand her, saying "le pauvre," and the tops of the spires a bit hazy in the fog.

Excursion Two: Jouarre (January 28-30, 1978)

Before I left home, I had written to the Abbey of Jouarre to ask if I could visit. Jouarre is a town about an hour's train ride northeast of Paris, and there is a famous Abbey, Notre Dame de Jouarre, founded in the seventh century by Saint Telchilde and home to Benedictine nuns ever since. It was from this Abbey that two nuns, Lady Abbess Benedict Duss and Mother Mary Aline, came to Connecticut in 1946 to found the Abbey of Regina Laudis. At first it was a priory dependent on Jouarre and lived under the constitution of Jouarre. In turn, Regina Laudis made a foundation in 1977 at Our Lady of the Rock, which is a dependent priory of Regina Laudis. Thus Jouarre is my grandmother, so to speak.

If my long life, and my time in France, have been typified by the contrast between light and dark, depression and joy, there is one single day when this contrast was at its most extreme. On the morning of Saturday, January 21, dark and rainy, I was as depressed as I ever had been. I was lonely and worried about my father, Carl, and Bill, having not heard from any of them. Life at the pension was getting me down:

Young people—very badly brought up, Americans and others alike. They make no attempt to greet strangers; the Germans converse in German, & the Americans in English, & to hell with the others who are at the table who understand neither. The Germans didn't know that there was a Brazilian woman who's been here for three months. Four more Brazilians arrived today. The Iranian girl is admittedly irritating; but the Americans are very mean to her.

Left at 1:00 to get the train for Jouarre. On escalator coming off Metro, 2 boys took my wallet. I didn't notice at the time, just that a boy very rudely stood on the same step as I. Later a young French girl stopped me & told me about it: it took me some time to figure out what she was saying. Found police, they sent me several blocks away to some headquarters. It took me a while in my panic to find out how to get in; they told me it had been found. I walked back to Gare de l'Est & 2 policemen met me as I came in. Money gone—well over $100, more like $150—why did I have so much?—but papers, passports, travelers checks, train & plane tickets, all there. I walked great distances to cash some travelers checks; long line in Gare de Nord; back to Gare de l'Est to catch train—this about 3—and no further trains till 6:15! Won't get to the Abbey until well after dark, certainly way past the souper when I am expected. I can't find their no. in book, so can't call; & telegraph office isn't open Saturday, so they will worry. All this—finding things, finding info—extremely difficult, frustrating, time-consuming. In tears much of the time. I CANNOT COPE WITH A FOREIGN COUNTRY.

What is the lesson, the message, of this theft? That I have not shared enough money with the poor? That I have been too trusting of people and have not been protective enough of my purse? That I don't want to be in Paris at all? Some truth in all these. I don't know. All I know is, it's been a hell of a miserable day, designed utterly to make me feel lost, alone, stupid, incompetent. I cannot describe the extent of the difficulty I have in finding out how things work over here. It's too much. And constantly having to figure out new environments, several places in 6 weeks! And in foreign languages and amongst strange people! Well, the police were fine.

But then: after the train ride and a short taxi ride, I rang the bell at the door of the Abbey of Jouarre. With great trepidation, I stepped into another world. A nun, Sister Aubierge, welcomed me warmly at the door and at once led me to the dining room where dinner was in progress. I was seated at a long table of young men and women. They were eating in silence and the music being played was a late Beethoven string quartet. Those late quartets of Beethoven are for me the most sublime, most contemplative music that has ever been written. I felt that this was heaven: the music, the good food and wine, the quiet.

I found out later that the Abbey had two guest houses, one for men and women, single or couples, who wanted to talk, and one (which thank God I was assigned to) for guests who desired more quiet. I was taken to what had been a nun's cell: narrow, high ceiling, the usual long windows with shutters, a small wash basin, and very cold.

At Compline I was appalled that there were microphones; but happy to see that the nuns looked exactly like the ones at Regina Laudis, except that the postulants wore street clothes. The music then and at Mass was all in French. They used the Gregorian Propers[48] only during Lent and at Sunday Mass, but they seemed to use the Gregorian Ordinary every day.

Music: accompanied by an organ. Sounds better than what I've heard thus far—a great deal better—Lauds almost entirely 2-part. At Compline the guests took full part; ample booklets are provided in the chapel, one for each Office. But I miss the Latin! It is so much better. Why O why give it up?

The next morning I looked out my window and saw the garden and the twelfth-century cloister. The day was filled with parlors, tours, and some time for prayer. Sister Telchilde welcomed me, gave me two booklets about the Abbey, and two memorial cards of Dom Gajard, the long-time choirmaster at Solesmes who had once made a visit to Regina Laudis to work on chant with the nuns. She showed me the tower, famous for being the place where Lady Abbess (then Mère Benoît) had received the inspiration to establish Benedictine contemplative life in the United States. After suffering beyond description during the Nazi occupation, during which Mère Benoît's presence in the Abbey had to be kept secret, and Nazi soldiers actually lived in the monastery, she, with a few other nuns, looked out from the tower and saw soldiers coming toward them. She alone felt that these soldiers were not Nazis, but Americans from General Patton's Third Army coming to liberate Jouarre. They were indeed Americans, and Mère Benoît, filled with gratitude, received her inspiration that has changed and affected the lives of so many.[49]

Sœur Telchilde invited me to a parlor that afternoon with a few of the nuns. The parlor lasted two hours. We spoke in French. They kindly tried to speak more slowly for my benefit, but soon lapsed into their normal speed. One or another nun would dash out now and then and come back to show me something. One Sister played the zither, very well. She often played at Compline. Sister Véronique had spent a year at Regina Laudis in 1960. She played the violin, and she and another nun played for me a Handel sonata. Mère Abbesse Aguilberte de Suremain de Bourgogne herself came in. She was very personable and not intimidating. She went out to her office and returned with two beautifully illustrated books on Jouarre and three postcards. I had some time alone with her during which she told me how different it was to live amongst all the history: the Abbey had suffered so much during the French Revolution and again during the Nazi invasion. We spoke of music, too, and the Church. I was truly overwhelmed by the kindness and generosity of these nuns. We exchanged news about our respective Abbeys. They showed great affection for Regina Laudis.

The Abbess told me that the nuns themselves composed the music for Vespers. I found it ravishing.

I get an idea what medieval polyphony would have sounded like in such a chapel; for their part music, in two parts, is similar: it goes along note against note, longer notes at the ends of phrases, consonances on strong rhythmic points, open fifths ending the phrases, 2nds happening in between these, sound utterly fantastic! Their music in French is much better & more tasteful than that in the cathedrals and parish churches, & is much better sung. It suits the language & the space very well.

But–I miss the Latin.

I had planned to leave that evening, but the nuns invited me to stay another night so that two women guests who were driving back to Paris the next morning could take me with them. They were lovely women, teachers, and took me right to my door at rue du Four.

To make the acquaintance of this Abbey, the mother of Regina Laudis, was a great gift.

Excursion Three: Solesmes February 3-19, 1978

What a blessed relief it is to be in quiet surroundings, after Paris. One hears a lot of birds; & roosters crowing as late as 9:30 in the morning, because the sun rises so late. On walks I've seen the local cemetery; many houses labeled, for example, "Villa St-François;" many walled gardens w/ incredibly beautiful old walls, niches w/ a religious statue, some lettuce, chives, leeks, cabbage, apparently growing & usable; the Abbey, looking from the river like an impenetrable fortress (which it is); the river itself, boats along it, gigantic wood piles, an old tub made of wood slats & in good usable shape; across the Sarthe, a littler village even, w/ a sculptor's workshop, a café, an intriguing narrow road going up a hill, turning quickly into a muddy path w/ stone steps; then the steps disappear & one comes to a gate barring the way beyond, some sort of chapel.

For the first week I stayed at the only hotel in Solesmes, the Grand Hôtel. I did not feel at home there. It was too expensive and too elegant. Breakfast was lovely; the *café au lait* was good, no drops of grease in it, the milk, whipped and warm, served in a separate pitcher. The first night I had dinner at the hotel. It was heavenly, but expensive, and was at the same time as Compline at the Abbey. From then on I had supper in the Crêperie, a restaurant run by two Portuguese sisters. They told me about an American woman who was living in the village, was a lover of Gregorian chant, and went to daily Mass at the Abbey. I looked forward to meeting her.

Next morning, Mass at around 9:30. As if Vatican II had never happened,[51] *no participation of congregation* *whatsoever, even to the Lord's Prayer. Music beautiful, I don't see how it cd be any better (except for the organ at Vespers).*

The monk in charge of taking care of me was Dom Jacques Hourlier, a scholar of chant, who had published several articles; tiny, frail, 60-ish, grey hair; very modest & selfless, great sense of humor, very discreet. He took me to see Dom Gajard's grave tho' it was in the enclosure.[52]

The Abbey did not receive women guests, nor were women allowed to work in the library, as male scholars could. But I found the monks as kind and helpful to me as they could be; they did not in any way hold it against me that I was a woman, and as a scholar, utterly a beginner. I was given a table to work at, and Dom Hourlier would bring me the huge, impressive charts that the monks had laboriously made in the early twentieth century, in which they could compare chants neume by neume as they were written in several manuscripts.[53] Honestly, I did not learn much from all this, but I was amazed and in awe of the huge project the monks had undertaken in their process of restoring the chant, which by the nineteenth century had degenerated to a drastic extent. In the meetings I had with Dom Hourlier I learned more about the Abbey itself and how they worked on the chant.

After a week in the Grand Hôtel I moved to the Crêperie, which had guest rooms upstairs. This was more my speed. The Portuguese sisters were wonderful in helping me with French. They were friendly and kind, supplementing the minimal French breakfast of bread and coffee with yogurt and fruit. It was here, too, that I finally met the American woman, Maria. She had been a graduate student in French at Yale and a disciple of Henri Nouwen.[54] Now she lived permanently in France. We became as good friends as people can become in just a couple of weeks. It was tremendously comforting to know someone with whom I could speak in English who also had an intimate knowledge of the French language and culture.

The Abbey has a sister monastery for women, Sainte-Cécile (Saint Cecilia's Abbey). I went to Vespers there a few times and liked it better than Saint-Pierre. The church was much smaller, lighter, warmer, more colorful. In Saint-Pierre one can't imagine anyone smiling. Sainte-Cécile is strictly cloistered; for this I envied them. I met the Portress. She was beautiful, radiant, happy, and whole.

Soon after my arrival at Solesmes came Ash Wednesday. I was grateful, for then the organ at the Abbey was silent. (Dom Hourlier had told me that they needed the organ to keep the monks from singing flat, but they seemed to do fine without it.) At Sainte-Cécile, however, the nuns had no parlors during Lent, no guests either, and the Portress was replaced by an eighty-year- old woman who was the sister of one of the nuns, and who actually lived at the Abbey in the winter. We became acquainted, had some nice conversations about *"la vie monastique,"* and, I was thrilled to hear, she thought I was doing very well in French.

I envied the nuns, and still do, for having a strict and quiet Lent.

France, summed up

One thing have I asked of the Lord, that will I seek after;
that I may dwell in the house of the LORD all the days of my life.

Psalm 27 (26):4

Throughout my stay in France my longing for a monastic life was overpowering, stronger than ever:

January 15, 1978, (Sunday 12:30 A.M., in Paris)

I haven't been able to sleep. I cried, to think of how Merton wrote to his Abbot that he hoped to be back by Christmas, and he was, though dead. The life to which I know I've been called seems so utterly far away. It seems selfish to want it. Yet those who are in it—they wanted it too; they are not there because someone told them it was their duty. I am no less fitted for it than many of them, and more so than some. Can I never have that which gives me the greatest joy? I will not be in a university for 20 more years!

January 31, 1978 (at Jouarre)

I question the value of all the running around I've been doing. A form of Avarice, surely: see as much as you can; learn French as well as you can—why? Do as much work in the library as you can—as if I were trying to embrace the whole Middle Ages, all of Gregorian chant. The acquisitiveness is intellectual as well. All this is an attempt to talk myself into accepting a life I don't really want. At all! To say that any activity one does in the world is, or can be, a way toward God, may be true; but I refuse to accept that it is equally true for everyone. It is true for those who are called to it. I am not. I am called strongly to a monastic life. How can I deal with this? I have never prayed to Saints before. But I have stood before St. Benedict's altar in St-Germain-des-Prés and asked for his help, that I may become one of his followers and live under his Rule. Again, all today, I have been sad & in actual agony, over the great desire I have for the monastic life. I wish the desire wd go away for I don't know how to cope with it. I know I ought to be patient & accept the Lord's will, but that's on an intellectual level only.

The happiest moments I've had in France have been the times of prayer, not in my own room, but in places where the accumulated energy of others' prayers is powerful. Namely: in St-Germain-des-Prés, especially by Our Lady & St. Benedict; at Chartres in the sunset; and especially the 15 minutes at about 7 A.M .in the 12th-c. Oratory at Jouarre, all alone until interupted.

February 16, 1978 (at Solesmes)

Talking w/ Maria today about dreams. Reminded me how little I've been in touch with them this whole year, how little I've been in touch at all with that intuitive side of my life. I feel out of balance, this way. Probably a lot has to do w/ the disruptions, the energy needed to be spent on other things, namely, the adjustments to many new environments. Within the last few days I dreamed that a woman whom I liked very much, & evidently felt comfortable with, had just joined the Abbey. But she was being sent already to go somewhere & get some sort of training leading to some degree. I also dreamed that I saw two beautiful streets forking ahead of me, very radiant light, & I must not have been totally asleep, for I thought, "Aha! This is going to be one of those Important Dreams. I'd better pay close attention." So of course, it stopped immediately!

After Solesmes, I spent another couple of days in Paris. I didn't write much in my journal, and I don't remember exactly what I was doing, except for some more exploring. I did write a bit: *I want to write so I won't forget, that garbage is collected 7 days a week; that men sweep the streets by hand w/ medieval brooms made out of twigs; that there are indeed a huge number of bums & beggars in the subways, some playing music, some w/ sign indicating a disease; women w/ babies. That there are a huge no. of dogs in Paris, and pigeons. The pigeons are very fat.*

I was extremely homesick all the time I was away. I had no news at all from Carl and Bill. One day more than halfway through my time in France I was thrilled and vastly relieved to receive all at once three letters from my father telling me of his six-hour surgery by the famous Dr. Mohs to remove a cancer from his nose. Also my stepmother Frances was ill. In that last week, I counted the days and hours until I would be home again.

I said good-bye to Saint-Germain: Christ crucified, St. Benedict, Sainte Geneviève, and Our Lady, and the beggar who is always at the door. Every time I was there I was struck by the contrast between the shrine to Our Lady and the one of the Crucifixion. The former was warm, bright, with dozens of votive candles and always several people kneeling there. But Christ on the Cross was alone, in darkness. People do instinctively want to avoid the Cross, suffering. They want the comfort that Our Lady gives. (But doesn't she also have a stern, fierce side? "... terrible as an army set in battle array"?[55]) In any case, I was drawn to Jesus and the Crucifixion on this farewell visit. *By Christ Crucified, I thought about His pain, and His Mother's, and our pains: mine, my father's, and the pain of others. Pain & joy all seem to become one; not that we ever go "beyond" or "outside" them; but we do not, either, go* <u>*from*</u> *one* <u>*to*</u> *the other; it is all somehow outside of time. I can't explain it because I don't understand it.*

I was deeply grateful for my time in France, despite the difficulties. Now I was ready to go home, to see my Dad and my sons, to be in my own country, and to begin my three-month stay at Regina Laudis. I was forty-six years old. My stay at the Abbey would be the culmination of the year's leave of absence from teaching, presumably to learn about and experience Gregorian chant. In reality, the purpose and function of this year, and especially these three months, was to discern the direction my life would take.

Ten

TURNING POINT

Thro' many dangers, toils and snares,
I have already come:
'Tis grace has brought me safe thus far,
And grace will lead me home.

—NEW BRITAIN (Amazing Grace)

From the perspective of eighty-four years, I can truly say that my three months at the Abbey were without doubt the most intense, challenging, and rewarding time in my entire life. The seasons of nature, the transition from cold bitter winds to warm sunshine, paralleled the liturgical seasons of Lent, Holy Week, Easter—of Christ's death and resurrection and my own death and resurrection. I was adrift most of this time, not knowing how things would work out. Treasured self-images and patterns of behavior were challenged. I had to die to so many things. Sometimes I was depressed, worried, fearful, untrusting. At the same time I was deeply happy to be in this monastic environment. Little by little I learned to trust—ultimately to trust God through the persons in the Abbey whom I related to.

My main contact person at the Abbey was Mother Mary Magdalen. Like me, she was a convert and a musician. I soon discovered that we shared the same birthday. Her father was a Methodist minister. Mother—MMM as she usually appears in my journals—had earned a Masters degree in sacred music at Manhattanville College of the Sacred Heart. Now she was deeply involved in catechetical work, especially working with new Catholics or people coming toward the Church. Through her I was placed into relationship with Lady Abbess, whom I seldom saw directly, and with the whole monastic community.

Everything worked together to bring about this decisive transition in my life: the daily liturgy of Mass and the Divine Office; the work I was given to do; relationships with other guests; frequent meetings with MMM and the things she gave me to read; and the homilies of Father Francis Prokes, S.J., the Abbey's resident priest. I took extensive notes on Father's dense and rich homilies. He brought together the readings of each day's Mass, his commentaries on the encyclical on the Mystical Body,[56] insights on community life (both religious and lay communities), and events in the world. These homilies seemed to be addressed exactly to me, in my particular situation; yet I knew that they could not be. Thus I realized that I was not that different from other people.

I lived at Saint Gregory's, the guest house for women, an old New England house with cast iron door latches and wide floor boards that reminded me of Flint Farm. Most of the time I had a room to myself; sometimes another guest would share it. We women guests ate at a guest refectory attached to the Abbey, close to the kitchen. Our meals were passed through an opening in a grille. Male guests stayed and ate at Saint Joseph's, another old house just across the driveway from the Abbey.

The Chapel gave me a strong sense of the presence of God. You could not enter it without entering a deep, tangible quiet, inviting one to pray. This Chapel has three main parts: the section for the monastic community, separated by a grille from the rest of the chapel; the sanctuary (the altar, the Blessed Sacrament, the Bishop's chair, and the lectern); and the section for the "people."

I went to Mass, Lauds, Prime, Terce, Sext, None, Vespers, and Compline every day. Matins, at 1:40 A.M., was the only one of the Hours I did not attend. In the Divine Office the Church is praying in the stead of and on behalf of those who do not pray. At any given time, somewhere in the world, people are praying these same words that have been prayed through many centuries. In this prayer, they are joining the prayer of the angels. The angels are praying all the time, and we, at Mass and at the Office, join them.

My main work, under the direction of Mother Patricia, was helping with the restoration of an 1896 Hutchings tracker organ that had been given to the Abbey. Mother Patricia was working under the guidance of Mr. Richard Hamer, an organ builder. I worked sometimes inside the enclosure, in the ground floor of the Novitiate, a sort of cloak room/work room combined. Here I remember gluing pieces of felt to other little parts. Sometimes I worked in the Crèche, a colonial barn that housed the Abbey's massive eighteenth-century Neapolitan crèche. This building would contain the organ until it was moved to the Abbey's church, *Jesu Fili Mariae*, in 1994. I hardly remember anything of what this work entailed, but I know that it was very healing and satisfying for me to be doing manual work instead of teaching. I could wake up worried and anxious and depressed, or tired and aching, and all these discomforts would vanish as I was working with something physical. I had other work, too: cleaning at St. Gregory's, helping in the vegetable and herb gardens, running errands.

March 10, 1978

My Lenten penance or task: to try to understand what is my basic problem. I am in the dark about it. I must get used to different ways of relating to people and adapting to the unexpected.

I have a good chance to learn 1) living in uncertainty, not knowing, but acting on faith anyway; 2) not talking indiscriminately; silence in the dimension of context & to whom one speaks; 3) If sad, not laying this on other people at all. All these are contrary to the way I've always been. I'd like to try them & see how things go.

All in all, the time from Christmas to now has been exceptionally hard. This last week especially. But it is healing to be here.

Incredible sunset out there.

Within a few days of my arrival in early March, I was told that I had been given the privilege of being "cloistered." What did this mean? Basically, it meant that I was to be under the direction of the Abbey in all things. I was not to leave the grounds of the Abbey without permission, or to visit Bill at Goddard, which I had planned to do, or to relate "socially" to other guests.

Most of the time I appreciated this: it put me into closer relationship with the Abbey, and it insured that I would be well protected from many diversions and temptations. It would be easier to focus on the main purpose of my being there. It would allow the necessary intensity of my development to happen. By analogy, water, to boil, needs not just heat, but a container to hold it. To turn to steam, it needs a pressure cooker. I too needed this strong container.

Yet sometimes I chafed at this, too:

March 16, 1978

MMMagdalen told me that this period is for me an instinctual & justice, preparation & incubation period—the justice level involves growth, the finding of one's place, one's identity.[57] *In answer to my question about the selflessness of the nuns & how this relates to my need to listen, to give: the nuns have their peer relationships, but none of them will relate to me that way; each in relating to me acts totally for the community & will not speak about herself or her problems or those of others. I am learning a new way of listening & of giving.*

Now, the thing I wonder most about is, can I survive for 3 months with all my human relationships being regulated? And with no peer relationships? That is the only really hard thing I perceive so far. The work & the regime are so healthy & good. It is the difficulty of learning discipline & discretion in relating to people, in what I say & don't say.

However, I want to submit to this process, to assume that I am not at this point the best judge of what is good for me, to be as receptive as I can possibly be to what I can learn here.

Around this time I was beginning to wonder what had happened to the formal study of chant that Dr. McPeek and I had expected would be part of my work for these three months. Originally it was proposed that Lady Abbess would work with me. It turned out that instead, Mother Pia would be my teacher. She was just a few years older than I, and amazingly, as Susan Lowe, had gone to Oberlin College. We shared one year there: she was working on a Masters in art history; I was in my freshman year. Our paths had never crossed. But in that year of overlap, she sang in the chorus, and I played in the orchestra, of a major choral work. My yearbook for 1950 has a photo of this performance, with both Susan and I visible.

Mother Pia was very musical and had spent some time with the Trapp Family in Stowe, Vermont. In fact, it was this experience that had led her to the Church. Now, we met weekly. Mother introduced me to the Solesmes Method,[58] helped me to deepen my understanding of the modes and the psalm tones, and, a little bit, chironomy.[59] This work was refreshingly practical: everything I learned was in reference to pieces from the Mass and the Divine Office.

Whither musicology?

Despite all my ambivalence about academic life, I still had not given up the idea that I might end up back in that world. I had not burned any bridges yet. At least not explicitly. In reality, I already had, by my very ambivalence.

From Father Prokes's homilies I learned that we must come into full possession of something, must enter fully into it, before we can let go of it and move on to a new level. As one example, Father compared the experience of a tourist in another country with that of someone who goes to live there, gets involved in working, living, making friends and acquaintances there, and learns the language; in other words, she has entered fully into that culture. In my life, it meant that I needed to enter even more deeply into musicology, truly possess it, before I would be ready to leave it.

March 11, 1978

I think I am beginning to get a clearer understanding of my real problem(s). First: I have not yet come into full possession of musicology. I have not achieved a mature relationship with it. As GM [Gwynn McPeek] said a good while ago, I need to develop my own style of scholarship & writing, & do work that is worthy of notice (in chant). I'm not sure what else, but I know there remains a lot of unfinished business. I have never really found my professional identity, my "place in community" there. I have no right to leave it before I come into real possession of it. Also, I must do this to be worthy of GM's confidence, and his thinking of giving to me the field he has tilled.

In addition to this level, there is my father, who has really only me as family who can be close to him; and I don't want to wait until his last illness to do that. And more: I see the possibility that I could love my sister, after all these years.

It amazes me to read of this hesitancy, after all my fervent longing for the monastic life and my deep ambivalence about the academic life. And it did turn out that in these three months at the Abbey I moved decisively onto the path of monastic life. How could this be? How could I be accepted into the Abbey (as I finally was), without ever achieving this full possession of musicology?

At first glance this interpretation of 1978 seems false: was I trying to please my father? Was I really wanting to go further into musicology so I would be "worthy" (as Dr. McPeek put it) of inheriting his territory? Was I really in doubt about my vocation? It is true, I have never really possessed the land of musicology. But I certainly believe that I have come into full possession of the land of MUSIC: not in terms of articles and books and public recognition by academia, not at all; but I have come to my unique relationship to music, in my own way, and this is recognized and respected by everyone I work with and have worked with in music.

My experience of Holy Week, not long after I began my time at the Abbey, affected me deeply and permanently. I wrote to Lady Abbess:

March 28, 1978

I would like to tell you something of what it means to me to be here at this time. The experience of the Passion, Crucifixion, and Resurrection of Christ is more real to me than ever before; and of myself with Him. It is no longer a matter of believing, but of knowing. His death and resurrection and mine. Everything contributed to this: Lent itself, the liturgy, my own life, and most especially Father Prokes' sermons, which invariably seemed directly to concern me; yet, since I know they are addressed to all, they greatly increased my awareness that I am one of many who share these experiences and feelings.

Then Holy Week: never have I felt so strongly the death of Christ: the words of the liturgy, the stripping down of the Offices to the bare essentials, the physical and visual stripping of the chapel, the absence of bells, holy water, lights and flame. The Crucified Christ on the floor, and most especially the absence of the Blessed Sacrament. The effect of all this was intensified a thousand times by being in the <u>*same place*</u> *all this time, so that the experiences in the chapel are reflected and reinforced by all the rest of life, including the weather and the seasons.*

Easter is a real Resurrection, beginning with the Pillar of Fire, with its dual life-and-death nature, an <u>*experience*</u> *for those who could be near enough to feel its warmth—and with the diffusion of that one Light, for which the Crucifixion was necessary, all over the Chapel and the world, without in any way diminishing the original Light.*

Then, I don't know if you can imagine how excited I am and how much it means to me, to hear the Chant here and now. The music of Easter has been familiar to me, some of it, for close to thirty years academically. I have waited all that time to hear it as I am privileged to hear it now, as it was intended to be heard, in God's house and in His praise. This makes me happy beyond words.

Chant lives in an "enclosure," that is, the absence of harmony & counterpoint, of the diversity & richness of instrumental colors, of the strong gravitational pull of tonality, and the tensions caused thereby, of regular meter and strong accent. This very enclosure accounts for the intensity, on a deep and subtle level, of things like the Responsories for Matins of Holy Week, the Gradual "Haec dies," the "Victimae paschale laudes." An outsider cannot perceive the variety and richness of expression in chant. It all sounds alike to him, just as he imagines that life in a monastery must be boring.

I hope this gives you some idea of what it means to me to be here for this extended time, and how much I appreciate the privilege of being allowed to share your lives so fully.

Of course, I had not suddenly become holy. I was still myself. On May 3 I wrote:

Today I am depressed. The <u>*hardness*</u> *of obedience, the lack of autonomy, the necessity of submission, really get me down sometimes. I am jealous of all the people who get to see Lady Abbess. The difficult thing & the thing I am most resenting now is not that I still don't know how the job situation will work out, but that it is hard for me to be as a child at the beginning, not to run my own life. And some suspicion & mistrust. And fear—of my Dad's reaction, his anger & hurt & complete incapacity to understand, that I know will happen when he hears I'm thinking of becoming an organ apprentice full time & not teaching at all. I'd better pray.*

Both aspects of life—dissatisfaction and acceptance—were present:

May 21, 1978 (Trinity Sunday)

Now, feel a lot better tho' everything is the same—all up in the air. I am suddenly realizing that the monastery itself is the only place that has enough intensity & strength & totality for what I need. The process of treating me like a beginner, & very rigorously, is part of the central process, the transition, that I've been involved in, from centering on self to centering on God, in community, & relating to that community in a proper & orderly way.

What happened about my future? Though I did not know it, it was pretty well decided already. One day I received a phone call from a professor at the University of Michigan at Dearborn. He told me I was one of three people being seriously considered for an appointment as Assistant Professor in their Department of Music. Would I come to give a public lecture? I was slightly tempted. But the appointment was just for one year, and did I really want to go to all that trouble with no assurance of future employment? I said no. The man was astounded, and said, "You're crazy." I replied softly, "I know."

My uncertainty about my future did not get resolved until my last week at Regina Laudis. I had been waiting for Mr. Hamer, the organ builder, to come so that I could ask him if I could be his apprentice. But I questioned this: it would be fine to work on organs every day; but did I really want this to be the center of my life? Did I want to study, and learn, all about organs, to be an expert? No. Finally, on the day when Mr. Hamer was expected, I asked to see Lady Abbess. I gathered up the courage to ask her if I could become part of the Abbey's new foundation of Our Lady of the Rock. I had heard of Our Lady of the Rock, and knew that it would appeal to me. I liked the idea of being part of a new venture. I knew that I would prefer a small community. I thought, too, that my chances of being accepted there were more likely than at Regina Laudis.

OLR was a newly established foundation of Regina Laudis. Three nuns had begun this new monastery on Shaw Island, located among the islands of the Salish Sea in Washington State near the Canadian border. I nearly fainted when Lady Abbess replied, "Well—you could go there in January [I owed Livingston a final semester of teaching], and see how you get along. Some people find the winters very hard there. You could stay as a guest for a few months, and then you could enter here for your formation."

Immediately I went to the Chapel and asked God for three things: that my father would come to be happy about my vocation, that my sister Nancy would come to have a better life, and that I could be with my father when he died. God granted the first two requests, though their fulfillment took several years. It was not necessary, after all, to see Mr. Hamer.

Preparations: Summer and Fall 1977

I'm on my way, and I won't turn back,
I'm on my way, great God, I'm on my way.

— folk song

I am driving my father to introduce him to the Abbey. I try to cheer him up, but it has no effect. We are spending the summer together at Flint Farm. On his way East he had stopped to bury the ashes of his dear Frances, with whom he had spent ten happy years, until she died of cancer. The first morning we were together, I burst out in all my naïve joy that I was planning to enter the Abbey, destined for Our Lady of the Rock. I genuinely thought that since he loved me, he would share my happiness.

But no. His dark depression was to last all summer. His fear and his feeling of loss, together with the loss of Frances, were quite overpowering for a long time. He had hoped so much that I would be able to be with him, or be near to him, in his last years. He feared that he would always have to see me behind "bars" (the grille). It didn't help much for me to tell him that there are no grilles at Our Lady of the Rock.

As we drove south on Interstate 91, I told him: "Just because you're eighty doesn't mean that you can stop growing." I told him about Lady Abbess, whom I wished him to meet. "You will like her. She is very cultured and well read and brilliant. You and she will have a lot in common." I told him that the nuns pray eight times a day. "That's too much," he replied.

He did have a parlor with Lady Abbess. He told me very little about it, but obviously it was not the polite, pleasant social visit I had led him to expect. It was not until many years later that he told me more. Lady

Abbess came right to the point the minute they met: "What about Martha?" she asked. Dad told her he thought I would be a good nun, that I would be obedient and helpful. But he was concerned, fearing I was making the wrong choice, and that I was going to regret it. Her reply pierced his heart: "You do not know your daughter." He left the parlor, bowing deeply.

Mother Patricia, a native of Norwich, Vermont, just across the river from Hanover, also met with Dad. I didn't hear much about that, either, but she was good for him. He asked her if she believed in life after death. "I don't believe, I *know*," she answered. I told Dad about Mother Mary Magdalen. "Her name is too long," came the reply.

His darkness was worse than anything I had ever seen, and it did not let up. I invited our neighbors, Charlie and Mildred Clark, over for tea one day. He did not come down to see them until I went upstairs and virtually demanded he see them.

His sister, my Aunt Jean, saved the day. She spent a month or so with us. She did share Dad's fears and apprehensions. She asked various friends what they knew about religious life, and it did not sound good to her. She had no idea, of course, what the Abbey was like. But she did have a strong faith in God, and went regularly to the Episcopal Church in Columbus, Nebraska. And she supported me completely, telling Dad that I had a right to decide my life's path (I was forty-six). "You, Merle, did what you wanted to do with your life, didn't you, despite your family's doubts? Yet they supported you." But we three sat awkwardly together, meal after meal, with my father refusing to take part in the conversation, totally unlike his usual self.

One day I couldn't stand it any more. The Holy Spirit came to my rescue, encouraging me to go to Dad's room and confront him. He was, as usual, lying on his bed, doing nothing. I remember only one of the things that I said: "You have a great love, respect, and admiration for Helen White, don't you? (Professor Helen White was a noted scholar of literature and a colleague at the University of Wisconsin.) But she is a devout Catholic. This is an integral part of her. Can you separate her faith from all the things about her that you admire?" Somehow this, and whatever else I said, helped him, and he began to make some effort to improve the atmosphere.

How did Carl and Bill react to my news? They were both living and working in Highland Park and New Brunswick. Clearly they supported me in doing what made me happy, but I am sure they shared many of my father's fears and apprehensions. Once I had moved out of our Highland Park apartment and left for Our Lady of the Rock, Bill, who had by now transferred from Goddard to Beloit College, expressed his feelings succinctly: "I don't have a home any more. When I am asked for my home address, I don't have one!"

Nancy, on the other hand, had no problems with my plans. Crazy as she was, she was religious. As I wrote earlier, she went regularly to a high Anglican church near her in Chicago. She loved it that there were nuns there, wearing traditional habits and carrying rosaries.

Leaving Livingston

Lady Abbess had asked me not to tell anyone that I planned to enter Our Lady of the Rock without her express permission. So I told no one at Livingston, even my close colleagues and friends. I went to tell the Dean I was leaving, and he was very curious, as was everyone else, about what I was going to do. Maybe I was going to get married. Maybe going off to some remote country for some mysterious purpose. I enjoyed the secrecy. And this secrecy was an excellent protection for me. I did not have to waste my energy defending my decision, explaining. But the other side was that a cousin in my mother's family was so offended when I finally told her that she cut off all contact with me. I lost a couple of friends, too, who thought they knew better than I how I should live. One, especially, was actually angry, and thought I should live with my father until he died. That would be nineteen more years!

I remember nothing of my professional life that semester—teaching, or playing music, or anything else. I was so happily looking forward to a balanced life of prayer, work, and study.

At the end of the term I gave a party for some of my colleagues, students, and friends. I asked them to bring a shopping cart or a shopping bag and help themselves to whatever they fancied in the apartment, anywhere except in my bedroom, where I had put whatever I wanted to keep or take with me. I was so exhausted from packing that I could not enjoy the party. My back ached, my facial muscles ached. But my friends had a good time. They were all still ignorant of my plans.

I suggested to my family that we all get together in Madison for one last Christmas together. I had not had Christmas with my Dad or Nancy for many years. Dad arranged for Nancy and me to stay in the house of friends who were away. Bill, already in Wisconsin at Beloit College, came, but Carl had to work. It was a rather painful and sad time. Nancy had her usual upsets, especially when our rented car got stuck in the heavy snow, and Dad was not feeling well. He had arranged to take Bill with him on a trip to Norway, and this was a godsend, in that it was he who did the leaving. I had a day or two alone in his apartment. I was all set to leave next morning for Seattle, planning to arrive at Our Lady of the Rock on New Year's Day 1979. A severe blizzard hit the city. The airport was closed. The following day I flew out, having called Reverend Mother Therese Critchley at Our Lady of the Rock to tell her I would be late. In the Twin Cities, where I was to change planes, there was also a blizzard and I had to stay in a hotel, calling Mother Therese once again. At last I reached Seattle, enthralled by the ranges of snow-covered mountains, the Cascades and the Olympics, on either side of the city, and by all the green amongst the buildings and houses.

Trying Out at Our Lady of the Rock

Mother Therese had suggested that I fly from Seattle to Friday Harbor so that I could see the San Juan Islands from the air. The plane was about the size of a VW Beetle with wings. It had seats for three passengers. I sat behind the pilot, who told me not to worry if the door by my seat flew open, for I would be held in by the seat belt. When the islands came into view, I asked him if we were seeing Shaw Island yet. I wished I had not asked, for he, with both hands off the yoke (the steering lever) gestured to show me the various islands. I did arrive safely at Friday Harbor, where Mother Prisca and Nate Benedict, an island resident who was a deacon, met me. Nate took us over to Shaw in his boat. Henry Ellis, who had given the land and buildings he owned on Shaw to the Abbey, met us and drove us to the monastery.

My first sight of Mother Therese was of her wielding a long-handled tool, chipping ice from the pavement just inside the gate.

At this time the foundation was only about eighteen months old. Mother Therese Critchley, Mother Miriam Benedict, and Mother Prisca Dougherty were the foundresses, sent from Regina Laudis. Mother Luke Parmigiani had been sent on a year earlier to supervise the workmen who were building the farm buildings and an addition to the house. She was a hermit, and lived in a cabin elsewhere on the property, and a couple of months after my arrival she returned, as had been planned, to the Abbey. I already knew Mother Prisca, who took care of the guests and the herbs,

The three foundresses: Mother Prisca, Mother Miriam, Mother Therese.

from my visits to the Abbey. I was happy to remember that she had been active in the Catholic Worker in her home town of Rochester, New York, before she entered Regina Laudis. She had known Dorothy Day, who was her sponsor when she received the monastic habit. I had met Mother Therese and Mother Miriam when they each made a short visit to the Abbey during my months there.

Besides the nuns, the small community had a resident priest, Father Louis Aufiero. He had come soon after the nuns arrived, and was to stay for sixteen years. I had already met him at Regina Laudis. He came from Brooklyn, with its wonderful accent. He had a great sense of humor, a beautiful singing voice, a thorough understanding of the liturgy, a love of gardening, and a love of people. His years with us were a priceless gift.[60]

The first thing that Reverend Mother Therese, superior of the little community, showed me was the chapel. It was under the house, cave-like, long and narrow. As we entered through a low arched door, we faced a large area of steep rock, down which ran a little stream that flowed under the concrete walk to the outside. Brother Jerome Blackburn, OMI (Oblates of Mary Immaculate, an order based in Canada and the Northwest) had built this chapel out of native driftwood. Turning right, the cave opened up into a good-sized rectangular room. Everything was driftwood. On our right stood a huge hunk of driftwood, taller than I am, holding in its folded arms a shell containing holy water. Planks and beams made up the ceiling. Carpeting of a deep maroon color covered the floor. Several lamps hanging from the ceiling were made out of coffee cans painted black. These lamps provided the only light, for there were no windows. The altar, a glass surface resting on a massive piece of driftwood, stood at the near end of the room. In the corner behind it was the tabernacle, made of a rusted iron box that may once have contained treasures, and now contained a far greater treasure, the Blessed Sacrament. The light next to it, always lit, had been a ship's lantern. The benches around the other three sides of the room were made of wood laced with large holes made by teredo worms, which had lined these holes with a white calciferous substance.[61]

All these details soon became familiar to me, but I was more or less in a daze when I first saw the chapel. At once I knelt before the altar, silently thanking God for being there at last.

I was not to see the inside of the house for a few years. As a guest and a possible future member of the community, I stayed alone in a small mobile home on the property of Henry and Marlyn Hoffman. Henry was a descendant of an old settler's family. I had my meals at St. Joseph's guest house, the house that Henry Ellis had stayed in, and sang the Mass and most of the Offices with the nuns in their chapel.

For the most part I was very happy. I could experience the balance that the three pillars of Benedictine life provide: prayer, manual work, and study. Since I could sing close to the nuns at Mass and the Office, I could feel more a part of things. My work was diverse: peeling apples, digging out wild roses from the pasture (the cows liked to taste my clothes as I worked), helping Mother Prisca with herbs, cleaning the guest house. The study part was mainly music. I was given regular time to practice the violin: I played a program of Irish tunes for the community on Saint Patrick's Day; I got together a few island people for a singing group; I prepared a series of classes for the nuns on the history of Passion music for Lent. The community—all three nuns—met with me weekly to introduce me to the Constitutions of Regina Laudis.

Of course, the internal struggles I had faced at the Abbey had not disappeared. One evening in Lent I was in my trailer preparing for the class on Bach's *St Matthew Passion*. I was listening to one of the two arias that have beautiful, elaborate obbligato parts for the bass viola da gamba. I sobbed. I had not realized at all how much I missed the viol. It is so easy to believe that one can enter religious life and give up many of one's treasured experiences. Sell everything and give to the poor. Sure. I can do that! But again and again we find that we are kidding ourselves.

And true to my nature, I longed for close relationships. I often felt left out of things, and I *was* left out, of course, because I was not in the community. On January 20th, the feast of Saint Anthony of the Desert, the community had the traditional blessing of the animals in the just-finished barn. I found out only afterwards. I was desolate. I could have been there—guests often come to such things—but for whatever reason, I had not been told about it. Now I understand how easy it can be for a guest not to be told about something: one person may assume that someone else has told her; or, with all the details we need to keep track of, it is very easy to forget some of them.

Another example that to most people would be insignificant: One of the nuns told me that the nuns did not like the way I snuffled my chronically runny nose. I privately fell apart at this, for somehow it brought back the dread that came when Nancy, about to explode with tension, would criticize me for "distending my throat."

But the nuns were always gentle with me, and often did wonderful, comforting things for me.

It was during this time at Our Lady of the Rock that I was suddenly overwhelmed with awe that God, who created the entire universe of which we are such a tiny part, and has given us all the beauty of nature, all the plants and animals, mountains and rivers, oceans and the stars, and life itself—all this and more than we can imagine—that this very same God knows each one of us, everyone who is alive now, has ever lived, and ever will live. He knows each; each is unique and unrepeatable, and he loves us! Realizing this, how could I do anything but give my life to Him?

Spring came. Lent was drawing to an end, and culminated in the Holy Week Seminar. This was the first such seminar that the Abbey used to have during Holy Week in conjunction with the two religious communities that were working with the Abbey in response to the call of Pope Paul VI for the renewal of religious life following Vatican II. Lady Abbess, Mother Dolores Hart, and Sister Noella Marcellino came from the Abbey. Father Prokes came, and representatives of the two other communities, the Religious Sisters of Mercy of Alma, and the Franciscan Sisters of the Eucharist. The seminar focused on developing the Holy Week Sequence—the sequence of the mysteries appropriate to each day of the week—as Father had begun doing while I was at the Abbey, in terms of chant.[62] Together we all rehearsed the chants, led by Lady Abbess. After that they had meetings, and my tendency to feel left out and my desire to belong were sorely tested. But the seminar ended, socially at least, with a dinner at the Franciscans' place.[63] At this dinner it was announced to all that I would soon be leaving to enter the Abbey, at which announcement all cheered and applauded.

So on April 25, 1979, the feast of Saint Mark the Evangelist, I left for Connecticut.

Eleven

THROUGH THE GATE

I am the gate.
Whoever enters through me will be safe.

—John 10:9

Often, when a new postulant enters the Abbey, she is given some unfortunate trial. Mother Philip Klein fell down the stairs and had a concussion. Martha Marcellino, later Sister Noella, got a bee sting in her eye. Catherine Lamb, later Sister Frances of Rome, fell while feeding the pigs and broke her arm. In my case, my body came through unscathed, but Northwest Airlines lost my suitcase and I never got it back. I applied for and received the maximum compensation, but nothing could make up for what was lost: my Confirmation cross, the only photo I had of my Vermont grandparents, my three diplomas, my *Graduale Romanum* and *Monastic Diurnal*, and my monastic clothes: the tunic—the floor-length, long-sleeved black dress which is the is the basic garment of the monastic habit—that I had just made, the new belt and sandals.

I suspect that someone had stolen my suitcase. What use they would make of my diplomas and monastic books and clothes I cannot imagine. It is a common assumption among religious people that the devil is behind these misfortunes, trying to block our vocations. I do not doubt this.

A sewing machine was given me to use in the guest house, and I tried to sew another tunic, but I am not at all good at sewing, and it just did not work in the short time we had. So Mother Pia quickly adjusted a tunic that had belonged to Mother Mary Simeon, who had died that year. I was thrilled to discover that the number on it (each woman at the Abbey is given a number to identify her clothing) was 14, which spells "Bach" in the number alphabet.[64] I took this as a sign that music would continue to be a big part of my life. The tunic was wool, and on the day I entered, the thermometer registered ninety-five degrees.

It was May 6, 1979, Good Shepherd Sunday. Mother Agnes took me to my new cell to change into my new clothes: the tunic and the short black postulant veil that allowed some of my hair to be seen. "Don't you want to remove your earrings?" she asked. They were so much a part of me—tiny silver balls—that I had forgotten them. She then took me to the big ceremonial gate, which is seldom used. I knocked on the door. Lady Abbess opened it and asked me: "What do you seek?" "To live under the Rule of Saint Benedict at Our Lady of the Rock," I replied. In I came, and instantly thought I was in Paradise. The abundance of flowers—on trees, on bushes, on the ground—the fragrances—were overwhelming. Lady Abbess and a few other nuns led me into the choir and showed me where to sit, and there was a little ceremony. Then I was taken out to attend Vespers and have supper in the guest refectory with some friends from Highland Park who had come up for the occasion.

Back inside the monastery, I was taken to the Novitiate common room, where the novices greeted me gaily. Following this, there was a work period for everyone in the laundry, folding clothes and talking. Then we went upstairs to the community's common room, where we had a rehearsal of Mendelssohn's "Lift Thine Eyes" in preparation for a coming concert. After all this there was "News:" a time when information, reports, and prayer requests are communicated, and here I was introduced to all. Compline followed, and at last to bed.

Was every evening going to be this full of things? It is a shock to enter the Abbey: one is suddenly thrown into a new culture, a whole set of different customs, forty women who look all alike at first, almost a new language. At my first meal in the refectory, the reader began reading something in Latin. Much as I loved Latin, I did not look forward to entire meals listening to it. Fortunately the language soon turned to English.

Now what? I could call this the end of my story. I am where I have longed to be. I have written what I said I would write about: how I made the transition from a Marxist atheist to a Benedictine nun. But I was not quite yet a nun. It would take me eleven years before I made my Perpetual Vows.

So there is more to tell. I cannot leave you with the several unresolved, unintegrated "issues" that I have introduced: the abortion above all; my marriage; my love-hate relationship with the violin; the depression, jealousy, and self-absorption that have caused me so much pain. I needed to grow a lot more before the dissonance of the Tristan chord could be resolved.

Ma fin est mon commencement,
Et mon commencement ma fin.
My end is my beginning,
And my beginning, my end.

—Guillaume de Machaut

PART TWO

RESOLUTION

Twelve

IN AT LAST

If there be some strictness of discipline,
do not be at once dismayed and run away from the way of salvation.

—Saint Benedict

The Novitiate had one bathroom on our floor and a smaller one downstairs for the ten of us. There was a small room that had an upright piano where we could practice our music. Another somewhat larger room served as our common room, where we could talk and have meetings.

Right away, postulants are immersed in the three pillars of Benedictine life: prayer, work, and study. My work consisted of helping in the laundry, cleaning, setting up the refectory for supper, and cleaning at St. Gregory's, the women's guest house.

Soon after I entered the Abbey I mentioned to Sister Hildegard that I was interested in wild edible plants. After Mother Prisca left for Our Lady of the Rock, Sister Hildegard replaced her as herb gardener and maker of herb products. My offhand remark led to a great gift for me. Sister Hildegard was looking for a disciple—someone with whom to share her interest in herbs and wild plants—and I turned out to be that disciple. She taught me for two years: basic botany, identifying wild plants, making a herbarium, planting and taking care of herbs, making herb vinegars and other products. On Sundays, after dinner, she would hurry me out of the monastery to spend the afternoon with her finding and identifying wild flowers and plants. Little did we know that Sister Hildegard would end up with me at Our Lady of the Rock. Her work with me was a perfect preparation for my future work here.

Lady Abbess and all the community encouraged me greatly in musical activities. During Lent I gave a series of lectures in the refectory on Bach's *Saint Matthew Passion*, as the community was rehearsing some excerpts of that long, complex work. Mother David, then the Prioress, worked with me on singing, and Lady Abbess asked me to prepare and direct the community's polyphony choir for the Abbey's annual Fair in August. I had never done such a thing, but I enjoyed it very much. The Abbey had never asked someone so new as I in the community to do this.

Another event, exciting for me, involved the organ I had worked on during my sabbatical year. I was picking blueberries one fine summer day in the large fenced-in berry patch. Suddenly I was summoned to get my bass viol and meet a visiting priest, Father Paul Fruth, who was an organist. Two days later on July 11, the Feast of St. Benedict, would be the celebration of the fifteen hundredth year since the birth of St. Benedict. This celebration, to which a large number of people had been invited, included the dedication of the restored organ, and featured a concert by Father Paul Fruth. But a crucial part of the organ was not finished—the foot pedals. My viol became the missing foot pedals for the occasion. I had to watch Father's hands very carefully as he played so as to keep in perfect time with him. We practiced, and all went well. I loved playing the bass part for the pedals, just as I had loved playing the double bass in the training orchestra at Oberlin.

When I found out that I could enter the Abbey, I gave my beautiful old Martin guitar and the violin I had used since the eighth grade to Laura Hawkins, one of my students at Livingston. I told her she could keep these instruments, or sell them, or give them away. I naïvely thought I would not need them. Thank God that Laura knew me better than I knew myself. On her first visit to me at the Abbey, she returned my violin. I was asked to play for the community. I played the Biber *Passacaglia* and some Irish jigs and reels.

I told Lady Abbess one day that I had complex and conflicting feelings about the violin. She replied, "Well, you'd better get those feelings straightened out." She must have known, years before I knew it, how important a process that would be for me.

For any postulant who has had a profession, one of the hardest challenges of religious life is to learn to submit her expertise to the needs of the community. This challenge hit me almost immediately. A Chant Seminar was planned by the Abbey to follow up on the Holy Week Seminar in April at Our Lady of the Rock. A month after that first seminar, in May, I entered the Abbey. The Chant Seminar was to take place around June 24, the feast of St. John the Baptist. Lady Abbess led the community in rehearsals of the chants for that feast, and told the community to plan to have a few days free for the actual seminar. The time came, and all were surprised to learn that the seminar had already happened, that is, the rehearsals *were* the seminar.

Only a few of the nuns were to take part in the formal seminar, and I was not one of them. My pride was wounded; I was furious. How could there be a music seminar at the Abbey that did not include me? I, a PhD in musicology! Lady Abbess explained that it might ruin my vocation if I were included, just as her own vocation had been severely threatened when, as a new M.D. and postulant at Jouarre during the Nazi occupation, she was called upon to be a physician to the nuns and to the villagers. I did not understand this, but I was somewhat mollified when I was asked to give a short presentation to the seminar on the role of Guido of Arezzo's role in the development of solfege.[65]

Study came in many ways. My postulant mistress was Mother Jerome. She was a beautiful, brilliant and elegant woman who came from a noble German family and grew up in Italy. In Germany during World War I she looked out the window one May Day to see her father shot by the Communists. She married a Muslim village chief in Dagestan, one of the former Soviet republics. She lived with him in the high society of New York City, and after his death entered Regina Laudis. I loved her. She worked with me on my genealogy and the Rule of Saint Benedict, and was a key person in helping me get used to monastic life.

Mother Columba,[66] a true scholar, worked with me on Latin. I had forgotten most of the Latin I had learned in high school, but instead of reviewing the basic grammar, we jumped right in to the hymns, which are much more difficult to translate than the psalms. Sometimes we would spend the entire hour looking up one word. I did review the grammar on my own for a few years.

Our prayer life is centered on the Divine Office. I went to all the Hours except Matins, for postulants were given six weeks or so to get used to the demanding monastic schedule before being asked to get up at two A.M. to pray. Private prayer came naturally to me. I had so much to pray about. I found many aspects of my new life hard to take. One of the biggest challenges was to live such a structured life with so little unscheduled time. I hated having to ask permission for everything. I could hardly bear the separation from my family, and to accept that our relationship would never be the same. I could not trust that a deeper relationship might evolve. There were times when I wanted to escape, to leave.

Carl and Bill, like my father, needed time to adjust to my new life. They both told me that they wanted me to do what would make me happy. But Bill, then a graduate student at Yale, lamented that he had no home address. Normally kids leave home. This time the mom left home, and indeed the home did not exist any more. Carl, on his first visit to me at the Abbey, was repelled. He said at once, "I'm going to get you out of

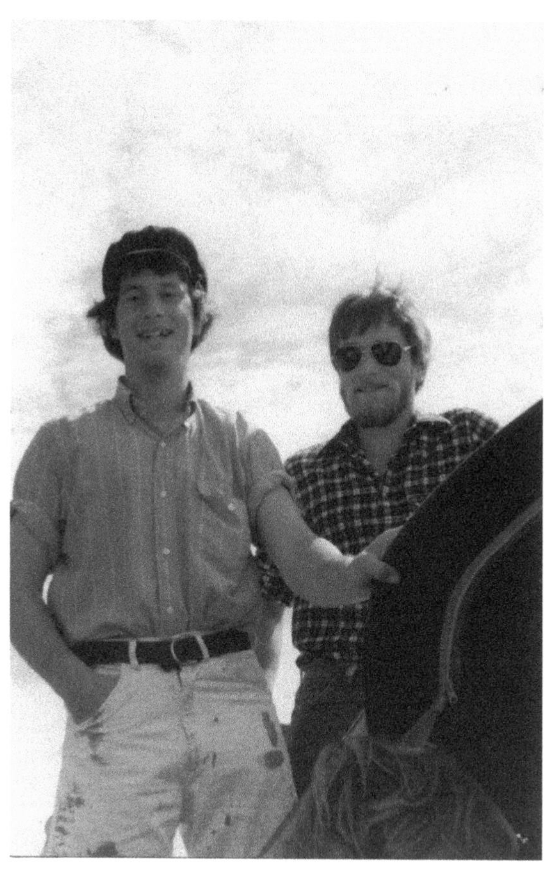

Bill and Carl sailing.

here! I'm going to take you up to New Hampshire to live." "But I *want* to be here," I insisted. On his few visits to the Abbey, he refused to set foot in the chapel.

Bill visited me several times, did come to Vespers in the chapel, thought the chant was "haunting," thought our clothes were "medieval," and agreed to see Mother Placid in the parlor a couple of times. I had hoped that by meeting her, he would be drawn into his own relationship with the Abbey, but this did not happen.

I now see that my entering religious life was harder on my sons than I realized at the time. And I missed them terribly. We all had to learn to relate to each other in new ways, and this took time. After Carl moved to California we did not see each other for four years. Bill, in a letter, mentioned that he and I were not the same people we had been two years earlier. I cried at reading this.

I was continuing and intensifying the changes within myself that had begun during my sabbatical. During my first two years at Regina Laudis it became much clearer how I needed to change. I found that I fiercely wanted to have my own way, to call the shots. I hated being asked to make sudden changes in my plans. I did not trust that I was loved or lovable. I continued to crave deep relationships. I formed deep attachments to those in charge of my formation. I wanted their attention. I wanted to be their favorite person. I resented the fact that these attachments were not and could never be reciprocated. I was still subject to bouts of depression and anxiety. I would often fall into a pattern of isolation, feeling totally abandoned, afraid to reach out for help. I called this a "Violent Vacuum." In coming chapters I will try as best I can to describe how I finally grew up and became more and more my real self.

Thirteen

THE POTTER AT WORK
REGINA LAUDIS 1979-1980

You are the Potter who makes me,
Pinching, patting, pushing and pulling,
Till I come out right.
You are always making me anew,
Persuading, enticing, sometimes having to punch and poke roughly
Because of the obtuse unyielding clay that I am.

—Mother Felicitas, OSB

How did the problems in my life get resolved? How did they move from dissonance to resolution? I can answer this in two words: religious formation. But what is religious formation? Church people, especially Catholics, speak often of "formation." We have priestly formation, the formation of deacons, and the formation of catechists. What is this, in a religious community? It goes much deeper than simply training to acquire a skill, to do a job, to learn the outward gestures and language of monastic life. All religious communities have vows, most often the "evangelical counsels" of poverty, chastity, and obedience. Many communities have added to these vows ones particular to their community. Our Benedictine vows come directly from Saint Benedict's Rule written in the sixth century. These are: stability, obedience, and *conversatio* (conversion of life). Poverty and chastity are included under obedience. The three vows are intertwined and interdependent. To live in stability, not only of a physical place but with an inward stability, and to submit to an authority who represents Christ, are impossible without a willingness, at least, to change oneself in many, often unforeseen, directions.

This explains, in essence, how my views on important things and my ways of interacting with others have changed over the years. We need others to help us. We cannot do this alone. Our families have helped us all they can, but it is not enough. The process of formation is adapted to the needs of each woman, who brings with her a number of issues from her family and her life that need to be redeemed. To help us with this *conversatio* the community works with each sister to discover her unique gifts, of which she is often not aware, and to bring these gifts into their fullness in the service of God.

To explain this further, I must describe the various steps that a sister takes on the way to becoming a Benedictine nun, and how I have gone through these steps in my own life.

First, a woman feels that she might have a religious vocation, or she somehow *knows* that she has a vocation. She may be attracted to a particular type of vocation—active or contemplative. Or she may simply be drawn to a particular community, as I was drawn to Regina Laudis. There was really no other community that I would have considered. Some women need to visit a few communities in order to find the right one.

But this feeling of hers must be tested. If a community to which I am attracted does not accept my desire to be part of it, then I do not have a vocation to that community. This period of seeking I have treated in Part One of this work.

If she is accepted, she enters the community, becoming a postulant. The Latin verb *postulare* means to demand, claim, desire. She is thus asking to become part of the community. The postulant is in fact a guest, who wears (at Regina Laudis and Our Lady of the Rock) a black tunic and a short black veil that does not completely cover her hair. She lives in the monastery and takes part in its liturgy and work. She is free to leave at any time, and the community can ask her to leave.

As a postulant, we begin our formation. Every postulant and novice is encouraged to delve deeply into her genealogy.[67] This enriches us, gives us a much deeper sense of our roots, and helps to explain some of the quirks and gifts that make each of us a unique person. In addition, we believe that by redeeming some of our own disordered tendencies, we are redeeming those ancestors who had the same tendencies. For an example in my own life, my parents, three of my four grandparents, an uncle who committed suicide, and others in the family—who knows how far back—suffered greatly from depression. If I could learn to accept that depression in myself, learn to live with it and to make good choices in spite of it, that would help my ancestors as well. Prayer is retroactive.

We begin to form relationships with our peers, the other postulants and novices. We begin to learn to practice obedience to our elders. All the members of the community, especially the Mothers in charge of our formation, and our fellow postulants and novices, help us to define our particular gifts and weaknesses. We learn, hopefully, to understand that our very weaknesses are also gifts. We begin to learn new ways of relating to our families and friends outside the monastery.

From the beginning I wanted to be at Our Lady of the Rock. But since OLR did not yet have a formation program, I spent my first two years of monastic life at the Abbey. It was hard for me to relate to my peers at first. I was twenty years older than most of them, but I began to see that in many ways they were wiser than I. We were encouraged by Mother Dolores Hart, Dean of Education,[68] to work together as a body and to help one another in resolving the inevitable conflicts that arise in a community.

Most of us, I am sure, spend this time in hope and fear. The postulancy can last as long as needed. Given my life-long propensity to anticipate rejection, I feared that I would never be accepted into the novitiate. The postulant writes a petition stating her desire to be received as a novice. This petition must be approved by each group in the community: first the novices, then those in First Vows, and finally the fully professed, the Mothers. Sometimes we are asked to rewrite the petition. Having gone through these steps, I was finally accepted on August 15, 1980, thirteen months after my entrance. I had to wait an agonizing two more months before my Clothing, the ceremony through which a postulant becomes a novice.

The Novitiate

In the Bible, receiving a call from God often involves the bestowal of a new name. Abram becomes Abraham; Jacob, Israel; Saul, Paul; Simon, Peter. In the Church, a new pope chooses a new name for himself. What would my new name be? I would not know until the Clothing ceremony. When we enter, we are called simply by our given name.

The first major ceremony, the first major step on the way to becoming a nun, is called Clothing, because it is then that the postulant is clothed in the full monastic habit and receives her new name. Canon law requires for all religious sisters a novitiate of at least one year. Beyond that, the novitiate can last as long as needed, until the novice is ready for First Vows.

Formerly the Clothing ceremony resembled a wedding. It took place in the chapel before relatives and guests. The postulant wore a wedding dress and had a godmother. But since the novice is nowhere near the spousal dimension that a wedding signifies, most communities, including the Abbey, revised the ceremony, substituting for the wedding dress clothes that represented the postulant's former life, or something else that symbolizes her uniqueness. I did not want to dress as a professor. For some reason that now seems strange to me, I had always wanted to be Sophisticated, an Elegant Lady. When I lived in New York City in my twenties, I envied the women I saw in the subways and on the streets. I thought that maybe some day I would look that way, sophisticated, when I was a little older. It did not happen. But this wish to be an Elegant Lady came true on my Clothing day, October 17, 1980: the feast of St. Ignatius of Antioch. Someone was sent out to buy enough satin material to make a gown. It was maroon, my favorite color. On the evening before the ceremony, Mother Prioress David Serna stayed up late to finish making this gown. What extravagance! It would never be used again, unless some day it might be useful in a play.

The ceremony, celebrated privately within the community, was to be in the afternoon. In the morning after Mass, Sister Telchilde inflicted torture on me by arranging my long hair on top of my head and using hair spray to hold it in place. From then on I could not turn my head freely. I wore my new gown and this hairdo to dinner, our main meal of the day at noon.

My Clothing day, October 17, 1980, before the ceremony. I'm still Martha Curti, postulant. Photo by Lady Abbess

The ceremony itself began with a Chapter, a formal meeting of the entire community in the Common Room. At this time I read aloud a few paragraphs I had written concerning my current spiritual state. Then I played a Telemann sonata, or one movement of it, on my bass viol. At last the moment came: Mother Jerome, my Postulant Mistress, and Mother Bernadette, who was to be my Novice Mistress, escorted me out and helped me to shed the gown and put on my newly made tunic. They led me back to kneel in front of

The same day, a few hours later. Now I'm Sister Felicitas, novice. Photo by Lady Abbess

Lady Abbess, who asked me to hand over my jewelry, a pair of garnet earrings that had belonged to my Grandmother Curti. She then cut my hair. I loved this part! It was deeply symbolic of a new phase for me, an offering of myself to God. Then I was led out again to put on the rest of my habit: the scapular, wimple, and white veil.[69] All these garments were newly made and had been blessed at Mass. Back to kneel again before Lady Abbess, who now handed me a beautiful card on parchment that said: "Tu vocaberis Soror Felicitas" (You will be called Sister Felicitas). At last, I was a Sister. After this, the community sang "Veni Creator Spiritus" while I handed out the card I had made to commemorate the occasion, and exchanged the Kiss of Peace with everyone.

Felicitas

The Abbess chooses the name for each new novice. This name is not revealed to anyone except the nun who makes the card. Everyone tries ahead of time to guess what the name will be, and usually no one gets it right.

I was immediately thrilled with my new name. Felicitas is the Latin word for "felicity." It means not a merely superficial happiness, a feeling good, but on a deeper level, good fortune, living one's true calling. The psalm that I chose to be read at my Clothing ceremony, Psalm 29/30, beautifully expresses the movement from sorrow to joy that we all experience over and over again: a little Death and Resurrection. I chose the final two verses for my Clothing card:

> Thou hast turned for me my mourning into dancing: thou hast put off my sackcloth, and girded me with gladness:
>
> To the end that my glory may sing praise to thee, and not be silent. O Lord my God, I will give thanks unto thee for ever.
>
> Psalm 29/30: 11-12

Saints Perpetua and Felicitas, by Ade Bethune. First published in 1937 in *The Catholic Worker.* Photo courtesy of Archives and Special Collections, St. Catherine University, St.Paul, Minnesota

Felicitas is a saint. In the year 203, when the Church was still very young, two young women were put to death in the amphitheater at Carthage in the persecution of Septimius Severus.[70] Perpetua was the daughter of a wealthy family and had a baby. Felicitas was a slave in the household, and was pregnant. (No mention of the fathers of these babies appears in any of the contemporary accounts.) They were friends, and part of a group of Christians.[71] Along with some of the men in their group, they were put in prison for refusing to renounce Christ and worship the emperor. Perpetua was permitted to bring her baby with her. Felicitas and her companions prayed that her baby would be born prematurely, for she wished to be martyred with her companions. Despite the cruelty of that age, a pregnant woman was not allowed to be martyred. Her prayers were answered: her baby was born in prison. Both women had to stand up against strong family opposition, for their families were not Christian.

I, though far from being or wishing to be a martyr, also had to stand up against the opposition and the sadness of my father, and I had to set my children free.[72]

The very word "felicitas" has great richness in itself. Its Latin root FE refers to fertility and so much else. Some Latin-based English words that show this are: female, feminine, fertile, fecund, femur, felix, fetus.

My name baffles most people on first hearing. I have to spell it for them. But I love it! It's such a musical name. It is so apt. Really, it encapsulates my entire life. During my novitiate I found my life written up in the Psalms and Canticles in so many places. Here is a typical one:

> The Lord makes poor and makes rich: He humbles and He exalts.
> He raises up the needy from the dust, and lifts up the poor man from the dunghill,
> That he may sit with princes, and hold a throne of glory.[73]

Felicitas, a slave, was lifted up into freedom and glory by her martyrdom.

As for me, I identified with the dunghill. When a woman enters the Novitiate at Regina Laudis, all the challenges she has met as a postulant are greatly intensified. For me, the emotional highs and lows became more extreme. I sat on the dunghill a lot of the time, feeling totally abandoned, believing that no one loved me because I was not lovable, that I simply could not tolerate the demands of monastic life any longer, that I wanted out. At other times I was ecstatic, amazed at the wisdom of my Sisters and the Mothers, in awe of their capacity to put problems into a contemplative framework, grateful to God for His goodness and mercy, knocked out by His interventions in our lives and those of multitudes of others.

This greater intensity is a normal and natural result of the tighter enclosure that a novice encounters. The first year after her Clothing ceremony is her "canonical year." She is totally immersed in the community. She is not to go outside the monastery, does not associate with anyone outside the community, may not receive visitors. I could write and receive letters and occasionally, with permission, speak with my father on the telephone. These connections did not, however, provide any real escape from the community.

In July of my canonical year, I was sent with Sister Anne Rushton and a young associate of the Abbey, Margaret Patton of the famous military family, who later became Mother Margaret Georgina, to attend a three-week summer session at the Catholic University of America in Washington, D.C. We took two courses, one in Gregorian chant and one in the Ward Method,[74] with Dr. Theodore Marier, the leading chant teacher in the country and founder of the choir school at St. Paul's Church in Cambridge, Massachusetts. We visited with some of Margaret's relatives who showed us the National Cathedral and its herb garden. We visited the family of the late Mother Mary Simeon, whose laundry number and several items I had inherited. But I was not allowed to see Elizabeth Midgley, the daughter of my stepmother Frances. In the canonical year you can associate with others if this is a mission of the community, but not with your personal friends and relatives. Elizabeth could not understand this, and I did not find it easy either.

Dr. Marier had recently begun to visit Regina Laudis to work with the nuns, and he helped them faithfully for the rest of his life. He was a very dedicated, energetic, and inspiring teacher. We invited him to Our Lady of the Rock, too, for a solid week of work on chant with us. Much as I had studied and listened and tried to apply the theories of Dom Gajard of Solesmes, I did not really understand them until Dr. Marier, a professional musician, explained them in language that I could understand.

These two years as postulant and novice at Regina Laudis were tough, but all along the way the moments of encouragement, joy, and wonder at the goodness of God, were more than enough to keep me going. Soon after my canonical year, I returned to Our Lady of the Rock, not this time as a guest, but as a novice on her way to be fully incorporated into the community.

Fourteen

ISLAND NOVICE
OUR LADY OF THE ROCK 1982-1984

Music uncovers the buried way to the heart,
to the core of our being,
where it touches the being of the Creator and the Redeemer.
Wherever this is achieved, music becomes the road that leads to Jesus,
the way on which God shows His salvation.

—Pope Benedict (as Cardinal Joseph Ratzinger)

In January 1982, soon after my canonical year, I returned to Shaw Island and Our Lady of the Rock. Why had I asked to be here? I knew I would be happier in a small community. I also knew that I was needed here. At the time I entered the Abbey there were fourteen postulants and novices, and about forty women altogether. Our Lady of the Rock had only its three founders: Rev. Mother Therese Critchley, Mother Miriam Benedict, and Mother Prisca Dougherty. These three sang the entire monastic liturgy, a most demanding work even for a large community. In addition, they did the farm work with very little help, and after the first few years began to receive guests. So I knew that whatever I could do would help. Moreover, I was drawn to the adventure of a new foundation.

ABBEYS, MONASTERIES, PRIORIES, et al

Monastery: a generic term for the residence of a community of monks or nuns living in an enclosure.

Abbey: a monastic community that has attained a significant size and influence.

Priory: a smaller monastic community.

Convent: a residence for active Sisters, often attached to a parish church.

Active Sisters take vows, as do nuns.

The Priory of Our Lady of the Rock owes its existence to the vision of a man named Henry Ellis. Henry Day Ellis came from a wealthy family, owners of silver and lead mines in the Coeur d'Alene area of Idaho. A convert to Catholicism, he harbored a strong desire that his land on Shaw Island might become the place for a Benedictine monastic community. He was an Oblate[75] of Mount Angel Abbey in Oregon and had become friends with Dom David Nicholson, the Abbey's organist and choir director. Since Father Nicholson was planning to visit Regina Laudis to help the nuns with their chant, Henry asked him to sound out Lady Abbess to see if her community might be interested in starting a foundation on his property on Shaw Island. This property, three hundred acres, consisted of three separate small farms adjacent to one another. Most of it was forest, with some open meadows and a short stretch of muddy shoreline on Squaw Bay. Henry's three siblings, Robert, Fred, and Elizabeth Ellis Jones, also had properties on Shaw. Henry's land had two cabins and one small house from the three original properties, but by the time he conceived the idea of a monastic foundation, he had built a beautiful house that he used for guests.

This house, built in the 1950s, has a Japanese look to it. This is for a good reason: Henry Ellis had spent time in Japan, where he had become Catholic under the guidance of a Professor Tagita, who had himself become Catholic as a disciple of Saint Maximilian Kolbe.[76] When Tagita and his wife came to visit Henry, who was living in an old farmhouse on his land, Henry asked Mrs. Tagita to choose the site for the house he planned to build. Most people would have chosen a site that gave the best view of Squaw Bay, looking at it across a wide meadow. But Mrs. Tagita chose a spot higher up and further back from the water, on an outcropping of moss-covered rock. She explained that this was the most sacred part of the property.

When the Abbey was preparing to establish a foundation here, Lady Abbess asked the nuns to suggest names for the proposed monastery. She rejected all their suggestions and announced that the new monastery would be called "Our Lady of the Rock."

Lady Abbess and Mother Mary Aline came out to investigate the house and land. They were impressed by the beauty and the peaceful environment of the island. After careful consideration by the Abbey community, Lady Abbess appointed three nuns to begin the foundation: Mother Therese, who was to be the Superior of the little community, Mother Miriam, and Mother Prisca. These three arrived on Shaw on September 1, 1977. Mother Luke Parmigiani, a hermit within the Abbey community, had been sent as a scout the previous year to get acquainted with the island, start a vegetable garden, and supervise the workers Henry had hired to build an addition to the house, a barn, a workshop, and a place for cooking and preserving food.

There was already a religious presence on the island. The Franciscan Sisters of the Eucharist, based in Meriden, Connecticut, had established a small community on the island a year or two earlier. They ran the store and the ferry landing, and as active Sisters "in the world" provided a complement to our small contemplative community. Besides the store and the ferry, some of them taught, on and off the island: music, computer skills, and kindergarten.

Before I entered the Abbey, I had some strange ideas about what it would be like. I wanted so badly to enter monastic life that I promised myself I would be willing to do anything just to be there. Clean toilets? Of course! By now I have cleaned hundreds of toilets, or rather, cleaned a few toilets hundreds of times. I even told myself I would undergo the torture of playing volleyball, or whatever the novices did for fun: I, who was totally inept at sports, who shrank from any ball coming my way, who didn't know if the World Series had to do with football, basketball, or baseball. Inside the monastery, the closest I came to that dreaded activity was one game of badminton.

Imagining life at Our Lady of the Rock, I nobly resolved to clean fish without complaint. Since OLR is on an island, I assumed we would catch and eat a lot of fish. I detest fish, with a few exceptions. In the early years of the foundation Mother Miriam did go fishing, caught a lot of cod, and cleaned it herself, to my great relief. I found that I actually liked that fresh cod. I did learn to clean the salmon that was often given to us by islanders, but I never have learned to like salmon.

I found that life here was essentially the same as at the Abbey. The nuns had made the same vows and were living according to the Rule of Saint Benedict, with the same liturgy, habits, and customs; the same commitment to raising their food, making their own clothes, and being good stewards of the land. The horarium (schedule of work and prayer) was basically the same. But here life was much simpler in one sense, and in another more complex, in that each of the Mothers had a multitude of various areas under their care. Their work was mostly on the level of survival. They weren't able to have specialties like raising fruit trees, weaving and spinning, making pottery or candles, raising bees, bookbinding, and so on. And because of their small numbers, they could not be as formal in the liturgy as at the Abbey.

My work as a new novice consisted mostly of helping the Mothers. I helped Mother Prisca in the herb garden and the guest house, ran some errands, took part fully in the liturgy, and made many of the suppers. At the Abbey and here at Our Lady of the Rock novices are encouraged to develop and take responsibility for the areas central to their call. For me, these areas are music, herbs, compost, and recycling. Henry Hoffman, whose grandfather had been one of the early settlers on the island, built several raised beds in a corner of the big vegetable garden for me to grow herbs.

Here at Our Lady of the Rock I came to understand better than I ever had the importance of music in my life. Through music I could turn the seething energies within myself into something constructive, something that could help others. I composed an "Angelus," a piece for women's voices, the best piece I have written. I played some pieces in public with Mother Kateri Visocky, one of the Franciscans on Shaw, a good musician, well trained in voice and in teaching. I began to direct the community in chant and polyphony. Two island women—Elizabeth Jones, sister of our benefactor Henry Ellis and a fine pianist, and Helen Storey—a very good cellist, formed the Shaw Island Trio with me, and we gave a few concerts.

Soon after my return to OLR, my sister Nancy turned up without notice. She had just quit her job as a clerk with the Railroad Retirement Board in Chicago and had no idea what to do next. I called her boss and pleaded with him to take her back. He declined. Nancy had made too many mistakes in entering numbers, which could cause great confusion in the accounts. If only she had waited to be fired, she could have collected unemployment benefits while looking for a new job; but out of her habitual impulsiveness, she had quit.

Nancy was her usual self. As I drove her from the ferry on her arrival, she looked out at our beautiful landscape and found it very stark and depressing. It was February, after all. No sun. We had no other guests at that time. Father Aufiero was very kind to Nancy. But her future was uncertain, to say the least. It was unlikely that she would ever have a job again. Dad rescued her as usual, supporting her as she stayed on in her Chicago apartment with her thirteen cats, enjoying church and volunteering at the animal shelter. Some time the following year Nancy moved to Alma, Michigan at the invitation of the Religious Sisters of Mercy. She stayed with them and responded well, for a time, to their dedicated and creative care of her. But inevitably, as she always had, she turned against those who had helped her. We had petitioned the proper authorities that a legal guardian be appointed for Nancy, but this request was denied. She spent the last years of her life on her own in Alma, with the help of her three churches—Episcopal, the Church of God, and the Salvation Army—and Dad's financial support.

Jean Morfesi, a postulant here who is now Mother Simonetta at Regina Laudis, helped me to take Nancy back to the Seattle airport, bound for Chicago. Amazingly, as we went up an escalator, we spied my son Bill descending on the neighboring escalator. I had no idea that Bill was anywhere near. He looked wonderful: handsome and neatly dressed. He was on his way to Anchorage to visit his Aunt Caroline and Uncle Eric Wohlforth. We had time to exchange a few words. He was working on his M.A. in International Relations at Yale.

Carl had moved to Mountain View, California to work as a computer programmer and was married to a woman he had known in New Jersey.

Inside a Pressure Cooker

These were the outward events of my life. My emotional life was volcanic. My old pattern of attachment to authority persons was as strong as ever. I honestly feel sorry for all the people who have been the objects of my attachments. I wanted to be their peer, their favorite person. Of course, and thank God, they could not and did not want to meet me at that level. I was jealous beyond measure of the other postulants. (There were always one to three postulants here—some sent from Regina Laudis and some from the West—who came and left.) We shared the kind of sibling rivalry, sometimes quite fierce, that typically takes place in a family. I was so full of anger at all sorts of imagined rejections that I feared the community would not want me to stay.

All this came to a head in December of 1982. Out of the crisis came clarity and great happiness. In my journal I described my pain—the grasping, voracious, insatiable desire that is turned in all the wrong directions and so can never be met. The cloudiness of perception. The darkness, the inability to see all the goodness and beauty around me.

December 3, 1982

So then I truly gave up. I said to God, "I can't stand this any more, but I have no idea at all what to do. I ask you to take me in your hands."

By this suffering, which is very severe and very real even though neurotically based, God is trying to tell me something. The suffering is part of His plan: not that He wants me to go on like this, but it comes from the body and the genealogy that He has given me. What He is trying to tell me is: if the suffering is so great, then the potential is also very great. I don't mean just the release of energy to get a lot of work done; or even the writing of some good music. Something else. And what could that be other than a religious *potential—for a deepening relationship with Him. At last, then, I can see that the built-in tendency to feel abandoned is, indeed, a fantastic gift.*

I had been in God's hands all along.

All this time I kept in close contact with the Abbey and experienced strong support from Lady Abbess, Mother Dolores, Mother Bernadette, Sister Noella, and others. Once at Mass I felt, though not in a dream or a vision, that I was at the Abbey. This experience was so vivid that I could see and even smell and sense the powerful aura of the chapel there. I could move at will from one place to another in the choir, the little dark passage leading to the side chapel, and the area for guests. I didn't see or confront any people, but I was there, and this made me deeply happy. From this time on there grew a great longing to return. In March I wrote to Lady Abbess asking if I could come back to prepare for my First Vows. I knew that through the community I had moved significantly in the direction of centering on God, rather than on myself. I knew now that I could give myself without reservation far more than I used to be able to do. I had been well tested at OLR, and felt that I was now able to live on more than one level at a time. The jealousy and anger were still present, but I could view them from another place, allowing me a greater freedom to choose and to act for the life of the community.

Mother Therese and the other Mothers agreed with this assessment and supported my request. It was time to go back.

Fifteen

PURGATORY ON EARTH
REGINA LAUDIS 1985-87

Restore us early with Thy mercy, that rejoicing we may delight in all our days.
Then shall we be glad for the days of our humiliation:
for the years when we saw misfortune.

—Psalm 89(90): 16-17

Humility, for Christians, is a good thing. It is not being Uriah Heep, beating ourselves on the chest and proclaiming that we are the worst sinners in the world. That would be boasting. It is, rather, an honest recognition of who we are in relation to God. It is accepting the truth about ourselves. It is the opposite of pride. Is anyone born with this virtue? Probably only Jesus, Mary, Joseph, and John the Baptist. The learning of humility is a painful process: it rips to shreds our self-defenses, our rationalizations, our resistance to change.

In the two years I spent at Regina Laudis preparing for my First Vows I learned a lot about humility. The word humility (Latin *humilitas*) comes from the word *humus* or soil. In his Rule, Saint Benedict speaks often about humility and devotes an entire chapter to it.[77]

It is fitting that during this time of preparation for First Vows (also called Temporary Profession) I was very involved in making compost. In my earlier life at Flint Farm I had tried to make compost, but since I knew nothing about it, the pile was a dismal failure, simply a pantry for raccoons. At the Abbey, I learned compost making in a professional way. Sister Perpetua taught Sister Rachel and me. We both needed and appreciated this grounding. We spoke of how the composting process is an analogy for the process we go through digesting all the nasty stuff within ourselves, physically and emotionally. Compost is an amazing process in which our food waste becomes good, sweet-smelling soil. We wanted to be turned into good soil, too.

The word compost comes from the Latin verb *componere,* to place together, and its past participle, *compositus*. In English we have composition, composite, component, compound, compote, composer, compositor. (In the old days of linotype printing, the compositor was the person who arranged the pieces of lead type to form a page.) I love all these connections. They reflect the medieval notion of the artist or composer not as a creator, since only God is a creator, but rather one who puts existing things together.

The Violin Challenge

The primary way I needed to learn to see and hear myself honestly was the violin. But singing was part of it, too. The problems in both were the same. It is always a challenge for a professional woman who enters religious life to learn to submit her professional self to the community. If our profession is music, we are involved with the central part of Benedictine life: chant, the choir, sung prayer. We are involved with singing—that is, we are involved with each member of the community in a vulnerable area.

Even before I entered Regina Laudis, I had my first challenge. At the Holy Week Seminar at Our Lady of the Rock, when I was still a guest, Sister Noella, then a novice, announced to me: "I work at the Abbey with people who need help with singing. So I will be working with you." A deeply threatening proclamation this was to me. How could I, a whiz at sight-singing, whom good musicians considered fun to sing with, who was highly trained in music, need help? From someone who wasn't even a musician!

Soon enough, one day after Vespers at the Abbey, Lady Abbess without warning summoned all of us who sat in the first row of choir—that is, the postulants and novices—to meet with her. Lady Abbess asked me to sing an Alleluia. Fear overtook me. My throat tightened. My voice froze. No sound would come out. Thus I learned compassion for people who are terrified of singing, and accepted that I needed help.

Gradually I was helped to realize that my voice stood out, did not blend with the other voices. I already knew that I was very tense when I sang. Just singing one piece at Mass, a Gradual or an Allelluia, left my face—all the muscles of my jaw and cheeks—in pain from tension. For years Mother Prioress David,[78] who was a trained singer with a beautiful voice, worked patiently with me to free my voice from all the tension. Working with her, then later in the 1990s working with Prof. Tomatis and doing the Tomatis Listening Therapy,[79] really did turn the tide. I am so grateful for all this help. Still, my voice is not what I would wish it to be, especially as I reach my eighties. We can always do better. We will always need help.

During the years of my formation, both at the Abbey and at Our Lady of the Rock, the Mothers and my peers spent a huge amount of time and energy encouraging me to develop musically and to do things I had never done before. During my college-teaching days I had always been shy about leading people in singing. The Abbey kept giving me opportunities to overcome this shyness. We had a Novitiate Schola, the Sadah Schola,[80] for people who had various difficulties with singing. Mother Prioress worked with us. I could help others with reading music—I had taught sight-singing for years—and sometimes led a whole rehearsal.

In my first year at Regina Laudis I was asked to direct the Abbey's polyphony choir for the annual Fair Concert. I chose the music, including two beautiful pieces by my former Livingston colleague Barbara Benary, and the canon "When Jesus Wept" by William Billings. Directing a choir was a totally new experience for me, and despite my vocal insecurity (I would often ask Lady Abbess to do the warm-up with the choir for me) I actually loved this work and enjoyed it tremendously. I think the choir did, too.

Lady Abbess was the first person to encourage me to write music. A stream of short compositions flowed forth: music for a Saint Hildegard play; songs, the best of which, the "Angelus" for two-part women's chorus, is often sung; pieces for violin and piano; a march for an ad hoc little band at the Abbey for the anniversary of the liberation of Jouarre. I had never written any music beyond assignments for theory and counterpoint classes. I simply do not have the training or the skill to write any extended piece. I can make up good tunes and good harmonies for them, that's all. But I have so enjoyed what I have done.

FIRST VOWS, OR TEMPORARY PROFESSION, is the next big step after Clothing on the way to becoming a permanent member of the community. The period of First Vows lasts for three years, but may be extended another three years if necessary. In the chapel, in public, the Sister reads aloud her Benedictine promises of stability, obedience, and *conversatio* (conversion of life). This statement uses the formula given by Saint Benedict (*Rule*, Ch. 58). The Sister has written this statement on parchment, and after reading it aloud in the presence of all, she signs it and shows it to all.

Despite all I had learned and done in music, I had to learn a different way of doing it. I had to submit to the needs of the community. I sat through many a polyphony rehearsal led by people who did not know nearly what I knew about music. In teaching sight-singing and theory, I was used to teaching one or one-and-a-half hour classes. Now I had to learn to see what we could accomplish in a half an hour a week, and to be open to having classes cancelled when the community had a greater need.

Once I was asked to write a short piece in three parts for three novices, including one who could not match pitches. Surprisingly, it worked! The need for bringing forth the novice who thought she couldn't sing took precedence over the normal professional requirements.

I even had to learn to read music differently, for we use the movable DO system for our music, and I had never learned that system. At first, I would look at a note and think, "This is D, so it's RE." Fortunately this process of translation was not needed for too long. Soon I could just think in syllables.

I remembered that soon after I entered Regina Laudis, I had told Lady Abbess about my ambivalent relationship with the violin. She said, "You'll have to get over that." She really meant it, but said nothing further. Now, on returning to the Abbey for my second stint to prepare for First Vows, I was informed that I would be given violin lessons. A huge surprise. My teacher was Jeanne Mitchell Biancolli, a concert violinist, who had recently entered the Catholic Church through her relationship with Regina Laudis.

Jeanne was then in her early sixties—a wiry, energetic, highly intelligent woman with a down-to-earth sense of humor. She had made her Town Hall debut in 1947 and had spent the next fifteen years playing concertos with the leading orchestras, giving three Carnegie Hall recitals, and appearing on television programs. Then she married Louis Biancolli, the music critic for *The New York Telegram*. He was considerably older than she, and by the time I met Jeanne, he was seriously ill with dementia. Her life with him and their two daughters was stressful beyond measure. She, Louis, and the girls all had health problems. She had had a heart attack, among other things. But Jeanne was totally given in her work with me. I had never had a teacher so dedicated.

But why, I wondered, would Lady Abbess want me to study the violin? What would this have to do with being a nun? As it turned out, it had everything to do with it.

Jeanne came weekly to the Abbey, a 45-minute drive, to work with me. I soon discovered that in her opinion, I was not playing in tune, I could not maintain a steady rhythm, my bowing was out of control, my tone was harsh and scratchy. This sounds really bad, but it was not quite as bad as it sounds. Playing in tune, for example: Jeanne was quoted in an article about her as saying that *she* had spent her whole life trying to play in tune.

I strongly resisted her evaluation of my playing. Somehow I had gotten away with all this for years. I had played with many excellent musicians, and no one had complained. In fact I had received many compliments on the beauty of my violin tone. It took a long time, many protests, arguments, and defenses, for me accept Jeanne's assessment of my playing.

After several weeks and many difficult lessons, I broke down and cried. I felt that it was impossible to do anything right in Jeanne's eyes. This crisis opened up a new way of working. Jeanne asked me if I wanted to go for perfection. "Yes," I replied. So we began at the very beginning, with open strings: just the four notes G, D, A and E. Jeanne would come to work with me three times a week, and I was not to go near the violin at any other time, for that would just be reinforcing all my bad habits. (Lady Abbess was very amused at this plan, for I had been complaining that I was not being given enough time to practice.) I now had to hold the bow in a very different way: right arm very high, fingers spread wide apart on the bow stick, arm rotated inward—the Russian style. This gives the player more strength and control at the tip of the bow. My left arm position had to be reshaped too: I had to pull my left elbow much farther to the right, under the violin, so that the fingers could come down on the strings with more strength. It hurt.

Somehow in doing all these things I was supposed to be relaxed.

Fairly soon a big breakthrough happened: Jeanne let me play "Amazing Grace" with her. What a treat! Another treat was that she let me practice alone a bit, playing a one-octave C major scale. Little by little Jeanne gave me real music to work on. She was pleased with my work. She told me that she had never been able to be as demanding, as hard on a student, as she was now being with me.

Originally I was supposed to spend six months at Regina Laudis preparing for my First Vows, and then go back to Our Lady of the Rock for the ceremony. But it was obvious to Jeanne and to Lady Abbess that I was nowhere near achieving the control and the freedom in my violin playing that Jeanne held out as the goal, nor was I nearly ready to make First Vows. At first I was devastated, but soon realized that I really needed and wanted to grow more in many ways.

The process went far deeper than merely improving my violin playing. It demanded submission, a thing that I found extremely challenging, both with the violin and in monastic life. What do we mean by "submit"? Certainly not external conformity, mindless obedience, as in the military. Jesus takes the First Commandment very literally and seriously: "Thou shalt have no other gods before me" (Exodus 20:3). Have no other gods. Leave father, mother, sister, brother, friends, all your property and possessions, to become His disciple. In short, be totally available God, to Christ, to the community, which represents Christ for me. Don't hold anything back for yourself.

Not to hold *anything* back really means not to hold *yourself* back. I was holding myself back in countless ways. I was afraid, most of the time, to be my real self. I was so concerned with being approved by others, being a "good girl," that I was either a conformist or a rebel. My emotions were so violent, and so bottled up in me, that I was afraid to let them loose. I could not let them flow freely into the violin or my voice (except when I was singing folk songs of Unrequited Love, or just singing for fun with others).

I had to work through all this inhibition in my relationship with Jeanne. I had to learn to trust her, to do what she asked without resisting, arguing, protecting myself. I had a bodily fear of her, as I do of anyone who comes too close to me. I visibly shrank back when she approached me. When she admonished me, I squirmed, I fidgeted, I could not look her in the eye. Yet I loved her, and was again in love with the violin. I loved talking with her, hearing her stories about the musicians she had known, about her own struggles, her keen insight into music. And where did her extreme dedication to my growth come from? She sometimes stayed awake all night worrying about me. She worked endless hours to make a tape for me to give to my father for Christmas. She recorded me playing the slow movement of the Bach Double Concerto, with herself playing the second violin part AND the piano accompaniment, and me playing "Song of the Birds" by Pablo Casals with her piano accompaniment. And this was when she was recovering from a stroke.

I realized that such a gift, such dedication, can come only from Jesus. Only when we have received such a gift from another person can we begin to know the love of Jesus. This work on the violin with Jeanne was torture for me. Jeanne managed to cut through thick layers of my pride and my many habits of self-protection. She stripped me of my emotional skin.

I'm behind my violin teacher, Jeanne Biancolli, and Dad at the reception following my First Vows ceremony.

Somewhere I had read that the monk endures a slow martyrdom. We in the community believe this, and also assure ourselves that the more purgatory we do on earth, the less we have to do after death. For purgatory is not a physical place, but the process of purification we all must go through.

Our work continued for another year and a half. It was primarily this work on the violin that brought me through to the point where I could make my First Profession of Vows on the Feast of Saint Benedict, July 11, 1986. My father came a few days early, and though I was on retreat, I was given permission to visit with him. What I remember most about the day itself was the familial celebration in the evening. Jeanne and Dad were there and sat side by side. I played something with Jeanne, I do not remember what. Then we had some silliness: the Sadah Schola sang "Twenty Froggies Went to School," a dear song my mother had taught me.

It was a very joyful and light time. Jeanne walked with Dad to St. Joseph's, the men's guest house, and they really enjoyed one another.

But I was still not ready to go back to Our Lady of the Rock. I had not yet achieved a consistent level of excellence on the violin. This was to come through my work on the Franck Sonata. I had been working on this sonata when I first met Jeanne. After my Profession we resumed working on this piece. My piano partner was David Stein, a young pianist who was close to the Abbey. Just before I left for Our Lady of the Rock, David and I played the sonata for the community. This was the verification of all the work we had done. Somewhere I have a tape of it: my spoken introduction is so happy, relaxed, and natural, and my playing is, though not technically perfect by any means, darn good. I am still very happy with it.

I could return to Our Lady of the Rock at last.

Sixteen

ON SHAW FOREVER

Then, when all these degrees of humility have been climbed, the monk will presently come to that perfect love of God which casts out all fear; whereby he will begin to observe without labour, as though naturally and by habit, all those precepts which formerly he did not observe without fear: no longer for fear of hell, but for love of Christ and through good habit and delight in virtue.

—Saint Benedict

Shaw Island

As the ferry from Anacortes approached Shaw Island, I could smell the land and the trees of the island. The Franciscan sisters were still here. A small group of Mercy sisters had come to live on the island. The postmistress, Mary Lou Clark, noticed that the very same boxes I had mailed to the Abbey two years before were now returning.

Happily back at Our Lady of the Rock, I wrote on February 12, 1987:

Remember what Lady Abbess told me in saying farewell: I have already—right now—what I've longed for.

So—the intensity of the seeking for the perfectly tuned tones on the violin—the joy & beauty of that seeking & finding—must for me as Benedictine be turned to religious life itself. I must seek & find that same intensity there—in the life, the liturgy, relationships & experiences that come because I have been released thru the violin, which can never be taken away.

When I walked into the midst of Vespers yesterday, having just returned from a medical appointment, I was so moved, so taken by the beauty, so grateful to be home & that this is my home & life.

Shaw is the smallest of the San Juan Islands served by the ferries. It is 7.7 square miles, mostly woods. Like many other parts of the country, the island has seen many changes since the nuns first came. At that time, in the late 1970s and early eighties, most of the roughly 130 inhabitants were old-timers from early settler families. They farmed, logged, fished, raised chickens, worked in construction. There were a few retired physicians, nurses, and teachers. The one-room schoolhouse had four students and one teacher. There were some young families, too. Everyone knew everyone else. Nothing happened that was not immediately known to all. Two women, Elsie Fowler and Gladys Alexander, were friends who lived across Blind Bay from each other. Each had a telescope aimed at the other's house. Once, Gladys called Elsie on the phone to tell her that she had dropped a stitch.

Within our community, the most important change had occurred during my absence: in 1985 the Holy See had raised Our Lady of the Rock to the status of a priory, and named Mother Therese as Prioress. This meant that we were now able to have our own novitiate. We had a couple of postulants who did not stay, but one woman, Catherine Lamb, did stay and became Mother Frances of Rome. From New Jersey, she had been close to the Abbey for years, but delayed her vocation to take care of her mother in her last illness. Catherine had been a chemist, and later was in charge of the USO volunteers under Cardinal Spellman in New York City. She was with us until her death in 2002.

It took considerable time for me to integrate all that I had come to in my work with Jeanne and with all who had helped me at the Abbey. My journals were still voluminous. I still had to work through many challenges and received tremendous help, often through very aggravating confrontations, from my formation Mothers, Mother Miriam, Mother Nika (a nun from the Abbey who was here for a few years); and from our Prioress, Mother Prioress Therese. These struggles did not cease even after my Perpetual Profession, July 11, 1990.

In addition, the late 1980s were a very tough time for our communities, a time of severe persecution, very tense to live through.[81] Our benefactor, Henry Ellis, had turned against us and tried to take back half of the property he had given us. He got together with anyone he could find who had a grudge against the Abbey and its lay communities and Our Lady of the Rock. They attacked us on TV, in the press, and even at the Vatican. But living through this time brought us closer together and strengthened us as a community.

I kept busy carrying out my mission of serving the Island through music. I collaborated closely with Mother Kateri Visocki, one of the Franciscans on Shaw and a fine musician, until the Franciscans left in 2005. We organized and often played in many concerts on Shaw Island. Most important, we started a little instrumental group with the few on Shaw who could play anything. As well as being conductor of the group, Mother Kateri was very good at getting people to fish their long-neglected instruments out from the attic and join the group, which we called the Island Consort. Gradually we attracted wind and brass players from Orcas Island

and became the Island Sinfonia. We gave concerts on Orcas, Lopez, and San Juan Islands as well as on Shaw. A few times we played Christmas carols, or the entire *Water Music* of Handel, on the ferry.

Besides all this, I have had the great joy of being in a string quartet that lasted at least ten years, until all its members except myself died.[82] For me, there is nothing as satisfying in music as playing quartets, and I got to do more of this than I had ever had a chance to do in my secular life.

During this time at OLR I began teaching violin, Ward Method,[83] and recorder to children on Shaw, Friday Harbor and Orcas Island, and to a few regular guests. I had taught violin occasionally in my secular life, but not regularly. From my students I learned a great deal, and I received excellent professional help from the two Suzuki workshops for violin teachers that I attended in Seattle.

One of our Barn Recitals, showing Aidan Shannon, Kendra Clifton, Mother Felicitas, Roni Woodard.

My Sisters

Both at Regina Laudis and at Our Lady of the Rock, I have been given the gift of strong relationships with my sisters in formation. Each woman is unique, and because of these differences we can learn so much from each other. No one can ever have a total comprehension of reality, but by listening and working with others who share the novitiate experience we can broaden and change our outlook. How many times I have discovered that my feelings of dislike of and conflict with a sister have changed to a deep appreciation of her. Has she changed? I do not know, but I do know that I have changed. My heart has become softer and more welcoming of others. And the bonds that my generation of novices formed have grown deeper through the years, in spite of our living on opposite coasts.

During all this time of monastic formation I was looking forward to making my Perpetual Vows, which would lock me forever into the community. I had grown in humility, in discovering my real self through all the work on music and the entire formation process. I will always need to struggle against pride. But I am truly at peace with the violin and with music in general. I have found my place. I do not play nearly as well now, in my eighties, as when I played that Franck Sonata, but I enjoy my playing, and through it I can be my real self and communicate with others. All along, God has offered tremendous gifts and challenges to bring me closer to Him.

But to make my Perpetual Vows, it was not enough that I had found peace with the violin at last. I needed to learn to live with depression and all its manifestations, to delve more deeply into my marriage and to come to terms with my abortion and my third son.

Seventeen

SOME KNOTS UNTANGLED

Welcome difficulty.
Learn the alchemy True Human Beings know:
The moment you accept what troubles you've been given,
The door opens.

—Rumi

When I fell in love with the Catholic Church, I knew full well that I disagreed with the Church's position on several matters: the celibate priesthood, abortion and birth control, an exclusively male priesthood. These differences with the Church did not bother me. I was a radical. I have always remained a radical in my heart. I still believe in the Communist motto, "From each according to his ability and to each according to his need." This is exactly what the early Christian community, as described in the Acts of the Apostles, was trying to do, and what many religious communities, including ours, actually succeed in doing. The IWW and union songs that so many of us sang in the fifties and sixties are still dear to my heart: "Which Side are you On?" "Joe Hill," "Halleluia, I'm a Bum," "Union Maid," among others.

All my life I had wanted to see a world transformed, but I learned that revolutionary socialism was not the way to a better world. I had seen an example of radical Christianity in the spirituality of Dorothy Day, who combined radical Christianity with a firm adherence to the traditions and authority of the Church. Christ himself is radical. His disciples did not understand what that meant. They hoped he would lead an uprising to free the Jews from the Roman occupation. It took them time to understand the nature of His radicalism.

Just think, for a minute, how the world would look if Christian values really took hold. The world as we know it would be turned upside down. There would be no war, no capital punishment, no abortion or euthanasia. All people would respect all other people, regardless of their state in life, their gender, their sexuality, their ideologies, their race, their physical appearance. People would not oppress other people, nor would they torture animals or destroy the environment. No one would be homeless. No one would have to die prematurely for lack of food or medical care. Love would have trumped ideology and avarice.

But this, the true Kingdom of God, is not going to happen in this life, because we are human. We cannot bring about this Utopia through our human efforts, crucial though it is for each of us, in whatever way we are called, and whatever religious and political views we hold, to work for a better world. We must seek this kingdom in the only possible way: by uniting ourselves with Jesus, the way, the truth, and the life.

I do not underestimate the tremendous contributions that people of all faiths and none are making to right the injustices of the world. The Church does not have a monopoly on the Christian values mentioned. These are shared in whole or in part by other faiths and individuals. Nevertheless, I must say what I believe: the Kingdom of God, while it exists here and now among so many, can come into being completely, universally, and permanently, only through Jesus.

Still, I need to explain how my positions on the matters where I disagreed with the Church have gradually changed to conform to the Church's teachings. It was not through intellectual argument that I was persuaded. Rather, I was transformed by seeing the examples of true Christians—ordinary people, and saints living and dead. My views on abortion, priestly celibacy, women priests, love and marriage have changed, simply through living in the Church and among the women of Regina Laudis and Our Lady of the Rock. These changes happened without any explicit discussion. About women, for example, I simply saw that the nuns were whole and happy human beings, giving themselves totally to God without any need or desire to be in positions of authority in the Church at large. We have always been encouraged and helped to develop our intellectual and professional capacities to the utmost, surpassing anything we had imagined for ourselves. We see ourselves as complementary to men, including bishops, priests, monks and brothers, without any trace of feelings of being oppressed or inferior. Admittedly, in the world, in our own country, and in the Church, we still have a long way to go before we can say that equal treatment of women has been achieved, even in the most basic area of equal pay for equal work. Speaking personally, though, I have never felt oppressed by the Church.

But my transformations on the huge questions of love, marriage, and abortion do require further attention. First, let me describe some of the miracles that God wrought for our family.

Flint Farm

In one of my very first meetings with Lady Abbess, I told her about Flint Farm: what it meant to my family, how I was pained that we were not able to take care of it as well as we wished, and how I fantasized that some day a community might live there. In the seventies I had envisioned a secular community living there, developing the land, living simply, maintaining the house. Carl and Bill did not want to assume the burden of the place. It was unthinkable to sell the house and have the land divided up for development. We all felt strongly that the land should remain intact. Dad had the house winterized to some extent, and various people, including Carl and his first wife, lived there in the winters.

Mother Mary Aline and Lady Abbess with Dad at Flint Farm

Ultimately it occurred to me to ask Dad if he would consider offering Flint Farm to the Abbey to use as a place where small groups of nuns could retreat for periods of study and prayer. After making sure that Carl and Bill would not ever want the property, he wrote to Lady Abbess, describing all the difficulties and deficiencies of the house. Lady Abbess was greatly impressed by my father's honesty and humility. She and Mother Mary Aline went up to visit Dad and look at the place. Dad put them up at the Lyme Inn and prepared lunch for them. Lady Abbess told me later that this visit was for her "a foretaste of the heavenly banquet."

Since then, nuns have gone to Flint Farm for varying periods of time. Mother Hildegard wrote her PhD dissertation there. Mother Luke, Mother Patricia, Mother Simonetta and other nuns have prayed and worked there. Mother Augusta and others go up now and then to cut the fields and do other maintenance. But the Archbishop did not give permission for groups of nuns to spend time there on a regular basis, as we had hoped. For a time a group of pre-postulants lived there as a first step in community life, and individual nuns came up to work with them. I was there for a month, working with them on music. Lay people, couples and small groups of two or three, have spent time there. In the winter of 2004 with a crisis involving a broken furnace, broken pipes, and extensive flooding, the Abbey realized that the house would collapse if basic revisions were not made. The very foundations were rotted. So the Abbey made a major decision to restore the house properly. This was going to require huge expenses. A couple related to one of the nuns came to the rescue with financial support and their own work, insuring that the house would not only survive, but be much more livable. In addition, many friends of Merle Curti contributed to this work in his memory.

For the Abbey, Flint Farm has been

> ... a tremendous gift to the community, a place where members of the community can go for renewal and retreat. With its surrounding woodland and gorgeous view of the mountains, Flint Farm provides a completely different environment from Bethlehem: quieter, simpler, closer to nature. In the 1980s, the community made the addition of a chapel to the upstairs, so that there is a sanctuary for meditation, prayer and recollection within the house itself. This adds a dimension of sacredness to the place. Thus ... it is not simply a house of studies, but rather a contemplative center for study.[84]

My father's remains are buried there. After his death in 1996, Lady Abbess, Mother Mary Aline, and Mother Irene, along with me, my sons and their families, and some close friends of my father, held a burial ceremony there, and the Abbey had a very beautiful gravestone made, whose motto is: "Now I know for certain"(Acts 11:12).[85] So he is at rest in his beloved land, in New England where his heart always lay.

Bill also came into a close relationship with Flint Farm and Regina Laudis. He has followed my father's footsteps in embracing with enthusiasm an academic career. When the time came for him to receive tenure, he had two offers: Georgetown, where he had been teaching, or Dartmouth. It was not hard to choose, especially when Dartmouth offered a position to his wife, Christianne Hardy, as Assistant Director of the Dickey Center for International Understanding.[86] Though Bill had not wanted to inherit Flint Farm, he had never lost his love of that land, of the beauty of the mountains, hills, streams and woods, and all the outdoor activities that one could pursue there. The family lived for several years in a house near Hanover, but then Bill asked me if I could sound out Mother Abbess[87] to see if the Abbey might sell him ten acres or so of the Flint Farm land on which he could build a house.

Mother Abbess was not only favorable to this idea, she said the Abbey would *give* Bill the land! However, according to canon law, the Abbey could not make such a transaction without the permission of the Archbishop.[88] Not surprisingly, it took considerable time before the Abbey received his reply. In the summer of 2005, I was visiting the Abbey, and Bill was to come down and pick me up to go visit the family. We were all getting anxious about what the Archbishop's decision would be. I was packed and ready to go—it was just after the noon meal—and Bill was waiting for me at the entrance to the monastery. At the very last minute I was summoned to meet with Mother Abbess and her Council in the side chapel just inside the entrance to the Abbey. To my surprise, there stood Bill. Mother Abbess had just received Archbishop Mansell's letter, giving permission for the transfer of the land.

I hope that this little drama made a deep impression on Bill. In any case, he and the Abbey are in a friendly, fruitful, and lasting relationship. Possibly that is the very reason my father gave Flint Farm to the Abbey. Bill himself is more than compensating for my having left academia, and is making my father very happy. And the Abbey, by preserving and renovating the

Bill, Chris, Charlie and Owen at their newly finished New Hampshire house.

house, respecting its history and its integrity, is carrying out its own mission of redemption.

Bill, Chris, and their sons Owen and Charles are happy in their new home. The boys are well established with friends, school, and sports winter and summer. Chris works hard at her Dartmouth job, has established beautiful gardens and landscaping around the house, and does all the things that mothers usually do: planning, organizing, arranging schedules. She and Bill share the cooking and other household work. Bill, in addition to his heavy work load, has truly become a New Hampshire native: he maintains a large, neat woodpile; makes maple syrup from trees on their land; goes hunting; loves his sailboat; climbs mountains. The whole family enjoys sailing and cross-country skiing together. It makes me very happy to see that the Abbey, and Bill and his family, love and enjoy the land that I and my family have always loved so much.

My Father

Father Aufiero and Dad at Our Lady of the Rock.

When I first knew that I would be accepted to enter the Abbey for Our Lady of the Rock, I prayed that Dad would come to be happy about my vocation. He was so negative and fearful at first that such an outcome seemed impossible; but little by little he grew to accept and even welcome my choice, seeing that I was happy and had by no means given up using my mind and my education. He did not lose me, as he had feared. We spoke weekly on the telephone, carried on an active correspondence, and had a good visit at least once a year. He came to visit me at OLR and Regina Laudis until he was ninety-one. After that I went to visit him in Madison for a week every year.

I loved those visits to Madison. Dad lived on the fourteenth floor of the Methodist Retirement Center, near the state capitol and right across the street from Saint Raphael Cathedral. I would go to the eight o'clock Mass each morning. When I got back to Dad's apartment, he would have breakfast ready for me, even in his very last years. He fixed oatmeal (always with real cream), eggs, or pancakes with maple syrup. He had cream on his cereal and in his coffee every day of his life, yet he lived almost to a hundred. We would spend hours talking about everything in the world. I would read the daily *New York Times*, which I never had time to do in the monastery. I would visit some of Dad's special friends in the building. We would normally have dinner in the dining room of the Retirement Center, but would have a nice meal or two at a good restaurant, and usually would be invited to dinner by some of Dad's numerous friends.

My former Madison friends had all moved away, but every time I went to Madison I visited my old violin teacher, Marie Endres. She was eighty-five when I first went to see her. I wondered what she would be like. Was she truly as wonderful a woman and as good a violin teacher as I had thought in my youth? Yes. She was a down-to-earth Midwestern Catholic, and had lost none of her sense of humor. I could tell by her conversation and her gestures that she had been an excellent violinist and a great teacher. I was delighted to see that she had a compost pile in her back yard and grew some vegetables. I went to see her on my subsequent visits to Madison until her death a few years later.

The Cathedral's bells rang the Angelus at 6:00 A.M., noon, and six P.M., and also announced the passing of each hour. These bells were a great comfort to me. It was also comforting to hear the voices of people on the bus and in stores and on the street. In my many years away from Madison, I knew that my voice was unique. But when I returned to Madison I was pleased to hear that other people sounded like me.

Dad came to revere Lady Abbess, with whom he carried on a good relationship by letter. By the time he was in his nineties, the prayer that I had made that he would come to joyfully accept my vocation had been fully answered. Just three months before he died he wrote:

"I am very happy with the way Our Lady of the Rock gives you a home and a vocation which is spiritually satisfying. You are very dear to me, dearer than the world, and your happiness makes my own." (December 1995)

Nancy in a New Light

It occurred to me recently to see what I could find out about encephalitis, the disease that my sister had as a baby. I had only a vague idea about this disease. It wasn't until the 1990s that I became aware that her disability had a name: encephalitis. This destructive illness is caused by an inflammation in the brain. It can permanently change a person's life, and that of her family. The long-term effects of the disease can very considerably. Some people can carry on with a fairly normal life. Others need to live permanently in an institution where they receive full-time care. Sometimes encephalitis results in death.[89]

Nancy fit toward the severe end of this spectrum. As I read descriptions of the possible effects of encephalitis, I felt I was reading about Nancy. I was relieved to discover that there are many people in the world who share Nancy's problems. I had always thought that Nancy was unique. It would have been such a comfort and support to our family if we had known and been in touch with others who lived with similar problems as she.

The Encephalitis Society in the United Kingdom presents a summary of common effects of the disease. Physically, the person is awkward: she has problems with coordination and balance. She "may appear to be more clumsy or careless." Nancy's sloppy appearance and atrocious table manners, her poor handwriting, and her general awkwardness, made it harder than for most people to do almost everything.

Hearing was one of the sensory changes that Nancy exhibited. I had never understood her total lack of tolerance to my swallowing, and her building up of that intolerance to a physical explosion of anger. A sufferer of encephalitis may be "extremely sensitive to certain noises. ... They may be unable to tolerate many environments we take for granted, for example shopping malls and pubs."

Emotionally, encephalitis can have devastating effects on a person. She may experience "uncharacteristic extremes of emotion, which are difficult to control. ... A person may act inappropriately and say or do things without thinking due to changes in frontal system functioning. It can be more difficult to control emotional reactions with an increase in anger outbursts. At the extreme, this may include acting with verbal or physical aggression."

Nancy's life was full of this inappropriate behavior, lack of control, and verbal or physical aggression: not only the two attempts to kill Mother, but the tearing up of her clothes hanging in the closet, the breaking of Dad's glasses, the attacks on me. No doubt this aggression sprang from Nancy's extreme anxiety, frustration and desperation. When we were getting ready to go somewhere, Nancy would become more and more tense, commanding us to get going faster. When she and I talked on the telephone, she would always hang up on me before we had a chance to conclude the conversation and say good-bye. When I was driving somewhere with her, I would not dare to express any confusion about directions, or any uncertainty whatever, for that would provoke uncontrollable tension and anxiety in her.

It was no surprise, then, that Nancy had a very low image of herself. She was convinced that she had been adopted, for she perceived that she was not like the rest of the family. At least twice she attempted suicide. Several times she called me and asked me to kill her. From somewhere I was given words to say that helped her on these occasions.

What could we have done, other than what we did do, to help her? A better understanding of encephalitis would have helped. It was a natural human tendency for us to blame her, to believe she could really learn to control herself better. There is no cure for encephalitis. But people have learned better ways for people to deal with it, and for their families to help. For example, when Nancy exploded in the car on our family's trip to Oberlin, instead of Dad's threatening to leave her on the side of the road if she did not behave, we could have, on noticing the buildup of her tension, pulled over, together taking a little walk, or together counting to ten, or taking deep breaths. Had we been part of support groups for encephalitis, and the help of professionals, we could have worked with Nancy to learn and practice meditation or other ways to deal with the anxiety.

My mother always wanted to have Nancy live as normal a life as possible. She tried, without success, to teach Nancy to drive. Perhaps my parents were somewhat unrealistic in their expectations. Perhaps to send Nancy to colleges (Goddard, and Rockford) just served to increase Nancy's frustration.

But whatever the new ways that have since been discovered might help, encephalitis presents an enormous challenge to individuals and to society. As for Nancy, the numerous things my parents did to help her—the specialists in medicine, psychology, psychiatry, relaxation—the special camps, schools, and institutions, from the Institute of Living to the mental hospital in Wisconsin—must have helped to some extent. But it's small wonder that nothing worked for Nancy; that there did not seem to be any solution; that she was thrown out of one rooming house or retirement facility after another.

What a huge relief it is for me to discover that Nancy's suffering was not her fault. Let us be grateful for all the help that she did have, and for all the people—family, friends, church people, professionals—who tried their best.

Carl

It was with Carl that a real miracle occurred. He was more open to spiritual dimensions than Bill. In my yoga days, he came down to Princeton with me for a session with Shyam. He could feel the different sort of energy that emanates from trees, if you stay quiet. He looked for transcendent experiences and found them, hiking alone in the California mountains, or watching a total eclipse of the sun. He had taken quite a different path in life from the rest of the family. He had a brilliant mind, loved to think and learn, but was never drawn to scholarship or teaching. He read and thought deeply, and he became well informed on matters of energy and on politics. He did not share the knee-jerk reactions of the rest of us in thinking that Big Business was a Bad Thing, nothing but greediness and selfishness. He made up his own mind about everything, and if he found himself mistaken, was willing to change.

He had an entrepreneurial bent. As a child he was always building things and leading other kids into his projects. Unlike his parents, he wanted to make money, and he did. He was totally honest and unpretentious, and though he was loving and kind to others, he could be very stubborn too.

The year 1987 saw a major crisis in Carl's life and in mine. When Carl had heart surgery at age eleven, the cardiologist told us that a second heart surgery would be needed when Carl was eighteen or so. This predicted interval stretched out until he was thirty-two. Now he needed to have an artificial valve. We were both scared.

Carl was living alone in California. His first wife had left him in 1985 on the seventh anniversary of their marriage.

I prayed intensely that whatever happened, I could submit to God's will. I would have preferred to die myself if Carl could be spared. His surgery was scheduled for December 8, the feast of the Virgin Mary's Immaculate Conception.[90] I told him how special this was, that Catholics all over the world would be going to Mass and praying. I was terrified that Carl might not survive the surgery. He wanted so badly to get married again, have a family, and to feel fulfilled in his work.

When Mother Nika answered the phone call from Carl, telling us that he had come through the surgery well, she told him we'd been praying a lot for him. He said, "Well, it worked! I'm recovering a lot quicker and better than is usual."

December 11, 1987

Carl is very happy & grateful to be alive. He said he looked forward to a good and long life! He said the surgery was extremely traumatic: indeed a close call because if any of the calcium in the heart had gotten loose it would have caused a stroke. The valve opening [before the surgery] was minimal.

My fear of losing Carl led me to think seriously about the fact that all parents must inevitably, in one way or another, suffer the loss of their children. All the nuns I know who are mothers have gone through this. Each mother's story is unique, but we all suffer the same pain and struggle.

February 27, 1987

I am sure that God wants me to give Carl into His hands. I have to do this in the darkness of faith. Mary is a model: standing by the Cross, she didn't know yet of the Resurrection. Really, I can't "give" Carl to God, since I don't "have" him anyway. But what I can do is recognize that I've done all I can humanly do. I see no resolution. I have been selfish & don't want to be. Since I'm at my wit's end, all I can do is let God take over. Even on a human nature level, mothers have to be disposessed of their sons. Look at all the times Mary suffered this, beginning in recorded history when Jesus was twelve.

Teresa, Carla, and Carl

Carl's view of the Catholic Church had always been mistrustful and critical. But after his first marriage of seven years ended, and after about ten years of single life, he married Teresa Dakis, a lovely, intelligent woman, a chemist, and a devout Catholic. In 1993 they had a daughter, Carla, and from middle school on they sent her to Catholic schools because the public schools in San Jose, where they lived, were not very good. Carl was very grateful for the Catholic schools, and though Teresa did not try to convince him to be Catholic, she adhered firmly to her faith, attending Mass regularly and taking Carla with her. Carl came to love Our Lady of the Rock and, like my Dad and Bill, was glad to see that I was happy and fulfilled in my vocation. When in 2011 he was diagnosed with pancreatic cancer, after a very scary hospitalization, he began accompanying Teresa and Carla to Mass every week. Just before his death, in the hospital, I baptized him. I will say more about him in a later chapter.

My Marriage Revisited

When I was in high school, I heard that the Sisters who taught at the Edgewood Academy, and also at the Blessed Sacrament high school, wore wedding rings, and considered themselves married to Christ. Like most Protestants, I thought that this was weird. Since I did not then believe in Jesus, though, I never thought further about it. Now that I was preparing for my Perpetual Vows, it was necessary to come to a better understanding of what Catholics mean by "marriage" and what that spousal dimension means for those living in a religious community. To do this I needed to look more deeply into my marriage with Tim.

Have I ever regretted that I married Tim Wohlforth? No! Not for one minute. We had many good times together. Considering who I was when I was twenty-one, he was exactly the right man for me at that time. And through him I got to know Bob and Mildred Wohlforth and the extended Wohlforth family, a good, interesting, and unique family with whom I maintain a friendly, if not close, relationship. Primarily, though, the reason I am indebted with every cell of my being to that marriage is that it gave us our two sons, Carl and Bill. I wish I could put into words what they mean to me, but I can't come close. I marvel at what fine men they have turned out to be. Mixed up as we were, Tim and I must have done some things right. They grew up, each found his own way in life, they became exemplary husbands and fathers and upright and responsible citizens. They both developed a strong work ethic, which was a pleasant surprise to me. They did all this despite the immaturity of their parents and our many mistakes.

Both Carl and Bill have chosen wonderful women as wives. They have always had a close relationship, and I have been deeply blessed in watching them grow up, in being able to relate to them as adults to whom I can look for help and companionship.

It is a tremendous gift to be both mother and nun. Motherhood is an excellent preparation for community life. One must love unconditionally, be open to the "otherness" of the child, be available to him 24/7. This is very hard to do, both as a mother and in community, but we all keep trying, and I am grateful beyond measure to have the experience of both physical and spiritual motherhood.

In the first few years after the end of my marriage I came to an elementary understanding of what had gone wrong. We were still children, not yet whole. We had not yet learned to assume the responsibilities of adulthood. We were still financially dependent on our parents, yet we insisted on escaping from them, and used each other as supports in this rebellion. I had worked and supported myself for a puny five weeks. We were both very needy people and looked to each other to fulfill our needs. In my years of psychotherapy I came to understand, too, that I had never come to terms with my sexuality, or to appreciate and enjoy and value my female body.

It took years of life as a Christian, and life in community, to deepen my understanding of love and marriage. I had been so hung up on romantic love. I longed for a total immersion of my being with another. I wanted to be Isolde and find my Tristan. From the Metropolitan Museum I had bought a pendant showing a twelfth-century image of that pair, with the chalice holding the love potion between them, and the dog that never left Tristan's side. At my Clothing I had this pendant mounted on a wooden cross—one of the nuns did this for me—and truly, this was my Cross, a burden that I had borne for so long. This burden needed to be transformed into a blessing. My whole monastic formation was really this. And it has happened, I can't say how. But I can say some things.

I had never understood—had no hint of an idea—what Christian love is. I learned, through the give and take of relationships in community, that you can love people without liking them. Even better, your feelings of strong dislike for a person can gradually turn into their opposite. You can choose, day by day, to opt for the good of another, to think about what she needs, what you and others can do to encourage her to be more and more the woman she is capable of being. In no way can I do this alone. It takes community. In the Constitutions of the Abbey of Regina Laudis it is spelled out that we commit ourselves to the becoming of one another.

That is the big challenge of monastic life. That is our desert, our prime ascetical practice, along with the unrelenting rhythm of the liturgy and monastic horarium, and obedience: to learn to love unconditionally, without hooks, without guile, people whom we would not have chosen to live with in our former lives. It is actually a miracle that we could never accomplish if we had not each one given ourselves over to God. He chose us. He, not we ourselves, put us with each other. We are united by our common love of Jesus and our commitment to Him. We are held together by our common life, too: our common prayer above all; our monastic clothes and customs. How else could it be that people of such different backgrounds and personalities could live together, in one place, until death? The perpetual struggles between rich and poor, between brothers and sisters, children and parents, North and South, East and West, introverts and extroverts, liberals, radicals, and conservatives—all these need to be worked out and redeemed in community.

To be ready for Perpetual Profession, the nun must have some conception of what a spousal relationship with Jesus is. For we do marry Him at that point.

The element of attraction has so much to do with marriage. We may be unaware of it most of the time, but we must experience a tremendous attraction to Jesus, to the community as a whole, and to individuals within the community. For Jesus seldom speaks to us or comes to visit us directly; He comes through the Word of God in the daily liturgy; in the Eucharist; and through other people. He is with us when we are receiving help, and when we are helping another.

Besides this attraction there is a more daily, humble requirement: we must come to feel *at home* and *free to be ourselves* in the community and in monastic life. This takes years. But we can't honestly make vows if we haven't been able to experience this. As a postulant, I felt so foreign. My cell was my home, nowhere else. Now, it's our bathroom, our kitchen, our refectory, our everything.

We must also feel at home with each other.

The most apparent difference, the one that first meets the eye, between the marriage of a man and woman and marriage into community, is: I didn't choose these people, and probably wouldn't, humanly speaking. But generosity of spirit *does* expand with the action of grace, and I do find antagonisms changing to tolerance, then appreciation, then love. It has happened, so I know it can continue to happen, and so I wish it. It is hell to hate people.

Further, all does not hang on any single relationship. Relationships are constantly in flux, growing, fulfilling particular cycles, lying in quiescence until a new cycle be revealed, subject to larger needs than our surface attractions and wants.

Most of my life I felt as if relationships were always ending, and with each one, something of myself died. To me it appeared that nothing would replace it. The spousal level looked like a negative, a NO to the ways I'd always lived. It's such a miracle, then, that I don't remember how this felt. It's gone! I think it's because I have begun to learn to relate to the reality of other people, not my own projections and transferences and expectations. And I have begun to learn to let the other be—not to second-guess authority or my peers, or try to manipulate or control them. And to accept that I don't understand them, and may never understand.

Concretely this means that any unresolved conflicts we bring to community as individuals need to be worked on and resolved within ourselves. So for me, it means that I have to work out my conflicts with my parents, my sister, my ex-husband, my sons, my lost loves, here and now, as they are manifested in my relationships with my Sisters. This work is never finished, but we can make tremendous progress. It is the work of redemption, and its effects are retroactive, helping all those who have touched our lives.

This meant that I had to grow up. I had to learn to be an authentic person, taking responsibility for my actions, able to speak the truth, able to live for others. With Tim, one of my big problems was what I call "fake feminine submissiveness:" that is, I found it difficult or impossible to tell him what I really wanted. I expected him to know what I wanted without my telling him. I did not know how to ask directly. Instead, I tried to manipulate. I complained, felt sorry for myself, felt misunderstood and downtrodden, bitchy and competitive.

This process of growing up was painful indeed. It was worked out in the ways I have learned to live with depression and all its manifestations, to clarify my relationship to music, and to come to peace with my abortion.

Baby Dreams: Mercy

Sleep has two gates, they say: one is of Horn
And spirits of Truth find easy exit there,
The other is perfectly wrought of glistening Ivory,
But from it the Shades send false dreams up to the world.

—Virgil

My baby dreams began in the 1970s, when I was living in Highland Park with Carl and Bill. It took many years before I came to realize that these dreams were about my third baby. I know that these dreams came through the gate of horn.

To convey the essence and the progress of these dreams, I will include several of them here.

February 22, 1976

Very restless nite; woke up many times, hard getting to sleep. Bad dream—my baby w its head cut off & eyes damaged; head put back but prob wdn't live long.

February 24, 1976

My dream of the baby was frighteningly prophetic, for yesterday Carl had such unbearable pain in his head that he said the only solution was to cut it off.

December 9, 1976

Upsetting dream: Looked out a window & saw below a baby, alive but quiescent in a coffin. Carl and Bill were w/ me: we stood up on a windowsill to see better. 3 men were killing the baby, injecting things into it. After waking up & going to the bathroom, 1-2 hours later, saw the baby sitting in my room leaning against the closet door, all mangled and bloody. I said, "O sweetheart!" out loud, and woke up.

What is this? The abortion? Not intervening when I saw it being killed & I am standing by?

February 19, 1977

This dream came after my weekend visit to Ann Arbor and the subsequent visit to Regina Laudis. It is the fourth in a set of very disturbing dreams indicating deep fears—of Tim's driving, of separation from the Abbey and Dr. McPeek, and of all the transitions in my life.

Tim has been injured or has a serious disease in his arm. They cut it open, wide, and I and another person are watching, horrified but fascinated as all the bones, veins, muscles, etc. can be seen. The arm is now the very middle central part of his body, with a big cavity. A rabbit is hanging down into this cavity, suspended from the upper area where the heart, lungs, etc. are. The Dr. cuts off the rabbit as one cuts off a baby spider plant. The rabbit has become a very bloody newborn baby. With horror I see that they are bringing it to me. They spread out a receiving blanket (I'm lying in a crib—a baby myself?) and lay the baby next to me, without cleaning it up. I immediately warm up to it, take care of it & hold it, trying somehow to cushion the shock of being born. It is completely articulate, so I ask it what it was like to be inside of Tim's body. But it can't remember, even tho it was there a few minutes ago.

A while later, I'm lying on another bed with the baby, facing in another direction. An Episcopal priest (why?) comes. He's a very big man with blond or light brown hair. He says that the baby's name, which was chosen with great care, is not right; that the baby has another name waiting for him, but he can't think of what it is. I throw out wild & ridiculous guesses, all wrong.

In this, the 3rd dream I've had of a mangled, bloody baby, the baby is articulate; and I'm gradually getting closer. This one I held in my arms & comforted. I predict this baby will return in future dreams, it will have its proper name, it will become incorporated into my life, it will grow healthy & strong, it will no longer be in danger of its life.

At this time I thought that the baby represented the new part of myself that had been emerging in the past few years, the creative, religious part, that was still fragile and had to be nurtured.

January 16, 1980, 2:55 A.M. (at Regina Laudis)

There was a baby emerging—not physically from me, yet it was my baby. It came entirely clean. Lady Abbess delivered it. A boy. I was lying in bed with the baby, & she was there too, standing at the foot of the bed. The baby was not going to settle down—it was full of energy—and L.A. was anxious to be off—so I said, "Why don't I just lie here with the baby, & you can go—after all, he's been inside of me for so long—and when he falls asleep, I'll—"... don't remember exactly, But this baby obviously was not going to sleep. It was extremely lively. Then we got up & the baby was all over the place. It could creep. I named it—a 2-syllable name—but immediately forgot the name! Then the baby & I together tried to remember it. He remembered his past life; he talked in complete sentences, and went on his own downstairs. I'd heard the doorbell ringing. He sat naked in the living room and as he was about to tell me the name of a 2nd book he'd been reading in his other incarnation, just yesterday, I said, "I must go & get my tape recorder. You sit here, and if you get cold, just jump up and down." I knew that, without proof, no one would believe that this baby was so articulate.

The emotional tone of the dream was, strangely, sort of jovial or lighthearted. And I was awakened by the 1st bell for Lauds—heard both in dreaming

& after waking—and it was the last thing I wanted to hear. But I geared myself to go—got up, & found to my great relief it was 2:45. I am very happy! It is the same baby—he has come through!

October 15, 1986

Another dream... I had a miscarriage, & caught the fetus as it came out. Only about an inch long, but definitely clear in its shape. I was tender with it & reverenced it. I don't know what I was going to do with it, but certainly was going to do right by it. Thank God.

I had spent all these years since the abortion feeling guilty. I had taken it to Confession, of course, so I knew intellectually that God had forgiven me. But I did not feel forgiven in my heart. How could such a thing be forgiven? I had more or less shut down my feelings of sadness and remorse. But my dreams told the real story: the abortion was barbaric; my baby was real, not a blob of tissue. He was a boy, he was intelligent, full of energy, alive and happy.

Several months later, about a month before my First Vows, Lady Abbess asked to see me. It was the Feast of the Sacred Heart, June 6, 1986. We spoke for about an hour and a half about my vocation and future, and about the violin. During this meeting I brought up the subject of the abortion. I had told Lady Abbess about it some time ago, but she had not remembered. She said I must give the baby a name before the end of the day. She said that I could be forgiven: I was "illiterate" when I had the abortion. Then she herself named the baby "Mercy." At that time I was not sure if it was a girl or a boy. She explained that the name Mercy works for either. She told me that Mercy was a gift of God to me; that I must pray to Mercy every day and ask him or her to forgive me. "This being lives," she said. On that same evening, and again the next day, we spoke of Mercy again. I told her of my dreams, culminating in her "delivering" him, and how in the dreams he needed a name but it was not yet the right time to name him. I also told her that Mercy had died on Good Friday. She replied, "That is very strong." Mother Bernadette, my formation mother, was present at this meeting. She immediately took me to the Chapel, where we both knelt and prayed and baptized Mercy *in absentia*.

June 11, 1986

I am so happy and grateful. This Mercy is now someone I can think of, pray to, hope to relate to. That he could forgive me is unthinkable; yet with Christ it is possible. What was sort of a sad blank in my consciousness, not deeply faced most of the time, is now, thanks to Lady Abbess, a living being.

This process of bringing Mercy into my life is what changed me from thinking of abortion as a perfectly acceptable thing to do, to the realization that a fetus is a baby, not just a blob of tissue, and that it deserves to live. Further, the process of monastic formation taught me that the abortion mentality extends throughout society. In so many ways, we are tempted to escape challenges and difficulties. If something is bothering us, or is a burden, we try to get rid of it. If a relationship sours, we can just refuse to see that person any more. If our husband does not live up to what we expected or imagined, we can just end the marriage. If life seems unbearable, the solution is simple: commit suicide. Of course in a religious community we do not have these options. We could put up an emotional wall around ourselves, but that would not help us or the other person. We are in this community together, forever. We must face difficult relationships and make them work. In families, the same choices challenge us.

In essence, this abortion mentality comes down to our human tendency to avoid the cross: to escape challenges rather than to face them; to refuse to be open to another, to new life, to God. To be open to Otherness—to people *as they are*, to circumstances as simple as being held up in traffic to more complex things such as a mean boss, a selfish relative, or whatever we do not want to happen—in other words, to be open to the will of God—this is very hard to do, and demands constant attention.

Music in Perspective

Music has been a constant thread in the various phases of my life. But until I was settled into my monastic life, I had not been able to discover my true place there. Now, I can see that music is for me a prime means of relationship with and service to others. My work on the violin with Jeanne Biancolli at the Abbey, and all my work with music in the context of community, has resolved my decades of ambivalence toward the violin.

For about nine years now, I have been playing regularly with a piano friend, John Brantigan, a retired spine surgeon who moved to Shaw Island with his wife Carolyn and some dogs, cats, and birds. John and I have given four concerts together so far, and it is in these concerts that I have felt free in playing the violin. I know that violinists who play far better than I can are a dime a dozen. But I am happy with my playing. I feel that I, with John, have something to give to those listening. I know that when we are playing for people, we and they are communicating on a deep level.

Sacred Harp, or shape note music, has opened up for me a wonderful new world. I had always been in love with its modal and pentatonic melodies and the archaic harmonies. I loved it that the tune is in the tenor, the next to lowest voice, as it had been through the Middle Ages and Renaissance. I was excited to discover that the four-note shape note system, in which the major scale is sung: FA SOL LA FA SOL LA MI FA sits right in the middle of the ancient hexachord system.

But it was not until I was at Our Lady of the Rock that I experienced Sacred Harp as it is traditionally sung, in large groups. I invited Stephen Shearon, a musicologist friend whose specialty is religious music in the Southern United States, to come to Shaw (his wife's family are old homeowners on Shaw) and give a workshop on Sacred Harp. This sparked our contact with Karen Willard of the Pacific Northwest Sacred Harp Singers, who brought a large group for an all-day singing on Shaw, joined by about twenty-five people from these San Juan Islands. It was a transcendent experience. I was hooked—on the music, the words, the history, the people, the culture. You really need at least twenty people to get this high experience, but I love singing Sacred Harp even with one friend, or a small group. Singing together unites people, brings them into a relationship that would not happen otherwise. In Sacred Harp, you will find Protestants of all stripes, atheists, Catholics, Buddhists, Jews, and people of all political persuasions. We leave politics and our personal opinions at the door. We are there to sing, not to talk. Food, a bountiful amount of it, is also important to this culture.

And now? In my eighties, I cannot play nearly as well as I did when I left the Abbey. My main involvement with music now is not to play myself, but to encourage and support others. I do not have any compulsion to play the violin; I can go for weeks without coming near it. But when I do play with others I enjoy it. The violin has accomplished what it was meant to do: bring about my rebirth into a grown woman and a Benedictine Nun.

Eighteen

PERPETUAL VOWS OUR LADY OF THE ROCK 1990

Now this shall be the manner of his reception. In the oratory, in the presence of all, he shall promise stability, conversion of his life, and obedience; and this before God and his Saints.

—Saint Benedict

At the time of Carl's surgery in October 1987, I was back at Our Lady of the Rock, having returned here from the Abbey earlier that year. Since then I have remained here, thankful for the Benedictine vow of stability. Every year or two I visit the Abbey and my New Hampshire family, or my San Jose family, but I will be here at OLR forever, God willing, buried in our own cemetery.

Everything that I lived through in the years between my First and Perpetual Vows was preparing me for that decisive step. In the statement that I presented to the community asking to make my Perpetual Vows, I wrote:

> There is a gulf, wide as wide can be, between existence in the human dimension of instincts, emotions, and thoughts, and the life of Christ, where all of a sudden nothing matters, nothing remains except the Christ life we are experiencing as a body. On my own I can do nothing to bridge that gulf. But every now and then, in a totally unexpected and indescribable way, I am propelled in an instant from darkness, worry, discouragement, concern with self and negativity towards others, to light: to forgetting myself, being able to enter totally into something immeasurably greater than myself, yet being more my true self than ever. The light comes as a total gift, offered not to me, but to us.
>
> Will I ever learn to accept the darkness, which is the more normal mode of life for me, as a necessary way, the only way, to the light? Will I ever find a bridge between them? Or could I ever unknowingly be myself a bridge for another? Even to ask these questions is to try to limit what can't be limited or defined.

But I desire more than anything else in life to learn to live peaceably in darkness or in light or in whatever state God bestows: to experience that peace which comes from doing His will.

For me, the way to that peace is to become a fully incorporated member of the community of Our Lady of the Rock: to offer myself totally and irrevocably to God under the Rule of Saint Benedict.

Four years to the day after my First Vows, on the Feast of Saint Benedict, July 11, 1990, I made my Perpetual Vows in our underground chapel. The celebrant was Father Louis Aufiero, our resident priest for the first sixteen years of the foundation. This ceremony of Perpetual Vows, like the ceremonies for Clothing, First Vows, and Consecration, takes place during Mass after the homily. Mother Prioress began the ceremony by singing from Psalm 33:

Veni, filia, audi me. Timorem Domini docebo te.

(Come, daughter, hear me. I will teach you the fear of the Lord.)

Then she held up the Rule of Saint Benedict and sang:

Veni, filia, audi me. Ecce lex sub qua militare vis; si potes observare, ingredere; si vero non potes, liber discede.

(Come, daughter, hear me. Behold the law under which you wish to serve; if you can observe it, enter; if you cannot, freely depart.)

As I had for the First Vows ceremony, I had written a petition on parchment, larger but with almost identical wording, but this time Mother Prioress had painted the initial letter with a lamb carrying a cross, a traditional Christian symbol of Christ. I read this petition, in Latin, signed it, and showed it to everyone present.

Then the signs of Perpetual Vows were blessed by Father Aufiero and given to me, one by one: the black veil, which Mother Prioress put on me; the ring, which Father put on the third finger of my right hand, symbolizing my marriage to Christ through the Church;[91] the Breviary (the book that contains all the texts of the Divine Office), and last, the cowl, now complete with long, full sleeves. After Mother Prioress put the cowl on me I stood, and with my arms extended, I sang Mary's famous words at the Annunciation:

Ecce, ancilla Domini, Fiat mihi secundum verbum tuum.

Behold the handmaiden of the Lord: let it be done to me according to Thy word.

At last, I was Mother Felicitas, fully incorporated into the community of Our Lady of the Rock. I am sealed into this community forever. Only with the direct permission of the Holy See could I leave or be dismissed.

We celebrated with a festive noon meal out on our deck. The music I chose for that meal was the final movement of the Franck Sonata for violin and piano that I had played with David Stein at the Abbey. After dessert I went down to the guest house to greet the several guests, spent a good bit of time with them, and when returning to the monastery was utterly delighted to find the whole community still sitting at the table, relaxing happily.

After this, life got very busy indeed.

Nineteen

TOWN AND GOWN: 2015

To one who has faith, no explanation is necessary.
To one without faith, no explanation is possible.

—Saint Thomas Aquinas

Our lives are shaped by the fact that we live on an island. It takes from one to two hours to reach the mainland by ferry. It is expensive: a round-trip from Anacortes, the nearest city on the mainland, to Shaw, costs $37.90 for a car and driver; for a couple with two children, the fare is $63.75. These are in the winter; the price rises in the summer. We spend a lot of time driving the four miles to the ferry landing to meet guests and to take them back for their return trip. When we need to go to the mainland, say for a fifteen-minute doctor's appointment, it takes all day. We have to organize our lives around the ferry schedule, which changes quarterly. The ferry system keeps raising the price of travel while cutting down on service.

Through the years the island's population has grown from 133 in the 1980 census to about 240 now. Most of the old people we knew in our first few years here have died, or have left the island to live an easier life on the mainland. Property has become very expensive. Many of the new people are quite wealthy, having been executives at Microsoft, Boeing, and other big enterprises. We also have families struggling to survive. One resident recently said, "Everyone on Shaw has either three houses or three jobs."

The school had about twenty children last year and two full-time teachers plus a part-time superintendent. There are many clubs, organizations and activities here: two book clubs, a monthly women's gathering, an exercise class, a Yoga class, a well-attended interdenominational Protestant Sunday service, a beautiful library, a post office and a general store. For twenty-seven years the store and the ferry were run by the Franciscan Sisters of the Eucharist. When they left, an island family took over. Concerts, lectures, and other presentations and meetings abound. Some people have come to be active in community doings. Others have come to be reclusive and escape from groups and meetings.

Saint Francis Church in Friday Harbor on San Juan Island serves the Catholics of all San Juan County, offering Mass daily in Friday Harbor and Sundays on Orcas and Lopez Islands. Shaw Island has very few Catholics. Besides ourselves and one Catholic couple, two Mercy Sisters (of the Religious Sisters of Mercy in Alma, Michigan) live on the island, taking care of their community's property and teaching catechism for the Saint Francis parish. The one Catholic couple who was here when we came died some time ago. As everywhere, there are many "used to be" Catholics. But we cannot even count the number of people who have come into the Church, or returned to it, through their experience with us. More than twenty-five people have been baptized in our chapel, many marriages have been blessed, and several people have entered or re-entered the Church elsewhere after their time here.

We have a definite enclosure, but we are not cloistered. The enclosure means that our house, areas of work, pastures, and most of our three hundred acres are off limits for guests and visitors. But we come and go easily on the island, and have many good relationships with islanders. Like them, we must be inventive in so many ways: we can't just get into a car and go to pick up a prescription, or a needed machine part, or anything else. We are part of the island people. Regardless of our religion or our politics, we look out for each other and help each other.

The community has grown, but slowly. Two of the three founders are gone. Mother Miriam, who took care of the sheep and the garden and did most of the cooking and baking, left in the early 1990s to help revive monastic life at the ancient Abbey of San Vincenzo al Volturno in Italy. Mother Prisca, herbalist and guest mistress, died in 1995. Thus, aside from Mother Therese herself, I have been here longer than anyone else. In the early years the Abbey sent postulants now and then, some of whom were expected to stay here permanently. But we did not have permission to have a novitiate at that time, so when these postulants returned to Regina Laudis for their formation, they never came back.

In 1985 the Holy See raised Our Lady of the Rock to the status of a Priory and named Mother Therese as Prioress. Now we were able to have our own novitiate. We have had several postulants enter who did not stay. Was our life not exciting enough for them? More likely, I think many of them had concrete ideas about monastic life, but found the reality of our life not what they had expected, just as a young woman might make a list of the qualities she wanted her husband to have, and thus could not be open to the real men she knew. Undoubtedly, too, many of our postulants simply were not cut out for life in community. The only way a woman can find out if she is called to monastic life is to jump in and try it.

But some did stay. Catherine Lamb, later Mother Frances of Rome, came in 1980 and stayed until her death in 2002. In the early nineties came Shirley Roy, a Seattle native who had been a housemother at a fraternity in Arizona and was already a grandmother. As Mother Martina, she was with us until her death in 2012. Both she and Mother Frances of Rome are buried along with Mother Prisca in Our Lady of the Rock's cemetery.

Susan Boulanger, originally from Springfield, Massachusetts but later a resident of California, entered in 1998 and is still with us. She was an office manager in a tax firm. Here she became Mother Mary Grace, a gifted seamstress, decorator, and shopper. She designed and maintains our beautiful Saint Polycarp Pond, and is in charge of the guest houses.

After me, four professed nuns from Regina Laudis came to Our Lady of the Rock at various times and stayed:

Mother Dilecta Planansky who, like Mother Hildegard, is a native Californian, came in 1985. She is the liturgist, mistress of ceremonies, sacristan, raises all our vegetables and most of our flowers, takes care of the beef herd, and is a poet.

Mother Hildegard George, a PhD in child psychology, came in 1987. She has given many lectures on animal-assisted therapy for children all over the country. She is our shepherdess (sheep, llamas and alpacas), guest mistress, portress (gatekeeper), econome (in charge of the cooking), and cellarer (in charge of all the property of the monastery). She has spent much time over the years working with island children on 4-H and independent projects. She is also a serious birder. She has a very popular blog: www.island life-inamonastery.blogspot.com.

Mother Catarina Boyer came in 1996. A former Dominican, she is an excellent teacher and very gifted in ecumenical relationships. She teaches a Bible study class on Orcas Island, takes loving care of the laying chickens, including several beautiful bantam chickens of rare breeds; does a considerable amount of cooking, baking, and shopping, and maintains many relationships with islanders.

Mother Ruth Barry, who grew up as a Southern Baptist on a small farm in Georgia and has not lost a bit of her accent, came in 1999. For years at Regina Laudis she was shepherdess, gardener and Subprioress. Here she does the laundry and some of the sewing.

As superior of the community Mother Prioress is in charge of everything. She keeps us together. She established our dairy, one of the first

Grade A raw milk dairies in the state. She makes and sells cheese, our most popular product. She takes care of the meat birds (chickens and turkeys), and as Infirmarian takes care of our health needs. As the Treasurer, she takes care of the taxes, permits of various sorts, and insurance. She helps with cooking and shopping and almost everything else. She puts the needs of others ahead of her own, and comes closest among us to the Christian ideal of giving ourselves totally to God.

Our community. Front row: Mother Ruth, Mother Prioress Therese, Mother Felicitas. Back row: Mother Mary Grace, Mother Dilecta, Mother Catarina, Mother Hildegard.

A giant step in our lives as a community was the building of our new chapel, which was dedicated in 1997. Our first chapel had been fashioned in a cave-like area under the house, on rocks, with streams of water running down the rocks when it rained a lot. It was furnished with driftwood. It served us well for many years, but it had no windows, little fresh air, and was cold, damp, and small. The acoustics were terrible. It was also impossible to have a good enclosure, because anyone who wished to attend Mass had to come right up to the house to get there. At last we acquired enough money to begin the new chapel. Many people contributed to the chapel fund, but the bulk of it came from New York City. Our first priest, Father Louis D. Aufiero, had two friends from Wall Street, Richard Marasco and Noel Peterson. They organized a yearly benefit dinner for our new chapel. It was built mainly by island people. This chapel deserves a book of its own, to acknowledge all the people who helped to build it and all the work that went into it. It is a jewel, an architectural gem.

Our architect, Joseph Giampietro of Seattle and a long-time associate of Regina Laudis, designed the chapel on the footprint of a building that had burned down between the initial visit of Lady Abbess and Mother Mary Aline and the arrival of the three foundresses. The plan had been to use this building as the basis for a future chapel. Ed Hopkins of Shaw Island was the builder. His very first act, with Mother Prioress and I assisting, was to bail out the water that had flooded the remaining part of the old building.

The chapel is in keeping with the Asian character of the main house. A Japanese garden at the entrance is enclosed with a bamboo fence and a tori gate. Inside, the grille separating the choir from the rest of the chapel is also made of bamboo. The four pieces of nineteenth-century Chinese furniture—a gong, a small table, a chair for the Bishop, and a seat for the priest—provide in their dark finish and ornate carving a stark contrast to the simple lines and light finish of the wooden walls, floors, pews, and choir stalls. Builders marvel at the superb workmanship. Various works of art complement and enrich the simplicity of the structure: a beautiful stained glass window, made here by one of our interns;[92] a large serigraph of Jacob wrestling with the angel by Schlomo Katz; the life-sized body of Christ crucified made by the Southwestern sculptor Frances Rich and mounted on a cherry wood cross; a set of brass Stations of the Cross from the Abbey of Maria Laach in Germany.

We were immediately thrilled to discover that the new chapel had wonderful acoustics. How much easier it was to sing here!

People are in awe of the beauty and the presence of God that permeate the chapel. After all these years I am still in awe of it, every time I enter it.

The entrance to the Chapel.
Photo by Tari Gunstone

View of the altar, the crucifix, and the choir.

The only way we can keep our property and our farm in good shape is with the help of many others. We always have one to three young people here on what we call our Land Program. They stay for a few months to a year, working and learning, and sharing in our spiritual life to whatever degree they wish. A large group of Mormons comes twice a year for one intense day of work. They bring their children and their own substantial lunch, and work hard for a few hours, accomplishing wonders. We all pray together before work begins. They love to come and are very cheerful as they work.

Nearly every summer for the past few years a large Catholic youth group from Ferndale in northern Washington comes for a week-long retreat and work. Led by skilled carpenters and builders, they also accomplish wonders. We are very energized by their faith, their generosity, and their communal spirit. And two or more men from the Knights of Columbus come several times a year to replenish our supply of firewood from the abundance of fallen trees.

Above all, we have a fine group of Oblates from various parts of the country. Each one helps according to her or his unique gift. This, then, is our life. Our prayer life, mostly together in our chapel, is the most important thing we do. More people than we can count, and many more that we do not even know, depend on our prayers. We pray for the whole world, and are part of it, sharing its pains and its triumphs.

Twenty

MARY AND MARTHA 1990-2007

A community is not an abstract ideal. We are not striving for perfect community. Community is not an ideal; it is people. It is you and I. In community we are called to love people just as they are with their wounds and their gifts, not as we would want them to be.

—Jean Vanier

The years leading to my Consecration in 2007 were full of visible outward activity. I was now fully incorporated into the Community of Our Lady of the Rock. I could confidently represent us publicly. All my public activity, and my daily work within the community, was the Martha side of my life, the visible side. At the same time, the hidden, contemplative Mary side was flourishing, aided by the Office of Matins. We pray Matins at 2:00 A.M. I love this time: a little extra day in which we do nothing but get up, pray in chapel, and go back to bed. Our minds are more open at this time, since we do not have to be concerned with chores and obligations. During these years of heightened activity, just when I most needed balance, the Holy Spirit put a lot of ideas into my head during Matins.

Sunday Matins in April

Stumbling out from disconnected dreams,
from warm cocoon, from tiny noiseless cell—
Will it be raining? Will there be stars?
Stars, yes! Shining at their posts:
"Here we are! Here to do Your will."
Tree-frogs, thousands—little, but so loud,
anticipating Matins.
Domine, labia mea aperies.
Woody chapel, wrapped in black blanket
blocking out the world beyond the windows
(all but that other chapel, doubling ours,
depending on the dark for its existence).

Darkness enclosing, drives thoughts inward,
infinitely outward;
Souls crying out to God—souls of all times and places:
People of the Psalm-world, of the Apostle-world,
Of my world, long life, girl and nunly grandmother.
Frogs suddenly silent. Cricket chorus comes.
Outside, still no ray of light,
But in, and out, rays of sound so many!
Te Deum laudamus. Benedicamus Domino. Deo gratias.

Chant Matters

In June of 1989, the year preceding my Perpetual Vows, I returned to the Catholic University in Washington, D.C. for the summer courses in Gregorian chant and Ward Method studies taught by Theodore Marier. This time my companions were Stephen Concordia, a fine composer and organist who later became a Benedictine monk, and David Stein, my former piano partner at the Abbey. I stayed again with the Sisters of the Visitation Monastery in Georgetown. Having by now had some experience in teaching chant and the Ward Method, I found the courses richer than ever.

In September I attended the annual meetings of the American Musicological Society, of which I was still a member. Professor Laszlo Dobszay, a musicologist from Hungary, was to present a paper. Years before, he had spent time at Yale, during which he visited Regina Laudis for Holy Week and thereafter kept up a correspondence, in Latin, with Lady Abbess. During my novitiate she had asked me to get in touch with him and establish a relationship. I was to write to him under my secular name as someone in relationship to Regina Laudis, expressing interest in his studies and recordings. He responded graciously, answering my many questions and sending me relevant material. In Austin, Texas for the meetings, I sought him out and introduced myself to him. It was great fun to see his astonishment on discovering that this Professor Martha Curti who had been writing to him was a nun. I spent the rest of the morning wandering about in search of a decent but not too expensive restaurant where I could take him to lunch. I was very nervous. I had never taken such an initiative. Professor Dobszay turned out to be as gracious as his letters had been. At this, our first meeting, he gave me a CD of the Schola Hungarica, of which he was the director. This was the first CD that Our Lady of the Rock owned. Carl bought us a CD player so that we could listen to it.

Professor Dobszay and I continued our correspondence. In 1993 he invited me to come to Hungary for an international conference of chant scholars. First I spent a week in Italy visiting our Sisters at the Abbey of San Vincenzo al Volturno, southeast of Rome. The Abbot of Monte Cassino, a famous abbey founded by Saint Benedict himself, had invited Regina Laudis to send some nuns to San Vincenzo to reestablish Benedictine monastic life there. The Abbey had been founded in the time of Charlemagne, but for centuries had not functioned as a monastic house. Mother Miriam asked to move there, a painful departure for us at Our Lady of the Rock. Mother Agnes from Regina Laudis went too, and other nuns came for short periods. It was my one chance to see Italy. I was fascinated to see the ancient church and the ongoing archeological digs revealing the vast extent of the original abbey—a virtual city in itself. I loved the hills, the sun, the color of the olive trees, the hill towns, and the Abruzzi National Forest. It was very good to see Mother Miriam and Mother Agnes again—and Mother Rachel, who was there at that time—and to discover, with all the differences, our own Benedictine life in a totally foreign culture. I got to see Rome, too, for a grand twenty-four hours, as the guest of the Franciscan nuns there.

Laszlo Dobszay had told me of a nun, Sister Vali Ancilla, OSB, who because of the Communist oppression in Hungary had spent all her monastic life at the ancient abbey of Nonnberg in Austria. Since Hungary had just become free of the Communist dictatorship, he invited her to return to Hungary and work towards re-establishing Benedictine monastic life there. She and I had written to each other and agreed that Latin would be our common language. With great trepidation and excitement I reached the Budapest airport three hours late, looking anxiously for her amidst a closely packed crowd. She had waited for me for all those hours. We soon discovered that German was much preferable to Latin as our common language.

I was to be the guest of Sister Ancilla until the conference began in Eger. The meetings were rather baffling for me, with papers presented in English, French, German, and Latin. But the food was wonderful and I enjoyed meeting a number of chant scholars. Prof. Dobszay, who was in charge of the conference, saw to it that we had many opportunities to visit, and sometimes to sing in, small village churches and other sites of interest. On the last day of the conference, back at the Academy of Music in Budapest, Prof. Dobszay showed us some of the work that he and the earlier researchers in Hungarian folk music had done.

One Sunday Sister Ancilla took me on a long drive south, to where her new monastery was under construction. I shall never forget this trip. I saw storks sitting in their nests atop telephone poles; gypsies among the crowds at a church fair; an old farmer driving a horse and cart, laden with hay, down a country road; houses with thatched roofs, old scythes, well sweeps; the ruins of an ancient monastery; Lake Balaton, with a single fishing boat battling the high winds and rough water; and the home of a young parish priest whose mother, with whom he lived, had prepared for us a very tasty Hungarian meal.

I fell in love with Hungary: its people, its food, its music. I fantasized going to live there permanently to help Sister Ancilla build a community. On my way back to Our Lady of the Rock I stopped at Regina Laudis and reported on my trip to the community. Lady Abbess put my feet back on the ground, telling me I belonged at Our Lady of the Rock.

In the year 2000 I attended the Colloquium on Sacred Music at Christendom College in Front Royal, Virginia. This was one of the first colloquia sponsored by the Catholic Musicians Association of America. We attended daily classes and lectures on Gregorian chant and sang the Gregorian Mass each day. It was a special joy for me to sing polyphony in the chorus, conducted by Paul Salamunovitch, director of the Los Angeles Master Chorale.[93] The work was intense, the weather hot and humid, but I received a strong dose of inspiration from the teaching staff and fellow participants. Here I saw Dr. Marier, now very frail, and Professor Dobszay, for the last time: two superb musicians, wonderful and devout men. Both of them had made enormous contributions to the challenging process of adapting the music of the Catholic Church to the changes of Vatican II.

33rd Sunday of the Year, 1996

You are my Shepherd, who brings me straying in,
You are the gate, the path, my sheepfold home,
You are those pastures green, to which and
from which you lead me.
You are the Potter who made me,
Pinching, patting, pushing and pulling,
Till I come out right.
You are always making me anew—
persuading, enticing,
sometimes having to punch & poke roughly
because of the obtuse stubborn clay that I am.

You are the Farmer who planted me,
The Gardener who tends me—
giving me water, food, sun, in just the right timing and proportion,
stirring up the soil around to give me room to grow.
The Weaver who wove me,
The Vinedresser who prunes me,
The Vine itself, whose tendril I am.
You are my Teacher, ever patient,
You, the Artist who conceived me,
The Composer who thought me up,
The Conductor of the orchestra in which I play,
The Maker of my violin, and of the sound
coming forth from it & from my voice.
You, Father, Son, Brother, Friend,
Lover, above all.
Husband who never abandons me,
who always takes me back,
who always forgives.
Physician who heals me.
You dwell in my inmost being, yet so far away—
That distance my own doing.
In You do I live, move, have my being.
Why, my Lord,
Why do I not stay always
In this awareness of You?

Physical Therapy for the Ear

The class was taking a break. I remained in my seat. People were chatting quietly. Gradually I became aware of one of the most beautiful sounds I have ever heard. It was the hum of a woman's voice. I could not identify the source, for it came from the walls. At last I perceived that it came from our teacher, Mlle Dominique Cannet, who was sitting on the raised platform in front of the room.

It was June 1994, and I was in Paris, at the Tomatis Listening Center near the beautiful Parc Monceau. The Abbey had chosen me to receive training in the Tomatis Method and then to administer the Tomatis Listening Therapy at Our Lady of the Rock. This therapy was developed by Alfred A. Tomatis,[94] a French otolaryngologist who had discovered, through his work with singers, actors, and workers in a munitions plant in World War II, that defects in the voice come from irregularities in the hearing. To correct these problems, he invented a machine he called the Electronic Ear. As one listens to music, mostly Mozart and Gregorian chant, through the Electronic Ear, the machine alternately tenses and relaxes the tiny muscles of the middle ear. This therapy does not restore the hearing loss that occurs naturally in most people as they age, or that is caused by disease or over-exposure to loud sounds; what it does is help us make the best use of what hearing we do have. Many people, both famous and obscure, have testified that the Tomatis Listening Therapy has improved the quality of their singing and speaking voices.[95]

At Regina Laudis, our curiosity about the Tomatis Method was aroused by an interview with Tomatis that was aired on CBC in Canada and then on NPR in the US.[96] Tomatis describes his experience with a community of monks in France who were exhausted, "slumping in their cells like wet dishrags." They had tried a change in diet, then in their schedule, without success. Dr. Tomatis had them resume their singing of Gregorian chant, which they had given up, and he treated them with the Electronic Ear. After several months of treatment their energy was restored, and they were able to return to the demanding Benedictine schedule.

So the ear does much more than simply allow us to hear. Given the input of higher frequencies, the ear can "recharge" our bodies. The music that best transmits these frequencies, according to Tomatis, is that of Mozart and Gregorian chant.[97]

I wrote to Professor Tomatis (he had by this time left his medical practice) and asked how we could obtain the Electronic Ear. He replied with a kind letter, saying, in effect, "Come to Paris and learn how to use the Electronic Ear."

That is how I got to that classroom and heard the sound that reached my heart.

Our class, lasting for three weeks, was given in French with an English translator. We had a Hungarian couple, two German women, a Swiss man, one other American, and several French people. Most of them were already involved in psychological counseling or various other therapies. We learned something about how our ears function; how the Electronic Ear works and how to use it; how to interview clients and administer the Tomatis Listening Test to them; and the many applications of Listening Therapy: to help children with learning disabilities of various sorts; to facilitate learning foreign languages; to energize older people; to calm pregnant women; to help people of all ages become better listeners and communicators; and, most important for me, to help singers and musicians enrich the quality of their sounds.

Mother Jeanne-Yolaine Mallet, a French woman who had entered Regina Laudis, had already taken the Tomatis courses. She came with me for my second training session in Paris, in which we took the Audio-Vocal Course (CAV) taught by Professor Tomatis himself. I greatly enjoyed working with him. It was like a master class, in that he worked with us individually before the whole class. He also played recordings of many famous singers before and after their work with the Electronic Ear. In November I met Mother Jeanne-Yolaine in New York and we flew to London for our third session of Tomatis training. This time, since the Professor was very ill, the Audio-Vocal course was taught by his assistant, Dominique Cannet, who had been our mentor all along. We stayed with the Benedictine Nuns of Tyburn, who extended to us gracious hospitality in the Benedictine tradition.

When the Electronic Ear and the Listening Test machine arrived at Our Lady of the Rock, Mother Jeanne-Yolaine came out from the Abbey for a few weeks so that we could practice using the machines together and give each other the therapy. I then proceeded to work with the Community one by one. Since the first phase of the therapy involves listening two hours a day for two weeks, it was quite a challenge to fit it into our schedule. But the listening process was very relaxing and gave us a sort of mini-retreat from our busy lives. We discovered that the therapy truly made it easier for us to sing, to stay on pitch, to reach the higher notes, and to greatly improve our vocal quality. I also found that playing the violin while listening to my playing through the Electronic Ear made it much easier to play, but it was awkward to play while wearing headphones and attached to the machine by a cord.

Later that year Mother Anne Rushton came out for several weeks to receive the Listening Therapy. Unfortunately, the Abbey did not send any more people, nor did they acquire the Tomatis equipment for themselves, and Mother Jeanne-Yolaine left Regina Laudis to join a Benedictine monastery in France.

With very first word of his Rule, *"Ausculta,"* Saint Benedict bids us to listen, to pay attention. This admonition has a deeper meaning than we might think.

April 14, 2000

Is it your fury, your rage, like the God of the Old Testament – flinging down such a violent storm, overpowering tender buds & flowers, newborn calves, and us? I prefer to think this, rather than ascribe the storm to impersonal forces of Nature. You care about us, so passionately! You gave us free will, and we have chosen the wrong things. It's not just "Them"—we, too, with all our prayers, all our work, our miniscule sacrifices—have let you down, in ways we do not even recognize.

In April—struggling for Spring—a wind so violent, so loud, so unrelenting—such as belongs to winter. The stream of water from the gutter, falling sideways instead of down. We recite Matins, expecting the lights to go out. The seven seals, the four living creatures, the four horsemen—swords, death. Rich & poor seeking shelter in caves, & praying to die. Mountains crumbling, sky disappearing. The spirits of the martyrs: "How long"? "Be patient—the quota is not filled up."

Israelis, Palestinians, consumed by hate & desire for revenge—children even. Eighteen guests this weekend, kids & teens & chaperones. Mother Hildegard, cutting up a chicken with a huge Chinese chopper, cuts a strip of flesh from the middle finger of her left hand. Imediate surgery, graft of flesh. Everyone already exhausted, tense, hurting. We are so much a part of the pain of the world.

So obviously You, not we ourselves, are in control. Sometimes it takes a storm to remind us. You are the bread, broken for us. We too must be broken for others.

Occasionally the wind takes a breath, & in this breath we can hear the frogs croaking. And we keep plugging along, and You are holding us.

Family Matters

When we enter the monastery at Our Lady of the Rock or Regina Laudis, we do not actually leave our families. We bring them with us, as far as they wish to go. Yes, the old familial life, living together, sharing our daily experiences, is gone. But we care about one another's families: we take on their burdens; we support them in prayer and in action. If they are unable to visit us because of age, we can visit them.

It was not always this way. When I entered the Abbey in 1979, one did not visit one's family unless a family member was seriously ill or dying. Several years ago we asked an Abbot who was making an official visitation to our priory: "Why can't we visit our families for a week each year, since men in monastic communities routinely make such visits?" Fortunately, he answered, "You can." So almost every year since then I have gone either to San Jose, California, or Lyme, New Hampshire, to visit Carl and Bill and their families.

On a visit to San Jose I had the joy of being with both my sons and my three grandchildren all at one time. On either side of me are Carl (left) and Bill. Standing behind us, from left to right, are Charlie, Carla, and Owen.

The years between my Perpetual Vows and my Consecration saw my family grow with the birth of three grandchildren, and shrink with the deaths of my father and my sister. On May 9, 1993, my first grandchild, Carla, was born to Carl and Teresa Dakis. Carl was afraid to tell me, since he and Teresa were not married. He called me and told me to sit down, then gave me the news. I cried. I was so deeply happy for him and for myself. I asked him what he was going to do. "I'm going to be a good father," he replied. And he was. Within a few months, Teresa and Carla moved in with Carl in San Jose, and in 1996 Carla was present at the wedding of her parents.

Another wedding had taken in 1995. Bill and Chris Hardy, who had grown up in Seattle, chose to be married at Roche Harbor on nearby San Juan Island. We had a party for them here, the day before the wedding. At this time I had the great joy of meeting my granddaughter for the first

My first meeting with Carla.

time. Since the wedding was so close to us, I was able to attend. It was a grand occasion, a big gathering of the Wohlforth and Hardy families and many friends, and a real treat for me since I had no responsibilities. I was nervous at the prospect of seeing Tim with his new wife, but the reality was better than I had expected.

Besides the wedding of Chris and Bill, the year 1995 saw another major event in my life: the death of my sister, Nancy. She died on February 25, the birthday of my father-in-law Robert Wohlforth. I have noticed many similar connections of dates in my life. My father and I came to Alma for her memorial service at the Episcopal Church. It took place on Nancy's birthday, March 3. I was surprised at how moved I was. This was my first experience of attending the funeral of a family member, for my mother had not wanted any kind of service. As I walked up to the lectern to read one of the lessons, I passed the black box that contained her ashes. In awe that this box held the remains of Nancy, I made the sign of the cross on it. I could hardly manage to get through the reading. Then Dad and I went to the last place she had lived and hastily gathered, from the mess of her belongings, anything that seemed important. I could see that all this was taking a heavy toll on Dad. At our hotel we ordered supper brought up to us, as it was obviously impossible for Dad to go out to eat.

The next morning, as we were about to leave for the airport in our rented car, Dad gently slid to the floor, cold, sweating. I asked him if I should call 911. No, he said. We sat there on the floor and rested a while. Then with great difficulty and very slowly we made it to the car. In Milwaukee, where we both had to change planes, I so badly wanted to help him get onto his little plane, but the officials would not let me. There was no time for me to appeal to their supervisors.

Not surprisingly, on reaching his apartment. Dad had a major stroke. He lived, with increasing fragility, another year.

We could criticize Dad's decision to make such a difficult trip, considering his ninety-eight years and frail condition. But he would not have missed Nancy's funeral for anything.

Everyone who has gone through the final illness of a loved one at a distance knows the anxiety and stress of it. My community was totally supportive throughout this year. Each time I visited Dad in his nursing home, not knowing if it would be the last time I would see him, my leaving was more and more difficult. It was a gift of God that Dad had a good friend, Jean Cronon, a nurse and the wife of a colleague. Jean was the one on the scene who could coordinate Dad's care with the staff, who could help to regulate the stream of people who came to see him, each one insisting to the staff that he or she was Dad's best friend. She was the one on whom I could depend to tell me straight how Dad was doing.

This was his second stay in the nursing home. This time he knew he would never get back to his apartment. His mind was alert until the very end. He wanted to live long enough to find out how the next election would come out. But he could no longer enjoy listening to music. He no longer laughed or smiled or told funny stories. Much as he loved all his friends, he tired very quickly when they visited him. Finally, very quietly, since he was being given morphine, he died in the night. Bill was with him, holding his hand, and the minute he died, Bill called me. I was so grateful that Bill was there, both for his sake and mine.

Dad knows now for certain that there is a God of infinite goodness.

October 3, 2010

> *On the way down the ramp to the chapel, I was filled with love for life and for this world. During Matins, the awareness of love for God consumed me, brought me great happiness with tears. He is in me and I am in Him. "In Him we live and move and have our being." Here, back at my desk, this awareness, this love of God & those tears are still with me. Every cell in my body is alive. Thank You, Lord. My love for You is so tiny, so inadequate. And though all my sins are forgiven (a miracle in itself), I still despise them. It is important that I do not lose the memory & awareness of my sins, past & present. They come from selfishness, a stony heart, excluding people & hurting them. Forgetting You, my God, my Jesus. You still want me, nevertheless. Your patience is endless. You are always mindful of me, even when I stray from You.*
>
> *"Unam petii, hanc requiram: ut inhabitem in domo Domini omnibus diebus vitae meae."*
>
> *My herinacii, Amos and Jerome, are looking at me, wondering.*

Teresa, Carla, and Carl at the Curti house in Rapperswil

(One thing I have sought; this I seek: to live in the house of the Lord all the days of my life." Ps.26.

Herinacii are hedgehogs. Amos is tiny, less than an inch long, pewter. Jerome is a little smaller than my clenched fist, wood.)

On March 9, 1997, one year to the day after the death of my father, my second grandchild, Owen, was born to Chris and Bill. Chris, a Catholic, brought him out to Our Lady of the Rock for his Baptism. Two years later my third grandchild, Charlie, was born, and again he was baptized here at Our Lady of the Rock.

At the end of the summer of 2000 I made my fifth European trip since entering religious life. When I entered Regina Laudis in 1979 I could not have dreamed that I would make more trips to Europe than I had made in my secular life. My Swiss family had invited me to the Curti reunion, held every five years. This time it was to be in Rapperswil, the city of the family's origin, and my father was to be honored, along with several famous Curtis of Rapperswil, by a plaque containing their names, and the re-naming of a plaza on the shore of Lake Zurich, to be called the Curti-Platz. My son Carl, his wife Teresa, and Carla, then seven, took me. We were in Switzerland about two weeks, and I shall never forget the wonders of that visit.

Matins: the Feast of Saint. Scholastica, February 10, 2002

Responsory 12 (from Matins of Saint Scholastica):
The soul of Scholastica went forth like a dove from the ark of her body,
bearing an olive branch, the symbol of peace and grace. She flew into heaven.

When she found no place where she could rest her feet,
She flew into heaven.

Scholastica flew, and finding no place to rest her feet,
figured she was meant to fly to Heaven, which she did.
Just then a large, airy, delicate spider
Lowered herself from a great height, five inches from my face
(somewhere from the lofty spaces of our chapel's ceiling).
She kept on her downward course, steadily descending.
At last, after pausing a brief second, eating up her fragile connection,
she went back up!
(All this happened as we were singing the Te Deum.*)*
God's humble, magnificent creature—
feared and despised by so many—
risked her very life to come down and give us such delight.
(Only Mother Catarina was in on this miracle with me.)

2007: Consecration[98]

As a dependent priory, Our Lady of the Rock abides by the Constitutions of the Abbey of Regina Laudis. These Constitutions specify an additional step in our religious life: the Consecration of a Virgin. This is a very old ceremony within the Church and has usually been given at the same time as Perpetual Vows. The Consecration of a Virgin, despite its antiquity, is seldom celebrated in today's Church. Even now, however, a devout laywoman can dedicate herself totally to God and the Church as a consecrated virgin.

But what of women who obviously are not virgins—those who have been married? When I entered Regina Laudis, I thought I might be the only divorced mother in religious life. I was sure that somewhere there must be nuns and sisters who had been married, but such a thing was then a novelty. Now, it is much more common. Originally the Abbey could not consecrate any woman who had been married. Mother Jerome was the only exception, and she was a widow, not a divorced mother. But after me the Abbey received, one by one, four other women who had been married, two of whom were also mothers.

I never expected to be consecrated, having been married and divorced. But the community of Regina Laudis "believed our lives (i.e., we five who had been married) needed the blessing that goes from forever to forever."[99] The Abbey found that within the Church there exists a ceremony, Monastic Consecration, that would cover our situation. The nuns at the Abbey of Saint Scholastica at Dourgne in France, and at many other European monasteries, had already used this ceremony in connection with the celebration of Perpetual Vows.

At our Perpetual Vows, we take the initiative: we write a petition offering ourselves totally to God through the Community and the Church. At our Consecration, the Church, represented by the local bishop, responds by acknowledging and blessing this offering. The day before the ceremony, the whole community met in a Chapter[100] in the Abbey's round stone chapter house. One by one we *consecrandae* (those about to be consecrated) made a statement. Several nuns spoke in response, expressing very movingly their strong support. Finally Mother Abbess spoke and gave each of us a mission. My mission was to "write my life." This Chapter was joyful, filled with laughter, tears, applause. I contributed tears of gratitude. I had never before felt such a total union with the community.

The next day, the Feast of Saint Benedict, July 11, 2007, His Excellency Henry Mansell, Archbishop of Hartford, consecrated us in the Abbey's church.

Each of the steps in monastic life involves a ceremony that takes the energy of the entire monastic community in preparation and on the day involved. But this one surpassed all the others in complexity, energy, and beauty. We had waited years after our Perpetual Vows—I for seventeen years—for this Monastic Consecration.

One of the material manifestations of the Consecration is that each nun wears a crown made of fresh flowers at the Abbey. Each of us had a crown that was tailored to our individuality. Mine had, among the gardenias and other flowers, blueberries, yarrow, and a seashell. At the end of the day I carefully put it into a special box and took it with me the next day to Lyme Center. Bill and Chris had come down for the ceremony and brought me home with them. When we got to the house, I showed my crown to my grandsons Owen and Charlie, telling them, "I was a queen for a day." Charlie responded, "You'll always be a queen." That is, in a sense, true.

The outpouring of energy, physical beauty, love, was so overwhelming that its effect will remain with me always.

I. My Hands

My hands are so old! They tell a long story: finger joints swollen, fingers misshapen from a childhood disease; three scars, two of them from inattention: meat cut too hastily; fingertip nearly cut off by my pruning shears, trying to prune while being besieged by constant questions from a co-worker; the third from surgery. Relics of burns. Bruises—a gigantic deep red one, turning purple, in the middle of my right hand up onto my middle finger, from a recent unremembered blow; another smaller one from a zealous acupuncture needle. Huge blue veins, 1/16" at least above the surface. Innumerable brown spots, red places, dry & itchy places. Swollen tender & sometimes jabbing-pained joints at the base of both thumbs, from sixty-three years of violin playing. Yes, my hands are old—they have worked hard, given & received, loved and comforted, struck out in fear, anger, helplessness.

II. The Choice

But life is so good! How can I enter into Christ's passion? Where are the fat bulls surrounding me, the enemies deriding, mocking, scourging me?

Where is our poverty? We are part of the richest nation in the world. We are far indeed from deprivation, cold & hunger, lack of medical treatment. We are safe, secure. We have each other.

But we have war, and all the other ills & messes of the world.

We have all the struggles to sing well, to pray well, to build a community of holiness. Hard though we try, we cannot fix these things. They will always be with us.

I could drown in this. I could be overwhelmed. But I could also make a choice: I could really try to pay attention to the Psalms. I could try to listen, to see if God has an answer, or just to see what He is saying.

III. What God Says

And oh! He says so much, in this never-ending dialogue between Him and us! It's far easier to enumerate difficulties, trials & troubles, than it is to describe the richness of God's Word in the Psalms, in St. Augustine, in the Gospel.

All I can say is that here, in God, in His Church, His people, His true temple (nowadays still full of sinners, money-changers, doubters, arguers, and all of us, or most of us, without the answers) the Mystical Body of Christ contains all, surpasses all. It contains the gung-ho supporters of the war, and the protesters, neither side willing or able to hear the other. Christ unites them. He absorbs all our troubles & worries. They still exist, and always will in this life. But they do not seem so important when we can rest in Him. He has not given us the answers. He has given us Himself. He is the answer.

IV. My Hand, Again

On my right hand, on the third finger, is a plain gold ring, a little dulled and scratched on the outside, but inside, as bright and pure as the day it was made. Engraved on this pure inside is: "Ego Christi Soror Felicitas 11.Julii 1990." (I, Sister Felicitas, belong to Christ. July 11, 1990). That's all I need to know. I am Christ's. He is my Spouse, I am His. He has everything figured out; I do not need to figure it out myself. I have only to trust Him.

Twenty-One

ENDINGS AND BEGINNINGS

I believe in reincarnation, but I am not a fan of death.

—Helen Weaver

Ma fin est mon commencement,
Et mon commencement ma fin.
My end is my beginning, And my beginning is my end.

—Guillaume de Machaut

I do not believe in reincarnation. But like my friend Helen Weaver, I am not a fan of death, and someone who is would be hard to find. As a child, I took death quite seriously. Someone—probably one of the women who took care of me from time to time—taught me "Now I lay me down to sleep, I pray the Lord my soul to keep; if I should die before I wake, I pray the Lord my soul to take." I did not know what it meant for the Lord to take my soul. I was not taught the comforting part about angels. So I must have been worried.

One day when I was four, I wanted to speak with my mother about death. Respecting the awe and mystery of it, I led her into a small, dark cloak closet in the hall. She told me death is a natural occurrence and does not hurt. We get very old and tired and do not mind dying. It is like going to sleep and never waking up again. The thought of never waking up again terrified me. A world without ME in it could not exist! Mother said that I would live a very long time and not to worry. I asked her how long? "Eighty years," she replied. This was a comfort to me, because eighty years was an infinity to me then.

Now, these eighty years have come and gone, and I am still here. Each of us is unique, and each of us will face our death uniquely and unpredictably. I do not fear death, and I fully trust that God will take me to Himself. I believe in the resurrection of the body and life eternal. I trust also that those I love, and all people who have tried to live good lives, will be safe in the hands of God even if they think they do not believe in Him.

Of course, I have the human dread of untreatable and unbearable pain, of total dependence on others, of dementia, and of dying without having taken proper care of all my papers. But I trust that the Lord knows better than I when I am "ready" to die. I pray for the grace to welcome whatever path He lays out for me.

How I came to this belief, this trust, was part of my overall experience of conversion. In the process of that conversion I had a dream about my mother. All I remember about this dream is that Mother and I were standing and talking in a large, empty auditorium; and that she was alive and very happy. She had died in 1961 when she was only sixty-nine and I was twenty-nine. Her death was very hard on me, and it took about ten years to integrate it, as our relationship had been very complex. She had not wanted a service of any kind, and was cremated and out of sight before I ever got to Madison. She had willed her personal and professional papers to me. Going through these papers, I realized that she really wanted me to *know* her. I feel very close to her now. I am more like her than I ever realized until recent years.

During my novitiate at the Abbey our dear family friend Louis Hunter had died, and in bed one night I heard his voice, trying to reach me. It was real.

I lived through my father's death for years, dreading it. While I was at the Abbey I had a dream in which we were walking together through a dark valley. He began to move very fast and I could not keep up. He went into that oft-spoken-of tunnel, with light at the end; and that was that. This dream in different forms occurred also at OLR. When it first occurred, Lady Abbess told me it did not mean he would die soon, but that the Lord was preparing me for his death.

He lived a good fifteen years after this, and all that time I had visions of him quietly and gently collapsing to the floor, dead. These were so real that I would check the time, as I was convinced that he was dying at that minute. He never was. When he really did die, I had no such experience.

As a guest at the Abbey I saw a dead body for the first time, that of Mrs. Lisauskas[101] in the Abbey's chapel. Seeing that body, even hesitantly touching it, and then experiencing later the death and burial of Mother Ida in Holy Week during my postulancy, struck a great awe in me.

At Our Lady of the Rock in the last few days before Mother Prisca died, I would often enter her cell to see her holding out her rosary in her right hand, and looking fixedly upwards to the upper right corner of the cell. She was clearly in the presence of someone on the other side: whether an angel, Our Lady, an ancestor, or Christ Himself, I could not know. I felt this presence so strongly that I had to kneel. Once another nun came in and started talking. I was upset because she had broken the spell, and Mother Prisca was very sad. Except for these times, Mother Prisca was totally immobile and passive, almost in a coma. (She had been bedridden for several years after her leg was amputated because of diabetes.) Her alertness before the Divine was a stark contrast.

Her funeral was truly a happy occasion. She died on a Saturday, just as Vespers was about to begin. We divided up the responsibilities. Some nuns prayed Vespers; Mother Hildegard got on the phone and called everyone who needed to be called; Mother Prioress and I prepared Mother Prisca's body. The coffin and the grave were ready. We kept vigil with Mother Prisca all night. Sunday afternoon we held a brief service in the monastery around Mother's coffin. The Franciscan Sisters and many friends and neighbors were there. It was a glorious bright and clear October day. The guests walked down the road to our cemetery, which is in a hay field overlooking Squaw Bay. Our neighbor Jack Rawls, who did logging with his fine team of Percherons, came with his horses pulling our hay wagon. All of us sat on hay bales on the wagon, surrounding the coffin. Jack took us around through the pasture into the field, and we approached the cemetery, singing psalms, at the same time that the guests arrived on foot from the road. Father Bernard Jonientz, a diocesan priest who was here for the weekend, stayed on to conduct the burial service at the graveside. Then we all, community and guests, began to shovel in the dirt. The men all stayed and finished the shoveling, which took a long time, and the rest of the guests went down to our guest house for refreshments. All our funerals follow this basic pattern, but this one was very special because of the glorious day and Jack and his team of horses.

My sister Nancy's death was remarkable. I had not spoken with her for two years because her behavior had become intolerable (for example, calling me up at two A.M., drunk). Shortly before her death, she was kicked out of the foster home she was living in. On a freezing night she was picked up off the street, very ill, and taken to the hospital in Alma. A nurse, who must have been Catholic, or at least Christian, called me and said that Nancy was declining rapidly and I should know about it. I called Nancy and we had an amazing talk. She was very peaceful, as I had never known her to be. We did not speak of love, or death, or forgiveness, but all three were there for both of us, I know. She said, "When I get out of here I have decided I will go to that nursing home (we had been trying fruitlessly to get her to go there). They have good activities there." She loved "activities." She had told a friend: "I used to think I was the queen bee. Now I know better." Within the hour, I received a call that she had died. I know that despite the terrible suffering that she had endured all her life, and the suffering she imposed on others, she is happy now in Heaven with plenty of activities.

All these experiences have strengthened my faith.

Welcome, winter wind!
Prune the dead limbs from the trees.
Blow away dead, destructive thoughts from our minds.
Let them float away, settle on the ground,
become sweet soil,
fertile host for seeds.
Clear the cobwebs from our souls.
Make our bodies a welcome home for God.

About Carl

Carl cannot tell his own story, so I must devote more space to him than to anyone else in my story. I quote from the letter I sent to family and friends after his death:

We used this picture on Carl's memorial card. Photo by Carl Wohlforth

Carl was born November 19, 1956 in New York City. Grew up there, in New Hampshire, Kentucky, and New Jersey. Earned a B.S. in Computer Science at Rutgers University. Headed out to Silicon Valley after graduation, worked as a software developer for several companies. In 1996 he married Teresa Dakis. The couple had a daughter, Carla, who is a student at UCLA. About the year 2000 he "retired" to work for himself, selling collectable coins on the Web (Carl's Coins.com), trading a stock account, building a magically beautiful and productive garden, learning to cook, and above all devoting himself to Teresa and Carla. In 2009 he earned Cisco certification, an advanced certification in the field of network technology, and returned to the software industry, working until he was diagnosed with pancreatic cancer in October 2011. On October 3, 2012, he died, with Teresa, Carla, and me at his side.

His prayer card shows the Arroyo Seco Gorge, where Carl loved to go backpacking alone. Backpacking was his great love. I see this as not merely a deep love of nature, which it was, but further, a spiritual search for the transcendent.

People have spoken of Carl as "the most honest person I have ever known:" a thorough optimist; affectionate, friendly, outgoing, but a private person; tenacious, simple, straightforward, unpretentious; highly intelligent, with an unending desire to learn. He loved to make others happy. He brought light to people's lives without realizing it. I would go with him to the post office, the supermarket, the cancer clinic at Stanford, and wherever it was, the people who saw him knew his name, shook his hand, and simply beamed.

He did not want people to know he had cancer, for then they would treat him differently. He did not want anyone outside of his family, even his best friends, to visit him in the hospital. Until the last two days of his life, when it became clear even to him that he was dying, he clung to the hope that he would somehow be cured, or at least have a few more months or years. But then, when he could scarcely speak, he said: "I don't want to die. But that is what's happening. I am sad." He loved life passionately, from the smallest wild flower to the stars, and most especially Teresa and Carla. If I asked him how his day was, even when he was quite sick, he would say "okay" at the least, and often he would say "great" or "fantastic." Why? Because he had taken a walk with Teresa, or talked with Carla on the phone, or spent a few minutes in the garden, or had a nice meal.

When I arrived in San Jose for what I knew would be my last visit with Carl, I found him in the hospital. He had not been able to eat, even a tablespoonful, for two months. The disease ravaged one part of his body after another. Now he found it increasingly difficult to breathe, and to talk, but he said to me on that first day, "Ask Saint John Vianney to pray for me." Remember, Carl grew up in an atheist family, one rather hostile to the Catholic Church. But after my own conversion, when he was in his twenties, I already saw in him a spiritual capacity.

Because Teresa is Catholic, and they had sent Carla to Saint John Vianney Middle School and Saint Francis High School in Mountain View, Carl became more and more open to the Church because of what it was doing for Carla. He volunteered to direct traffic as parents dropped off their children at Saint John Vianney Middle School, and loved greeting the parents. He went with Carla and Teresa to various events at the Church, and occasionally to Mass. After he was diagnosed with pancreatic cancer, he began to go to Mass each Sunday

> with Teresa. He noticed that people were praying. He asked me, "Can people like me pray?" "Of course, I said. "Just do it."
>
> Earlier, during his third from the last hospitalization, at Stanford, when it was already hard for him to speak, he said to me in our last real conversation on the phone, "I have some questions about religion I'd like to talk about with you when you come." We never were able to have that conversation. But the morning after I arrived in San Jose, I did call Saint John Vianney Church and asked for prayers for Carl. The next day, Father Steve Kim came to see Carl at the hospital. He spoke with Carl briefly, then prayed with us, using the beautiful prayers that the Church has for the sick. Carl responded to Father, becoming totally alert, and Father said, at the Memorial Mass for Carl, that he had a look of great longing in his eyes.
>
> Carl asked if Father could come again, but for various reasons it was not possible. So on October 1 I said to him: "Carl, I can baptize you if you would like me to." He nodded "Yes" very decisively. So with Teresa helping, I baptized him. He was now ready to pass into eternal life with God.
>
> Perhaps most of our lives, for those of us who try to live in faith, consist of a struggle between our heart and our mind. So with Carl's death, I know that he is with God, he is happy, he lives. But that does not fill the big hole in my heart and in my life. That hole will never be filled, as long as I live. And I don't want it to be.

When Bill was in high school, a classmate of his died from a dive. Either the water was not deep enough, or the boy hit some sort of barrier. Then the father of one of Bill's friends in the neighborhood died suddenly of a heart attack. Bill said to me something amazingly wise and mature. He said he never wanted to forget his sadness about the deaths of these two people, because then he would forget his love for them. That is true. Grief is the flip side of love.

Exactly three months after Carl died, I dreamed about him. I had been longing and praying to see him in a dream, but now the dream came. I was standing at the bottom of a long, straight staircase, and I saw Carl and my father at the top, playing together, and both very happy. Dad saw me and started to come down, and I yelled out, "Be careful!" That's all. But I was very comforted by this dream. I know it came through the gate of horn.

Shortly before he died, Carl wanted to see how he looked. There was no portable mirror, so I took a picture of him with my iPad. He was literally skin and bones. His glasses looked huge on his face. His deep suffering and pain were reflected in his eyes. There are people close to Carl who cringe at the very thought of this picture, who violently abhor it. But I will always keep it and treasure it. It is the face of the suffering Christ. Carl was heroic in his suffering. I deeply respect and honor him for the way he handled the suffering of his disease.

So I wanted to hang onto Carl and let him go at the same time.

Carl was the most authentic person I have ever known. He was without guile. He said what he thought. He usually said it tactfully, but he could be very stubborn. Like most children, he was fascinated by everything he encountered; he took great joy in discovering and learning things. This joy and excitement never left him. Many of his interests—in coins, water and energy, math and science, hiking and camping, building things, and above all, friends—were evident very early in his life.

He took risks. He was always optimistic. He had faced death four times before his final death: his osteomyelitis at ages three and four; his open heart surgery at eleven; a serious car accident at sixteen. Not long after, he hitchhiked across the country alone, sometimes joining up with men riding the rails. (I am glad I did not know about this at the time); and in his thirties, a second heart surgery. In his youth and as a young man he went through some dark times. But later, and especially after Teresa and Carla entered his life, he was supremely happy.

Have I written about his and Bill's relationship? How, as children, they built dams with such delight at Jacob's Brook in New Hampshire? And when we all returned to that spot decades later, those two fully grown men immediately rushed across the rock to build a dam and try to divert the stream, all over again? How they crawled along the high beams in the old barn at Flint Farm? How they made trails in the woods? How, on a hike in Vermont, when we discovered that Carl was missing, Bill said: "Who will there be to burn the trash with me?" Carl soon appeared, having come down his own way.

Dear Carl, I miss you more than I can say. I long to see you again.

The Long Road

It's been a long road, and I am coming to the end of it. God has given me a long time to find Him and to work on all that was blocking my way to Him. He, through my community, has given me the time to "write my life," as Mother Abbess David asked me to do. In doing this, I have learned to see my past, with my many serious mistakes and failings, in the context of my present. I did not know Christ. I did not know how to live in a Christian manner. I was, as Lady Abbess once told me, "illiterate." Had I known Christ, I would have behaved very differently toward my parents and all others. I would not have closed people out of my life.

I still have all the tendencies that I had before I was baptized. But I recognize them now, and I have learned, and am still learning and striving, to live in a more Christ-like way. All I can say, with my whole being, is: "*Deo gratias.*"

**Hollyhocks in our herb garden.
Photo by Barbara Penningroth**

Walking down the ramp to chapel early on a misty morning: ahead of me two nuns, one behind the other, silent narrow black pyramids. It looks like they are gliding along, since their feet are not visible.

Many people in the world would probably see them and think, "They look ridiculous." Some would be curious. Others would be pleased or even excited, as they would be to find an artifact from the Middle Ages, or an antique from colonial America. A few would be in awe of the women's dignity, mysteriousness, other-worldliness. I am in awe, too, even though these are my Sisters whose every mannerism and quirk I know well. They are signs to me of something beyond the ordinary—of a life, unimaginably beautiful, with God.

THE CHORD IS RESOLVED

APPENDIX

GENEALOGY

Our family history has a huge influence on us. How this happens, scientifically, I do not know. Some skeptics about the current craze for genealogy claim that it has very little meaning, that the number of descendants of one person in just a few generations is so vast that nearly all of us have a common ancestor. But whether by means of genes or some other way, I believe that our ancestors play a large role in who we are. Somehow, we each bear the unfulfilled longings, the conflicts, and the joys of our ancestors. We build on their achievements, their breakthroughs. Whether we know anything about them or not, they are in us, and we are called to redeem or resolve some of their burdens.

The Swiss Curti Family

In the year 1665 a silk merchant of Milan, Giacomo Maria Baptist Curti,[102] who had been making regular trips to Rapperswil in the canton of Zürich, settled there permanently and became a citizen. One of his nephews, Giovanni Battista Curti, became Johann Baptist Curti, citizen of Rapperswil, in 1689. With his wife Judith Fuchs he had seven children and so was the progenitor of the Swiss Curti family. He and some of his descendants continued in the silk trade. They were Catholics, and enjoyed competing with the silk traders in Zürich who were Protestants.[103]

Rapperswil is a small city on Lake Zürich, due east from Zürich. Its old center is well preserved, with a castle, churches, many old buildings, and twisting narrow streets. The town climbs up a hill from the lake to the castle. Along the lake there is a wide promenade, where families and single people of all ages, and numerous dogs, walk under the huge old trees and watch the swans in the lake. Near the end of this promenade is a little square, formerly named Endinger Platz. Two old houses on this square are Curti houses, inhabited by many generations of the family. The older house, more than six hundred years old and still owned by members of the family, bears the family's coat of arms above the front entrance. Behind one of the houses is a vineyard, the wine from which I have tasted in the Ratskellar of the old town hall.

In the year 2000 the square was re-named Curti Platz at a grand ceremony, with the town band, the mayor and other town dignitaries, and a large gathering of Curtis, including my son Carl, his wife Teresa, their daughter Carla, and myself. A new plaque, attached to the corner building, was unveiled and dedicated. This plaque bears the names of eminent members of the family who came (except for my father, Merle Curti) from Rapperswil.

My father's grandfather, Dr. Boniface Curti, (1828-1901) left Switzerland in 1866 with his wife, Frances Leder, and their children, including my grandfather, John Eugene, age three. [104] Boniface had studied medicine at the University of Zürich, then Wurzburg, then in Prague and Vienna, receiving his diploma at Zürich. He practiced in Rapperswil, Switzerland, for eleven years, and in Illinois for several more years.[105] The family settled in La Salle County, Illinois. Boniface, who had had a fine practice for several years in Switzerland, did not succeed as a doctor in America. According to my father, Boniface wrote to his half-sister in Rapperswil:

> ... that the people in LaSalle seemed unusually healthy and that the native-born English doctors had the edge on him. He came with his share of the family wealth and bought a farm. No one in his family had ever farmed; they were merchants, lawyers, doctors, magistrates, journalists. He was a complete flop in farming. His cows died. His corn crop failed.
>
> His frail young wife ... [Frances Leder] was also of the Swiss patricianship, convent educated, her own lady's maid, a devout Catholic. He was a free-thinker, becoming one as a student at the University of Zürich, sympathetic to the revolutions of 1848, and out of line with his conservative family, none of whom had been touched by the Zwinglian reformation. My grandmother had to all but give up Catholicism, though she insisted on the baptism and training in the catechism of her four sons.[106]

After some twenty years they moved to Papillion, Nebraska where Boniface ran a drugstore, and where his grandson, my father, was born. The Curti family and the Vermont family of my grandmother were both early settlers of Papillion, which was founded in 1870, just twenty-seven years before my father's birth.

The Swiss Curti family was, and is, a distinguished family. They are mainly middle class professional people—many in prominent positions in law, politics, medicine, and business. There are musicians, too, most notably Anton Curti (1820-1887), a singer at the Dresden court opera, and his son Franz, a dentist and a composer, who wrote an opera, "Das Rösli vom Santis", first performed in 1897. Anton's grandson, Antoine of Montreux (b.1922), was an hotelier, member of the cantonal council and organist. The youngest of the five children of this Antoine, Jean-Marie Curti (b.1950), is the distinguished conductor of a chamber orchestra. Unfortunately I have never met Jean-Marie and his wife and four children, all of whom are musical and play various instruments. I am delighted to read that Nelly Curti calls him "about the most cheerful person I ever knew."[107] Yet another musician, concert pianist Silvio Curti, lives in St. Gall.

As for religion, a look at the genealogy reveals several Catholic priests and nuns. The family was strictly Catholic until Pope Pius IX in1871 promulgated the doctrine of papal infallibility. Ferdinand Eugen Curti (1836-1921) was one of the founders of the Old Catholic Church.[108] At present, I estimate that about half of the family are regular Catholics, and the rest agnostics.

One interesting connection of the Curti family with the Church concerns the island of Ufenau, the largest island in the lake of Zürich, near Rapperswil. For centuries it belonged to the Abbey of Einsiedeln. "But when Napoleon became dominant in Switzerland and changed the aristocratic system to more modern forms, he ... [took away] the ownership of the island [from] the Abbey of Einsiedeln. ... And it was a Curti who bought it. But as a good Catholic, when the time of Napoleon was over, he re-sold the Island to the Abbey of Einsiedeln."[109]

I imagine that most families who can find records of their European forbears will find several Catholic priests and nuns in their family. But then I wonder: did the Curtis have an unusual number of these? When I became Catholic I was thrilled to find them listed in the genealogy. Aside from this mention of them, we know virtually nothing about them. The nuns all died in their early twenties, and my father's guess is that they probably died of tuberculosis. Those monasteries were terribly cold in the winter. I like to think of my long life, much of it lived as a Benedictine nun, as perhaps fulfilling, or living out, their all too brief vocations. To remember them and keep them in prayer, let me list them:[110]

Maria Elisabeth, nun in the convent of Solothurn, called in religion Maria Judith; died in 1769, age 22.

Maria Salome, nun in the same community, called in religion Maria Isabella; died in 1767, age 24.

Maria Magdalena, OSB, in the monastery at Fahr, called in religion Benedicta; died in 1781, age 22.

Louise Beatrice Curti, nun at Zug; died in 1868, age 27.

I am proud to claim a Benedictine monk in my genealogy. Born Franz Curti in 1880, he entered the Abbey of Disentis and received the name Notker, after the famous Notker Balbulus of St. Gall (c. 840-92), known especially for his composition of numerous sequence texts.[111] Pater Notker Curti died in 1949; there are family members living today who knew him and liked him very much. His brother was Dr. Alfons Curti, who showed my father around Rapperswil in 1924. Pater Notker seems to have been a Renaissance man, with much learning and many skills. He had a degree in mathematics; he restored several frescoes at Disentis and elsewhere, some of them dating from the fourteenth century. He traveled around the country gathering hundreds of artifacts, works of art and religious objects of great historical and aesthetic interest for the Abbey. I saw many of these things in the Abbey's impressive three-storey museum and in the Abbey's church, when I visited there in 2000. Disentis is located in the region (the Grisons) where Switzerland's fourth language, Romansch, is spoken. This language was close to dying out when Pater Notker took on the task of teaching Romansch to local children and collecting several folk tales in the language, which were published in a book. Thus he was a key person in the survival of that unique local language and culture. In his last years he became blind.[112]

This is the bare essence of my Swiss family. Much more could be told, and has been told, in the 1925 letters from my father to his family; in Dr. Arthur Curti's history of the family; and in many newspaper articles and other documents. I owe a great deal to this family, and am very grateful that I have had the opportunity to visit twice: first in 1970 as the guest of my most gracious cousins Dr. Eugen and Nelly Curti of Zürich; and then for the family reunion in 2000 as guest of my son Carl and his family. I love Switzerland. On the 2000 visit we went to St. Gall to see Sidonia Curti and her husband Wolfgang Korte. Wolfgang treated us to a visit to the Abbey of Disentis, where he had gone to school. At the family reunion we met our Milwaukee, Wisconsin relatives, Marianne Curti and her husband Hansruedi Kull, and their daughter Annemarie and her husband Franz. My father loved this family and they had many visits together.

In college I had a German friend who criticized Switzerland as "boring and bourgeois; not congenial to bohemians." I found the country to be anything but boring, with its incomparable mountains and forests that invite one to believe in dwarves, trolls, talking trees, elves; its neatly arranged pastures and meadows and villages; its rich history and evidences of times long past. Bourgeois? Undoubtedly, and that I find most attractive, manifested in what seems to me a rational, sensible, democratic political arrangement; cleanliness; love of good food; friendly people.

My Father's Parents

The sun was shining and all was peaceful as I was playing Indians by myself in our back yard in Bronxville. All at once someone from the house came out and told me that my Grandpa Curti [113] had died. I cried. Strangely, I remember these moments so clearly, yet I do not remember my grandfather at all. I know him from photographs, from what I have heard my father tell about him, and from the bird house he made for us. This house sat for decades in a crook of the old apple tree outside the living room of Flint Farm, our New Hampshire house. It had two storeys, four "rooms" on each level. It was a traditional New England house, white with green shutters and a shingled roof. No birds ever made their home there, to my great disappointment, for it seemed such a beautiful, generous, almost palatial, dwelling for them.

The photos, often with him holding me in his arms and my sister Nancy by the hand, show him a sweet, gentle man. But his life was hard. He suffered from depression; he supported his family in various changing ways. He was a very skilled carpenter, and had little patience with my father's lack of mechanical aptitude.

John Eugene Curti, son of Dr. Boniface and Frances (Fannie) Leder Curti, was born in Rapperswil, Switzerland in1863 and came to the United States with his family at the age of three. He lived for twenty years in Ottawa, Illinois; then in Papillion, Nebraska, and then for the last twenty-eight years of his life in Omaha. My father's own words describe him best:

> ... my father, who regarded himself as a failure and who, in business, was certainly marginal. But he kept us going. He had, as it turned out, TB in his young manhood and it became overt shortly after he married my mother. ... My father worked in the drugstore [of his father, Boniface in Papillion] and finally took it over, having ultimately to hire a woman pharmacist. He was very much liked by everyone, being kind, generous, over-considerate, and deeply worried by the alcoholism of his father, fearing he would make a mistake in filling prescriptions. My father had also to look out for a brother who, by report, had been kicked and irretrievably injured in the head while he was trying to milk a cow. At the best he could only do the cleaning-up part about the drugstore. The family lived upstairs, without a toilet or running water, until, finally, my father was able to buy a very nice house on Main Street. I was born in it and remember it as being one of

the 'best' houses in Papillion – a town of 500, 5 churches, and 5 saloons. The only thing that was bad was that when the Papio creek flooded, Main Street was a lake and the water filled the lower part of every downstairs room – we vacated the place for the cleanup, staying with neighbors up the hill.

Finally my father felt he had enough of the drug store and we moved to Omaha as he had got a job in a farmers mutual insurance. He liked going about the state adjusting losses and settling claims and, until [when] his tenure was unbearable because of the doings of his "friend" the treasurer, [got into] the lightning rod business, driving his Ford and equipment all through western Iowa and east-central Nebraska.

Shortly after I began teaching at Columbia it was found he had advanced prostate cancer and though my brother, an Army medical doctor, got leave and took him to the Mayo Clinic, it was too late. My understanding of and respect for him came very late. My mother always had great appeal. Unlike my father, who openly said on birthdays he was sorry to have been born, my mother was light-hearted, full of fun, party-loving, a water-color and oil painter of considerable talent which she managed to do with bringing up four children…[114] looking out for her father-in-law and brother-in-law, fleeing of summers to her parents' farm in Vermont, with all the children, expenses being paid by her father, who also sent us each winter a barrel of apples from his orchard and plenty of maple sugar. I was a mix of both my parents.[115]

Grandmother Alice Curti[116]

Grandmother Alice, as we called her, was the only grandparent I really knew. Even now I can visualize her. She had bright blue eyes, neatly permed white hair, and had a good sense of humor. She was a staunch Episcopalian; she had her children baptized, took them to church regularly, and saw to it that they received their religious education. She smoked and enjoyed playing cards. Her Methodist forbears in Vermont would have been scandalized. They did not trust "those Piskies" (Episcopalians). Grandma visited us every so often, staying a month or so each time. I remember her visits to us in Bronxville, Madison, and New Hampshire. She made pies and helped in various ways, until, at the mere age of 70, my father would not allow her to wash the kitchen floor any more. My father must have inherited his insomnia from her. I recall her saying once, "I haven't slept in twenty years." I loved her, and there is so much I would like to ask her if I could see her now: how she met my grandfather; what her life was like as a child in Vermont, and as a young wife and mother in Nebraska. She had a sort of innocence about her. In grade school, the children were preparing for the visit of the regional superintendent of schools, and each child had to "speak a piece." Grandma's classmates taught her the following verse, which she actually got up and said to the visitor:

Oh Lord of love, look down above,
And bless our school committee.
For hiring a fool to teach our school
Right here in Junction City!

Vermont Ancestors

Her genealogy is much simpler to relate than that of the Curtis. There is the information one can gather on the gravestones of the cemeteries in northern Vermont around Essex Junction; a paragraph of my mother's notes; a draft in faded ink of Grandmother's application to join the Daughters of the American Revolution (DAR); and three double spaced pages, a blurry carbon copy, of a statement about family history for my father by one of the children of Levi Warner, M.D., whose brother, Benjamin Warner, M.D., was my father's great great grandfather.

My grandmother never followed through on her application to join the DAR. Here follows her draft:

> "I, Alice Curti, apply for membership in this Society by right of lineal descent in the following line from James Nichols, who was born in ______, on the day of _____ 1755 & died in Richmont Vt. on _______ 22 and who served in the War of Revolution.
>
> I was born in the town of Essex, County of Chittenden, State of Vermont. I am the daughter of Eliza Nichols Hunt and her husband, Jason Hunt and granddaughter of Charles Nichols and Abigail Warner Nichols his wife and great granddaughter of Charles Nichols and Rachel Peck Nichols his wife and great great granddaughter of Jas Nichols and Sally Shal.. Nichols his wife … .. .. ancestor who assisted in establishing American independence while acting in the capacity of private in Co. 7th
> – Captain Daniel Lyons – Conn.
> [the ellipses indicate writing too faded to decipher]."

From the three typewritten pages we find that John, Eben and Israel Warner came from England "in a very early day" and settled in Roxbury, Connecticut. John Warner had three sons, Seth, Daniel, and John, who were all soldiers in the War of Independence. Seth was a Colonel, John was a Captain. John and Daniel fought in the Battle of Lexington (April 19, 1775). Daniel was killed in that battle. Captain John Warner was with Colonel Ethan Allen at the surprise attack on and capture of the fortress of Ticonderoga.

After the war, Captain John Warner settled on a farm near St. Albans, Vermont and became a "noted physician." The three-page document by the son or daughter of Levi Warner contains a few stories about the prodigious strength of Dr. (Captain) John and his son, Dr. Benjamin Faye Warner. The document describes Dr. John as

> a man who stood six feet two inches high in his stocking feet and weighed over two hundred pounds. ... He went to Plattsburgh to get a load of salt, and there were men called Torys [*sic*] gathered around him and asked him if his name was not John Warner. He said it was and they said we are going to capture you for the British Government. He replied, 'Gentlemen, please wait until I load this salt, and if you ....[blank space] you will have the whole team salt and all. They waited for him to load the salt. Dr. John took up the salt, two hundred lbs, in a sack and tossed them six or eight feet onto the sleigh with apparently as much ease as though they were bags of bran. After he had put on seven sacks he jumped onto the sleigh himself and said 'Gentlemen, now I am ready for you.' And one of the nine men said. 'I don't believe we want you.' So Dr. John drove off and left the nine men looking at him in amazement.

The document contains other stories of this nature about Dr. John. Benjamin, my great-great-great grandfather, is described in a similar fashion, with another story about carrying salt, this time a barrel. Dr. Benjamin was also six feet two, but weighed fifty pounds more than his brother. One cannot help wondering how well one can trust the memory of the writer. The typing looks exactly like my father's; I would guess he transcribed it from handwriting.

In any case, Benjamin had by his second wife a daughter Abigail, who married Charles Nichols. Their daughter Eliza Nichols married Jason Hunt. This couple were the parents of my grandmother Alice Hunt Curti. Of them my mother wrote: "Mr.& Mrs. Hunt of Essex Junction, Vt., a farm family. Grandmother Hunt a great character, very intelligent, lively, fond of music."

My Mother's Family: The Woosters[117]

Amidst the political and religious turmoil in England, two brothers, William and Edward Worcester, took ship for the New World in 1638[118] in search of a better life. William, the elder, settled in Massachusetts. Edward, a young man of sixteen, soon moved to Connecticut where he changed the spelling of his name to Wooster. He was the first permanent settler and founder of the town of Derby, Connecticut, originally named Paugasset. In the deadly conflict between Puritans and Roundheads, culminating in the beheading of King Charles I in 1649, Edward must have been a Royalist, for he had his children baptized in Christ Church (Episcopal) and he was buried there.

Among Edward's numerous descendants was my mother, both of whose parents were of the Wooster family. In between came a huge number of people in many walks of life. It would seem that every young male Wooster in the colonial period served in the military during the War for Independence and the French and Indian War. Of these, the most famous was General David Wooster, who was killed in 1777 in the Battle of Ridgefield, Connecticut. He was the family historian, and unfortunately the papers concerning the English heritage of the family were lost when the British burned down his house. There were many preachers, mostly Methodist; there were farmers, small business people, adventurers, and of course the absolutely essential but virtually ignored wives and mothers.

My grandfather, Charles Wooster (1843-1922) was probably the most well known member of the Wooster tribe since General David. Born in Hillsdale, Michigan, he was one of the six children of John Edward Lacy Wooster (1809-1884) and Abigail Fowler (1811-1892). Charles fought throughout the five years of the Civil War and was wounded in action. After a few false starts in various places, he settled in Merrick County, Nebraska, on a claim of 300 acres. This land, located between the Loup and Platte Rivers, was rich and never cultivated. Silver Creek ran through the land. When my mother took me to see the place in about 1940, we could still detect traces of the Oregon Trail, which followed the course of the Platte River. With unending hard labor, Charles started a farm, built a sod house, and then sent for his young wife, Helen Hitchcock, whom he had left behind in Michigan. Helen died young, and my grandfather then married a first cousin, Lillie Margaret Todd Wooster. With Helen he had two daughters; with Lillie he had six children, of whom my mother, Maggie Lillie Wooster, was the next to last.

Charles and Lillie had a difficult marriage. Lillie felt that her husband never gave her the affection she craved. In fact his heart remained with his first wife; he married Lillie mainly for the help she would offer in the household. They differed in their view of religion: Charles was a confirmed atheist, Lillie a Methodist. They differed in their ideas about how the children should be educated. Charles waged a continuous battle with the public school, at last pulling the children out of school and educating them at home. He was a brilliant man. He had a library of five hundred books and in the evenings would read to the children from the classics. Besides settling the land, planting many trees, building a frame house, and farming, he edited the Silver Creek newspaper for years, finally turning it over to the daughters of his first marriage, Edith and Pauline. He studied law on his own and argued many cases in court throughout the rest of his life. At one point he took on the Union Pacific Railroad and, arguing his case in court, took his case all the way up to the Federal Court, where the company won the right of way right through his land. The attorney for the railroad considered him one of their ablest adversaries." Charles Wooster became very involved in politics, sharing his firm opinions with all in numerous letters to the editor of local and statewide papers. He served a term in the state legislature as a Free Silver Republican. He loved to argue, and would seek out arguments with one and all, taking whatever position contradicted that of his opponent.

He was deadly opposed to any sort of organized religion, regarding preachers and believers alike as hypocrites. He may have granted the existence of a Supreme Being, but he was "down on the God of the preachers. … [he regarded their God as] a supernatural and despotic ruler of the universe."[119]

My mother described her father thus: "Tall, with white hair and white side whiskers, black suit, Prince Albert coat, black broad-brimmed hat, white silk tie, with his gold false teeth in his mouth. His Omaha tailors wanted him to try more modish garb. but he would have none of such. I still see him sitting at his roll-top desk. His office was a mess. … He was an extremely tender-hearted person, and dearly loved his grandchildren. On the other hand he was a strict disciplinarian. He believed in obedience. He was a just judge in disputes between any of us and the neighborhood children."

But my cousin Daniel Dean Swinney, who loved his grandfather Charles Wooster, wrote: "I remember very few occasions when I ever heard or saw him laugh."

Lillie Todd Wooster

My maternal grandmother was an entirely different person from her husband. Despite her very hard life—living most of the time in poverty, raising six children, of whom two lived only a couple of years, being a stepmother to Edith and Pauline, who never accepted her as their mother, and in a very difficult marriage—she had, according to my mother, "a fine voice" and an "exceptionally lively and happy disposition." From her, through my mother, I learned many of the old songs: "A Frog went a-Courtin'", "Green Bay Tree", "Twenty Froggies Went to School." My grandmother's versions are ones I have not heard anywhere else; and of course I think they are the best versions. Lillie was a great practical joker, especially on April Fool's Day. She once made pancakes on that day. They looked enticing, but hiding in each was a round piece of paper. When my mother and her older brother Charles complained that they never got enough honey, she sat them down and invited them to have all they wanted. They had more than enough and got sick. The same thing happened with pie.

Daniel D. Swinney knew his grandmother, and writes of her:

> Lil was a highly intelligent woman who loved to socialize and who had a broad range of interests. She liked books but had little time to read. Gardening was one of her favorite pursuits, particularly her flowers and their arrangement in the house. She visited her neighbors and participated in the Grange, the Eastern Star, and to a limited extent in activities sponsored by both the Episcopalian and Congregational Churches in Silver Creek. Charles always opposed any church activities and tried to forbid both her and the children from engaging in such. ... She loved parties and the celebration of holidays and birthdays. They were always festive occasions for which she made imaginative decorations and beautifully wrapped presents. There was no money for such luxuries so everything was simple and homemade. She spent hours with the children, teaching them how to make things and to fix them attractively. She had a merry disposition, appreciated jokes and humorous situations. Evidence of this was her fondness for wrapping up potatoes or other unusual items and placing them in the Christmas stockings. She loved to give parties on Saint Patrick's Day and April Fool's Day, and would arrange funny games and presents for the children. To my knowledge, Grandpa

seldom participated in any of these activities or showed any real appreciation of her efforts in these respects."[120]

To know Charles and Lillie Wooster is to know my mother. The contrast in their personalities, the conflicts between them, are present in her.

In concluding this section on my ancestors, two things come especially to mind. First, the connection between my father's and mother's American ancestors: most of them were farmers, and passed on to my parents their love of the land. And some of them undoubtedly knew each other. Colonel Seth Warner and General David Wooster, for example, were both in the battle at Crown Point and it would hardly have been possible for their paths not to cross.

Secondly, I was flabbergasted when I discovered that a great many of my ancestors lived in Connecticut the neighborhood of the Abbey of Regina Laudis. Among the Warners were:

John Warner (b.1615 England, d. 1679 in Farmington, Hartford)
John Warner (1639-1706-7) d. in Farmington
Ebenezer (b. c. 1677, Farmington; married, practiced medicine, and died in Woodbury
Benjamin (1709) lived most of his life in Woodbury
Seth (1743-1784) born and died in Roxbury
John (b.1745) in Woodbury

Among the Woosters were:

Lt. Peter Wooster, Oxford
Ensign Jabez, Bridgewater
Col. Joseph, Stratford
Gen. David, Stratford
Henry, Woodbury
Pvt. Elijah, Waterbury
Pvt. Samuel, Oxford
Capt. Thomas, New Haven
Sgt. Ephraim, New Haven
Sgt. Joseph, New Haven
Pvt. Herman, Woodbury
Pvt. Clark, New Haven
Rev. Pvt. Benjamin, Waterbury
Pvt. Nathan, Waterbury
Pvt. Hinman, Waterbury
Pvt. Lemuel, Litchfield

Did all these connections somehow "pull" me to the Abbey? Was it in the plan of God that my birthplace and childhood in religious life are there? Or is it just a coincidence? How many nuns, either at Regina Laudis or Our Lady of the Rock, have large numbers of ancestors on both sides living in Waterbury, Woodbury, Roxbury? The facts exist, whatever one might think.

Endnotes

[1] For an amusing and insightful description of my father by one of his early graduate students, see G.D. Lillibridge, "So Long, Maestro: A Portrait of Merle Curti." *The American Scholar* Spring 1997: 263-270.

[2] "Memorial Resolution of the Faculty of the University of Wisconsin-Madison on the death of Emeritus Professor Merle Curti." http://history.wisc.edu/people/memorial_resolutions/curti.htm. Consulted November 5, 2013.

[3] Letter to M. Felicitas. February 6, 1992.

[4] Dr. William R. Emerson differentiates between shock and trauma, and focuses his professional life on the treatment and study of the influence of prenatal and neonatal experiences on the personality of the individual. Dr. Alfred Tomatis, throughout his career, anticipated these findings: prenatal conditions can show up as irregularities in a person's hearing. Emerson. "Shock: a Universal Malady: Prenatal and Perinatal Origins of Suffering." Six audiotapes with booklet, n.d. [after 1999]. Alfred A.Tomatis. *The Conscious Ear: My Life of Transformation Through Listening* 1991. Trans. Stephen Lushington. Trans. and Ed. Billie M. Thompson. Barrytown, New York 1991. Trans. of *L'Oreille et la Vie 1977.*

[5] For a detailed account of my first five years, see Margaret Wooster, "Ann's First Five Years," *Child Psychology.* New York: Longmans, Green, 1939.

[6] The entire cost of travel, including the Glacier Park visit, was $229 for both of us!

[7] Later, Archbishop Sheen.

[8] Debs spoke these stirring words at the hearing for his sentencing under the Espionage Act of 1927 for his opposition to World War I.

[9] Palestrina was the leading composer of church music in the sixteenth century.

[10] Many Internet sources supply information on the various socialist groups. Tim Wohlforth gives a detailed account of the movements he was involved in, in his memoir *The Prophet's Children: Travels on the American Left.* New Jersey: Humanities Press, 1993. See also Dennis Tourish and Tim Wohlforth, *On the Edge: Political Cults Right and Left.* M.E.Sharpe, 2000.

[11] Winter Issue 1957: 25-27.

[12] Dorothy Day is on her way to recognition as a saint by the Church. A writer all her life, she became a Communist as a young woman and never lost her identification with the working class and the poor. After her conversion to Catholicism she founded the Catholic Worker movement.

[13] Daniel Berrigan was a Jesuit priest who throughout his long career as a prolific writer and anti-war activist was arrested several times for civil disobedience.

[14] Big Bill Haywood was one of the founders and leaders of the IWW—the Industrial Workers of the World, whose members were known as "Wobblies." The IWW's motto was "one big union" organized by industry. It was founded in 1905, reached its peak of membership in the early 1920s, and still exists today.

[15] I was asked at an interview with all the psychiatrists at the New York School of Psychiatry to name my favorite book. It was Trotsky's *History of the Russian Revolution.*

[16] Some of the theories were that the USSR was a Workers' State, a Deformed Workers' State, a Degenerate Workers' State, or a State Capitalist regime.

[17] Tim Wohlforth, *The Prophet's Children.*

[18] Martha Curti Wohlforth, *Orlando Gibbons' Chamber Music*. Master's thesis in Music Library of the City College of New York, 1967.

[19] Medieval and Renaissance bowed stringed instruments.

[20] Dr. George Buelow (1929-2009) was an eminent musicologist who specialized in the Baroque period.

[21] The word "gamelan" refers to a style of music centered in Java and Bali, and to the collection of instruments and the performers of that music. The gamelan ensemble consists of several instruments, mostly gongs and xylophones. A Javanese gamelan performed at the Paris Exposition of 1889, thus introducing this music to the Western world. Debussy was fascinated by this music and it was an influence in his own compositions. Gamelan has also influenced many other twentieth-century composers, including John Cage and my composer friends at Livingston College.

[22] The Kiss of Peace occurs during the Mass or Sunday services of many Christian churches. The congregation is invited to exchange a sign of Christ's peace, usually a handshake or a brief hug.

[23] This is a bass viola da gamba, with six strings and frets like the rest of the viol family. It is smaller than the modern string bass. The player holds it between her knees; it does not rest on the floor as do the modern cello and bass.

[24] This book, by Frances Moore Lappe (1971), was very influential in promoting vegetarianism, as it showed that by combining various grains and beans one could obtain complete proteins without meat.

[25] "Saddhana" is the word that Shyam used to cover all the practices of yoga: asanas, diet, meditation, and so on.

[26] The Eucharist is that fundamental core of the Mass in which Christ, through the person of the priest, turns the bread and wine into His body and blood, offered for the salvation of the world. Jesus instituted the Eucharist at the Last Supper by offering bread and wine to His disciples, saying, "This is my body ... this is my blood."

[27] For the Biblical references to these, see: for "Love your enemy" and "Bless those who persecute you" in the Sermon on the Mount, Matthew 5,6,7; for Mary and Martha, see Luke 10:38-42; the fig tree, Mark 11:13-14.

[28] Compline is the last of the daily prayers of the Church.

[29] The very word "exorcism" is scary to many people. It summons up images of demons, magic, superstition. True, some sort of exorcism, a driving out of demons, has existed for millennia in many forms and in many cultures. The Catholic Church performs a simple exorcism as part of the sacrament of Baptism, as it has done since at least the third century, and as Jesus often did. The new rite of preparation for Baptism, inaugurated with Vatican II, calls for one or two simple exorcisms of catechumens (the candidates for Baptism). These exorcisms are preventive: they do not mean that the candidate is possessed by the devil. They are meant to protect the catechumen from attacks of the Evil One. For the solemn, or major exorcism, see *Catechism of the Catholic Church,* Libreria Editrice Vaticana 1994, #1673.

[30] "Duodecimo" refers to a book size, 13x19 cm.

[31] Martha Margaret Curti, *John Playford's 'Apollo's Banquet' 1670*. PhD dissertation, Rutgers University, 1977.

[32] These are popular dances of the seventeenth century.

[33] For an excellent presentation of this necessary break of a new Christian from his or her family, see Joyce E. Salisbury. *Perpetua's Passion:*

The Death and Memory of a Young Roman Woman. New York: Routledge, 1997.

[34] See Acts 2: 44-45 and 4:32-35 for Biblical descriptions of the early Christian community.

[35] The Abbey of Regina Laudis, in Bethlehem, Connecticut, was founded in 1946 by two nuns from the Abbey of Jouarre in France: Mother Benedict Duss, OSB, an American with a French mother, and Mother Mary Aline Trilles de Warren, OSB. Mother Benedict had envisioned this first contemplative Benedictine monastery for women in the United States in grateful response to the liberation of Jouarre from the Nazi occupation by the American army under General Patton. For a rich description of this foundation and its history, see Antoinette Bosco, *Mother Benedict:Foundress of the Abbey of Regina Laudis*. San Francisco: Ignatius Press, 2007.

[36] Mother Mary Magdalen was the nun assigned to be my contact person at the Abbey. She, like me, was a convert (her father was a Methodist minister) and a musician: she had a master's degree in music from the Manhattanville College of Sacred Music. I discovered later that she and I shared the same birthday.

[37] The founder, with Dorothy Day, of the Catholic Worker movement.

[38] The publisher of the book on which I wrote my dissertation.

[39] Solesmes is the Benedictine Abbey that instigated the revival and reformation of Gregorian chant in the late nineteenth and early twentieth century.

[40] See footnote 21 above.

[41] Sacred Harp: so named after a book first published in 1844. The more general name for this style of music is "Shape Note Music." For further information see the website fasola.org.

[42] Neumes are the characters in the notation of chant that represent individual notes or groups of notes. They developed in the ninth century, and by the twelfth had evolved into the square notation still used today.

[43] An interval smaller than a half step.

[44] A Gradual is a fairly long chant sung as a commentary on the first reading (usually from the Old Testament) at Mass. A large grouping of these Graduals is in Mode V, one of the eight Gregorian modes, sometimes called the Lydian Mode.

[45] A professor of art history who was one class ahead of me at Oberlin.

[46] Organs have existed in one form or another since ancient times. There is evidence of organs in churches in Europe from the 8th century, but whether, or how, they were used with the chant is not known. However, "By the 15th century, the organ was widely used at least for … [playing verses alternately with the choir] in the liturgy, and it has been widely used (if not universally approved) in the accompaniment of chant ever since." *The New Harvard Dictionary of Music,* 1986, 354.

[47] Jouarre: the village in which the Abbey of Notre-Dame de Jouarre is located.

[48] The Latin Mass music consists of the Ordinary (Kyrie, Gloria, Credo, Sanctus, and Agnus Dei), whose texts are the same in each and every Mass, and the Proper (Introit, Gradual, Alleluia, Offertory, and Communion) which has different texts for each week, the feasts of saints, and the liturgical seasons of the year.

[49] For a vivid and authentic account of life at Jouarre during the Nazi occupation and the vision of Mere Benoît, see Bosco, *Mother Benedict* , 113-134.

[50] Solesmes, on the river Sarthe, and near the town of Sablé, is an abbey of monks most known for its diligent work in the late eighteenth and early nineteenth century on the restoration of Gregorian chant.

[51] But of course the Mass was of the Novus Ordo established by the Council.

[52] Dom Gajard, choirmaster at Solesmes (1930-1971) *Plainchant and Medieval Music Society,* 17.2 (October 2008). He spent some time at Regina Laudis, helping the nuns with chant.

[53] The characters used in chant notation. See footnote 42.

[54] Henri Nouwen (1932-1996) was a priest, professor, and a prolific writer, interested in psychology and social justice.

[55] From the Benedictus Antiphon on the feast of the Assumption.

[56] Pope Pius XII "Mystici Corporis Christi" June 29, 1943.

[57] The Abbey had adapted the theory of "Creative Process" proposed by an academician: stages of Preparation, Incubation, Illumination and Verification. From this, Fr. Prokes and the Community began looking at things—anything that grows or changes, like individuals, violins, gardens, et al, in terms of levels or stages: Instinctual, Justice, Eucharistic, and Spirit.

[58] The approach to chant, especially in terms of rhythm, that had been developed at the Abbey of Solesmes by Dom Mocquereau in the

early nineteenth century and carried on by Dom Joseph Gajard, who had come a few times to Regina Laudis to work with the community on chant.

59 Chironomy is the method of conducting Gregorian chant, and is also useful, indeed essential, for instilling in all the singers an awareness of the rise and fall of energy that gives life to the chant.

60 Father died on Pentecost Sunday, May 24, 2015.

61 The teredo, also called "shipworm" or "termites of the sea" is not really a worm, despite its worm-like shape. It is a mollusk. It bores into submerged wood for sustenance.

62 These mysteries are: the Saturday before Palm Sunday: Commitment. Palm Sunday: Procession. Monday: Intimate Extravagance (Mary Magdalen pours precious ointment onto the feet of Jesus). Tuesday: the Compulsion to Completion (the word *peragere*, to carry through, complete, appears in the prayer for that day). Wednesday: Aloneness (Jesus predicts that one of His disciples will betray him. Only Jesus can accomplish his mission; no one else can do it for him. Just so, each of us must, alone, complete our own mission). Holy Thursday: Body Given (Jesus institutes the Eucharist at the Last Supper). Good Friday: Non est lex (there is no law). Holy Saturday: Night. Easter Sunday: Resurrection. All these are based on Scriptural references or the main liturgical action of the day.

63 The Franciscans of the Eucharist, based in Meriden, Connecticut, had established a small community on Shaw Island even before the Benedictines came. For twenty-seven years they operated the general store and the ferry landing, finally leaving in 2004.

64 B-2+A-1+C-3+H-8=14. Bach uses the number as his "signature" in many of his compositions.

65 The monk Guido of Arezzo, eleventh century, invented the four-line staff and the use of solmization syllables to name each pitch. He took these syllables from the first verse of the hymn for St. John the Baptist, in which each phrase begins one step higher than the previous one: Ut (which later became Do), Re, Mi, Fa, Sol, La. Pope John XIX summoned Guido to show him this new system, which made it so much easier to read and teach music.

66 Mother Columba Hart, OSB, a prodigious scholar, was a nun at Regina Laudis for forty years. Her numerous publications include translations of the *Scivias* by St. Hildegard of Bingen, and of the complete works of Hadewijch.

67 For a complete genealogy of my ancestry, see Appendix.

68 This office and the dimension of Education are explained thoroughly by Mother Dolores in her recent book *The Ear of the Heart.* San Francisco: Ignatius Press, 2013.

69 The postulant wears a tunic, a floor-length plain black dress with long sleeves, worn with a belt. At her Clothing the Novice receives the rest of the monastic habit: the scapular, the wimple, and a long white veil. Her hair is now completely covered.

70 Septimius Severus was the Roman emperor from 193-211. He was unusually bloodthirsty and cruel.

71 The martyrdom of Felicitas and Perpetua is amply and brilliantly described and placed in the context of the religion, culture, and politics of third-century Carthage by Salisbury, *Perpetua's Passion.* Marie-Louise von Franz gives a Jungian interpretation of Perpetua's dreams and visions in *The Passion of Perpetua.* Irving, Texas: Spring Publications, 1980.

72 During my time at the Abbey I was greatly comforted by the fact that I had a "twin martyr," Sister (later Mother) Perpetua. She helped me greatly in so many ways, among them, acquainting me with material written about Felicity and Perpetua. Sadly, she is suffering as I write this from a fatal illness.

73 I Kings 2:10-12. This is a foreshadowing of Mary's *Magnificat.*

74 A proven method, prevalent in Catholic schools especially in the 1950s, to teach children how to read, hear, sing, write, and create music in a way that prepares them for singing Gregorian chant. Mrs. Justine Ward, a devotee of Gregorian chant and of the Solesmes approach to its rhythm, developed this method.

75 Oblates are lay people who associate themselves with a particular monastery for life and follow a Benedictine spirituality.

76 St. Maximilian Kolbe (1894-1941) was a Polish Franciscan friar who was killed at Auschwitz.

77 Abbot Justin McCann, edit. and trans. *The Rule of Saint Benedict in Latin and English.* Chapter 7, "Of Humility." London: Burns,Oates, 1952, Series: The Orchard Books.

78 Later, the second Abbess of Regina Laudis.

79 For a description of the Tomatis Listening Therapy, see Chapter 16 below.

80 A schola is a small group of people who sing certain parts of the Mass by themselves. The Abbey has three or four scholas that alternate week by week.

[81] For a good description of this time, see Bosco, *Mother Benedict*, Chapter 14.

[82] Besides me, the quartet had Katie Weed of Friday Harbor, a wonderful and forthright woman, on second violin; Evelyn Rodrique, from Orcas, a superb viola player who had recently retired from twenty or so years in the Seattle Symphony; and Helen Storey, here on Shaw, who took up the cello after decades of neglect. We had a coach, Tom Rodrique, Evelyn's husband. Tom had been in charge of the entire music program of the Shoreline schools for years, and in the early days of the Seattle Youth Symphony was its Assistant Conductor. He is still a dear friend.

[83] See footnote 74.

[84] From a letter by Regina Laudis thanking donors, December 19, 2005.

[85] The slate for the stone was selected by Mother Praxedes Baxter; it was designed by Karin Sprague of Rhode Island, and carved under the direction of Mother Praxedes by Adam Heller.

[86] Chris received a PhD from Princeton in the same field as Bill, International Relations. She works at Dartmouth in administration.

[87] Mother Prioress David Serna was elected as the second Abbess of Regina Laudis in 2001.

[88] At that time, the Archbishop of Hartford, Henry Mansell.

[89] See www.encephalitis.info. Consulted July 11, 2015.

[90] This feast celebrates the conception of Mary: God gave her, alone of all human beings, the gift of being born totally free from the burden of original sin.

[91] About the ring, see "My Hands" in Chapter Twenty.

[92] Martha Hanson, who with another intern, Janet Parker, later formed a successful stained glass business: see www.PanedExpressions.com.

[93] Paul Salamunovitch died in 2014 after a long illness.

[94] Tomatis ,*The Conscious Ear.* Paul Madaule,*When Listening Comes Alive.* Noval, Ontario: Moulin, 1994.

[95] Maria Callas, Sting, and Gérard Dépardieu are among the famous ones.

[96] *À l'Écoute de l'Universe: an Interview with Dr. Alfred Tomatis*. Washington, D.C: The Dom Mocquereau Foundation, 1986.

[97] But Tomatis never claimed, as did some of his followers, that listening to Mozart would make babies, and the rest of us, more intelligent.

[98] For a deeper treatment of the ceremony of Consecration at Regina Laudis, see Bosco, *Mother Benedict*, 221-367 *passim*.

[99] Letter from Mother Olivia-Frances Arnold, OSB, to Mother Felicitas, September 29, 2014.

[100] A formal meeting of a religious community.

[101] Mrs. Lisauskas, who belonged to one of the several Lithuanian families in Bethlehem, had prayed for years before Lady Abbess and Mother Mary Aline arrived that a monastic community might come to being in Bethlehem.

[102] The most comprehensive source for the Curti genealogy up to 1936 is Arthur Curti. *Durch drei Jahrhunderte: Geschichte einer Familie.* Zürich: Orell Füssli, 1936.

[103] Dr. Eugen Curti, letter to M. Felicitas Curti, November 24, 2008

[104] From a letter of Merle Curti to his father, August 18, 1924, based on his investigation of records in the Rapperswil Court House.

[105] *History of LaSalle County* (Illinois). Vol.2. Chicago: Interstate Publishing Company, 1886. 289-90.

[106] Merle Curti, letter to Robert Nesbitt, February, 1990.

[107] Nelly Curti to Merle Curti, August 9, 1995.

[108] Eugen Curti, letter to M. Felicitas, November 24, 2008.

[109] *Idem.*

[110] Arthur Curti, *Durch Drei Jahrhundert.*

[111] The sequence is a genre of Gregorian chant, usually following the Alleluia in the Mass.

[112] A good article about Pater Notker, "Der Monch und die Stickereien," appeared in the Rapperswil newspaper, probably sometime in 2005, the 125th year after Notker's death.

[113] John Eugene Curti, b. Rapperswil 1863, d. Omaha, Nebraska 1939.

[114] Merle Curti, letter to Robert Nesbitt , February 1990

[115] Ralph Elmer 1890-1948; Jean 1893-1982; Erma Frances 1892-1894; Merle Eugene 1897-1996.

[116] Alice Hunt Curti, b. Essex Center, Vermont 1869-1952

[117] The main source of information on the Wooster family is the privately published book *Charles Wooster: The Sage of Silver Creek, Nebraska: His Forebears and Descendants* by my first cousin and my mother's nephew, Daniel Dean Swinney. This book contains a) "Genealogy of the Woosters in America" by Edward R. Wooster, 1973, a mimeographed paper by the then Historian of the Edward Wooster Family Association; b) Edward R. Wooster: "Major General David Wooster of the American Revolution; c) Selected letters of Charles and Helen Wooster, 1872, describing the difficult conditions of Charles

as an early settler. Swinney's book also includes the entire M.A. thesis of James E. Potter, "The Political Career of Charles Wooster," which describes in detail Charles' political and editorial activities. An earlier and very rare book, *Genealogy of the Woosters in America* 1885, gives a detailed account of the family, including a copy of an exchange of letters between General David Wooster and George Washington.

In addition, Wikipedia entries under "Wooster Family History," "Edward Wooster," "Derby Connecticut," "Immanuel Saint James Episcopal Church of Derby, Connecticut," were consulted.

118 There is a discrepancy in all the sources about the date of Edward's birth, of his coming to America, and other dates. All dates in this genealogy must be regarded as tentative. For example, in Swinney, in general a masterpiece of research, the author surmises that Edward must have been a Royalist, and left England in 1639 as a reaction to the execution of Charles I. But King Charles' execution did not take place until ten years later! Swinney also gives my mother's birth date as 1893, when in fact it was either 1890 or 1892.

119 Swinney 22

120 Swinney 19f.

CPSIA information can be obtained
at www.ICGtesting.com
Printed in the USA
LVHW02s1233060118
561998LV00008B/12/P

9 781457 549540